OTHER BOOKS BY RICHARD TELOFSKI

Fast Food for e-Business Marketers

Dangerous Competition - Critical Issues
in eCompetitive Intelligence

Conehenge - The Story of a Jersey Schlub

Insidious Competition - The Battle for
Meaning and the Corporate Image

Living on a Meme

How Anti-Corporate Activists Bend the Truth, and You, to Get What They Want

R I C H A R D   T E L O F S K I

iUniverse, Inc.
Bloomington

Living on a Meme
How Anti-Corporate Activists Bend the Truth, and You, to Get What They Want

iUniverse books may be ordered through booksellers or by contacting:

iUniverse
1663 Liberty Drive
Bloomington, IN 47403
www.iuniverse.com
1-800-Authors (1-800-288-4677)

Copyedited and proofread by Nena Weber.

Original cover concept by the author.

ISBN: 978-1-4620-7198-2 (sc)
ISBN: 978-1-4620-7199-9 (hc)
ISBN: 978-1-4620-7200-2 (e)

Printed in the United States of America

iUniverse rev. date: 1/09/2012

Dedicated to Stephen, who never let a meme bother him.

Contents

INTRODUCTION

Truth. Belief. Falsity.

As strange as it might seem, these are difficult concepts to grasp. They are especially difficult to grasp for anyone living in the highly fragmented media environment that is today's America. Reality is up for grabs. And what you allow to go into your head either challenged or unchallenged makes up your reality. You're the judge on what is real and what isn't with many organizations standing ready to bribe you for your verdict. Have you been living in the United States during the past 30 or so years? Yes? Then none of these ideas should come as any surprise to you.

The idea of truth is of great interest to me. Of even greater interest is how various organizations "bend" your reality for you, with the intent of "bending" it in their favor. Do you think I am speaking of corporations who have long been accused of hijacking our minds for the benefit of their bottom lines? No, I am not. There have been many, too many, books written about the ins and outs of corporate marketing and its effects on society. This book is not another one of those. Rather this book, *Living on a Meme - How Anti-Corporate Activists Bend the Truth, and You, to Get What They Want,* is a look at the organizations, the "anti-corporate corporations," that engage corporations in a continuous battle.

On my Web log (blog), Telofski.com, I "keep an eye" on a certain category of those anti-corporate organizations and how they use memes to help further their agendas. I'm speaking of non-governmental organizations (NGOs) and activist groups, specifically the ones that engage corporations adversarially. Examples of this type of anti-corporate corporation are Greenpeace, Rainforest Action Network (RAN), Friends of the Earth, Corporate Accountability International, and others about which you may read on Telofski.com. These are organizations, with an agenda of their own choosing, that compete for the image of the corporations which they target in order to further the agendas that they themselves have chosen. And they don't miss a chance to use a meme to help make their case. Trouble is, those memes aren't always true. By using those unchallenged memes to persuade people to their side of their anti-corporate argument, they're bribing people for their verdict on reality. Bribing? Yes. By leveraging a meme, these groups are giving people something, a way to feel better about themselves, in exchange for their tacit agreement with, support of, or active participation in their agenda, all with scant or no support of that meme. In doing this, these anti-corporate corporations are no less a threat to the modern company than are a company's traditional competitors. Through their "meme-mangling," these NGOs and activists who compete for the image of a company can impose undeserved damage on corporate reputations, costing market share, revenue, and jobs. These organizations are truly competitors, not only to the individual corporations that they target, but also to the economic system in general. I call them "irregular competitors."

Now, as I mentioned in the above paragraph, on Telofski.com you can read about Greenpeace and RAN, etc., but I've long known that some folks just don't like reading articles on computer screens. Quite frankly, I can't blame them for that dislike. Poring through a lengthy and meaty article while staring into a computer screen isn't my idea of a good time either, even though I do far too much of it. On the other hand, reading very short posts, as those found on many Web sites, might be an acceptable activity to many, including me. But many of my posts are not what I would classify as short and likewise those same posts are definitively meaty. They don't make the stuff of a quick and light read. They make the stuff of something that folks probably want to "hunker down" with and contemplate or, at least, I hope they do. So, to make my articles about "irregular competition" more easily readable by the hunkering segment of the audience that isn't readily attracted to screen-staring, I have put together *Living on a Meme - How Anti-Corporate Activists Bend the Truth, and You, to Get What They Want*.

Living on a Meme - How Anti-Corporate Activists Bend the Truth, and You, to Get What They Want is compiled from a selection of articles published on Telofski.com between August 10, 2009 through August 3, 2010. But, many of these articles are really more than articles. Many of these writings are more essay than article because many of the writings are more analytical in nature than that which you would associate with the word "article." Within the essays in this book, you'll find insights and theories, as well as specific facts, and analysis on how certain irregular competitors operate online and offline to sap a company of its vital reputation. These are essays (or articles if you prefer) that provide observations found nowhere else and that explore new territory; that of combatting the adversarial NGO and anti-corporate activist in cyberspace. Essays, yes, many are. But, so as to use a vernacular with which more people are comfortable, I will also be referring to them alternatively as articles.

Given the increased influence of the social web on the corporate image, people working in the area of corporate reputation management will find these articles/essays to be of value. In the process of reading *Living on a Meme*, you'll get a look at some of the strengths and weaknesses of irregular competition. Oh yes, they have weaknesses; they are not as invincible as people have come to believe. The belief in their invincibility is just another meme, one usually generated by the irregular competitors themselves. Through reading this book, you'll discover how those irregular competitors make use of existing cultural memes, true or not, and how they contribute to those memes, strengthening them and contributing to the degradation of a company's image.

For irregular competitors, "living on a meme," or rather should I say, having *others* "live on a meme," is critical to their strategies. Many of these new and non-traditional business competitors simply could not survive without the memes that exist out there. Nor could irregular competitors succeed unless they perpetrate and simultaneously exploit the memes within our culture. But hold on. Before we go any further, to be sure we are all on the same page, so to speak, let's put an answer to the question "what exactly is a meme?"

A meme (say it as "meeeeeem," by the way), according to the current version of the Merriam-Webster Dictionary is "an idea … that spreads from person to person within a culture." More accurately described, memes are meanings that are spread across a society, often now due to the ease of access to the Internet, and are taken as truth regardless of their veracity. I'm reminded of the adage, "Tell a big enough lie and everyone will believe you." That's a principle on which meme creation and propagation depends. I've noticed that people, as busy as they and we all are, will often not "vet" the information that they ingest. They'll accept a meme as true and run with it. They'll often base much of their daily reality upon it. Do you see why for irregular competitors it is important for them to have people live on a meme, especially *their* meme? Memes are important to the success of the irregular competitor, especially so since they can be so easily created and transmitted.

This book is divided into 12 chapters, one for each month of the year of my insights. The chapters start in August. Why do the chapters start in August and not January? As you'll come to learn in the two parts of the essay entitled "You Could Say That This Post Serves as My Annotated Resume," it was in mid-2009 that I integrated my competitive intelligence expertise with my social media monitoring research experience and transitioned my consulting business from monitoring what consumers were saying about companies to what NGOs and activists were saying about those same companies. Why? Because I found that what the irregular competitors were saying about companies was far more damaging than what their customers were saying *and* no one had comprehensively studied the NGO and activist and characterized them as the irregular competitor that they have become.

My fourth book, *Insidious Competition - The Battle for Meaning and the Corporate Image*, broaches and explores this idea. Prior to August 2009, being more of an "ordinary" social media consultant, most of my blog posts were about the more run-of-the-mill problems in social media marketing. However, starting in August 2009, I devoted my blog writing to this uncommon problem within social media, this insidious business problem of irregular competition. So, in this book, I take you on a journey of what irregular competition is, how it is effective, how it evolves, and how you might want to start thinking about it. Do you want to live on the meme provided by irregular competition? Or do you want to consider another reality?

Now, this book isn't just a repackaging of my blog postings. Don't worry. You're going to get more than that. After all, you paid for this book and therefore I want this book to bring you more than just comfortable reading. I want this book to bring you insights and critical analyses. So to give you that bonus, that exclusive supplement, I've done two things. First, I've removed from the blog 23 of some of the most popular articles on Telofski.com. Those 23 articles appear only here in "Living on a Meme." Each of those 23 articles will be flagged with an "Exclusive" note next to it. Second, at the end of each chapter I augment the salient points of that month's postings with "Take-Aways." Those Take-Aways are a critical analysis of the essays and articles in the chapter, pointing out for you how what we just discussed relates to irregular competition's reliance of living on a meme or their hope that people are living on that meme for them. The better to help you manage irregular competition, I hope.

Here's a housekeeping note before you depart on your journey of *Living on a Meme*. Because this is a book and not a Web site, there will of course be no hyperlinks. However, to maintain the sourcing integrity of these writings, where a sourcing hyperlink originally appeared in the post, I have used the good, old-fashioned method of a reference note. All references run sequentially throughout the book and may be found referenced in the References section. You will also notice that in some of the pieces there is the phrase "click here." As I mentioned above, there will be no clicking. But because I wished to maintain the editorial content of the original posts, I have left those "click here" references in. Where you see the phrase "click here," if there is no reference note indicating a source, it will be quite clear from the context of the sentence as to where "here" refers.

For comments about this book, you may certainly go to Telofski.com and make a comment.

With this Introduction out of the way, I thank you for picking up a copy of *Living on a Meme - How Anti-Corporate Activists Bend the Truth, and You, to Get What They Want* and hope you enjoy the trip through the following pages.

Chapter One

The Ideas Begin to Coalesce

Psychic Profit is as Powerful as Monetary

August 10th, 2009

Category: Activism

There are many different types of competitors out there. The most well-known is the "garden variety competitor," or the company with which you go "head-to-head" in your industry. This is the one that is the easiest to wrap your mind around. There are others, too many others. Some of which I'll discuss in later posts. Today, let me discuss the most obvious.

Direct or indirect competitors, are companies which offer a product or service that can also fulfill the needs, wants, and desires of your consumer/customer. These types of competitors could be head-to-head product rivals, like one brand of television against another brand. Or they could be indirect competitors like television programming versus video gaming versus online gaming.

This is basic marketing theory. But what's not so basic is this:

> **The realization that direct or indirect competitive forces can be at work within social media to affect your brand negatively. And these forces don't always take the form of the "garden variety" competitor.**

Let's bring in the concept of the "brand evangelist," the person or persons who carry on and on with glowing testimony and opinion about how good a particular product or service is. Call them fans, devotees, disciples, evangelists or whatever you like. They're out there and much has been written about them. But there is always a yin to a yang. If there is a hot, then there must be a cold. If there is good then there must be evil. If there are evangelists, then there are "anti-evangelists."

I know you may not want to "hear" this, or more accurately put "read" this. But, there are "brand anti-evangelists" out there. I've read them. You've read them. And we'll learn more about them in future articles that I will write here. They come in different flavors and sizes. Their motivations are all over the map. They're not all just peeved consumers. There's one thing they all have in common, their objective. They want your brand image. They want to control that brand position.

Yes, their motivations may be all over the map, but what isn't hard to discern is that their profit is "psychic," not monetary. They feel complete when they take that monetary profit you want and move it elsewhere. They are atypical, irregular, uncommon competitors. They're out there and they want control of that brand image.

Social media is the tool they can use to achieve their psychic profit.

A Web of Activists?

August 21st, 2009

Category: Activism

Here's an interesting quote regarding activists and their efforts to influence corporate policy:

> *That a one-man NGO armed with just a laptop computer, a Web site and a telephone calling card can, with his allies, influence a huge multinational corporation illustrates the role social activists can play in a world that's going increasingly online.*

This quote refers to a June 2005 WSJ article published on the GlobalPolicy.org website. To read the entire article, click here.[1] Think about that: a world that is going increasingly online. That article was written four years ago, before social media was little more than a glimmer of an idea to take the human jones for interaction into the cybersphere. And the online state of that world today looks, in comparison, very under-connected. So you can imagine the power that social activists have with social media at their fingertips.

Prior to the social web, organization was one of the roadblocks to activism. But now, with much of the developed world online and growing every day, activism has gotten a shot in the arm. The foundation of activist organization is held together by social relationships based on a common interest. Without that social glue, activism would fall apart. And it's that social glue that's put into hyperdrive within social media.

For corporations, social media provides a double-edged sword. Companies want people to discuss their products and services in social media. But the rise of the social web allows people, activists, the opportunity to discuss those products and services within the context of forming a political or social action against them.

That saying is really true, "You can't have your cake and eat it, too." Yin and yang.

Chapter One - The Ideas Begin to Coalesce
——— Take-Aways ———

As I said in the Introduction to this book, it was in August 2009 that my thinking about the business threats I saw in my social media monitoring work were greater from activists than they were from customers and consumers. This is the time when various thoughts I had about the activities of activists on the social web began to converge into thoughts about calling them irregular competition. I had not come up with the term "irregular competition" as yet, but I felt that there was a force out there that was potentially more powerful and threatening than most other business factors that companies face daily.

Through my mind ran the line from the Bob Dylan song, "Ballad of a Thin Man," where the line goes "Something is happening here, but you don't know what it is, do you, Mister Jones?" I was Mister Jones; I didn't know what it was. But I could sense that whatever it was, it was important, and my "jones" was that I wanted to know more.

I wanted to know more because in my travels across the social web and in my monitoring of conversations in that environment, I saw that the activists were more committed than consumers in their brand detraction, more vitriolic, more in it for something other than personal satisfaction to be gained from the kvetching about purchasing a faulty product or service. At that time, the social media adage "Velocity, Virality, Veracity" was bantered about frequently in the mainstream and business press, as well as repeated ad nauseum in social media. That saying was coined to express how fast, how far, and how truthfully a thought, or meme, could or would propagate through social media, and in the social media monitoring businesses, mine being one of them, the adage was used as a measuring model to test meme propagation for clients. In my own social media monitoring work, I thought it appropriate to add to that saying the word "Vitriolity." (Yes, I know "vitriolity" is not a word, but it sounded and fit better than saying the correct word which would be "vitriol.") So, I used it and it picked up interest from my clients. Why did it pick up interest?

Well, I think that term, and the augmented adage gained traction with my clients (many of whom weren't experts in English grammar, anyway, so they never even noticed) because there seemed to be something spiritual behind what the activists were doing online. The word vitriolity was primal and related to the activists behaviors. There was no money in for the activists, so there must have been something deeper, some sort of personal satisfaction. There must have been something they gained psychologically by trashing a company mercilessly online. A greater sense of self? Proof that they could "stand up to the man?" A feeling that they were helping society and thereby achieve self-validation for taking up space in the Universe? All of these things, or others?

I didn't know. But I wanted to find out. It was these feelings and thoughts that were in my mind when I wrote "Psychic Profit is as Powerful as Monetary." These people that I saw writing about the perceived wrongs of companies didn't all come across as nut-jobs. They, and even the nut-jobs amongst them, seemed to be driven by an inner motivation that wasn't going to be compensated in dollars and cents.

In August 2009, I was about two-thirds of the way through the writing of my fourth book, *Insidious Competition - The Battle for Meaning and the Corporate Image*. That book was based on my experiences with social media monitoring to that time and, based on my social media monitoring experiences, contained a look at how meaning was manufactured and manipulated on the social web by many different types of players, activists being only one of the nine types of groups that I identified as "insidious competitors" to the corporate image.

When I was doing research for the activist chapter of the book, I found the source that appeared in the "A Web of Activists?" post. It was then that I was struck with how powerful social media could be in the achievement of the objectives of activists who had companies in their sights. And what I felt was particularly disconcerting was how those activists could use so easily the "meme-mangling" tools that abounded in social media. I discussed in *Insidious Competition* the ways in which reality is created and how it is "bent" on the social web by various groups, activists being only one of those groups. The creation of the meme, the leveraging of existing memes, the bending of the meme I saw as being important and highly available to activists on a social web that was growing by leaps and bounds.

CHAPTER TWO

Taking It to the Marketplace

Online Activism an "Affirmative" Action?

September 1st, 2009

Category: Activism

In reading recently about political campaigns online and about the activist actions that spring up around them, I was struck by a quote [2] from Carol Darr of the Institute of Politics, Democracy, and the Internet which is at George Washington University. She is quoted as saying:

> *Given that the Internet is interactive and requires an affirmative action on the part of the users, as opposed to a passive response from TV users, it is not surprising that the candidate has to be someone people want to touch and interact with.*

What she means is that in online activism, no matter it's objective, the Internet users must actively engage with the topic, seek it out, affirmatively, and be attracted to it in the first place. Whether the issue with which you choose to engage is a candidate or an abstract concept, the process remains the same. She compares this Internet process to TV which she describes as a more passive medium. But let's consider this idea instead of accepting Internet media as wholly affirmative.

What about Twitter?

True, with Twitter you must take an "affirmative" action and sign into the thing. It doesn't just appear before your eyes without doing so. Neither does TV, for that matter. You must at least turn the TV on. And you do the same with Twitter. You turn it "on." And then, based upon your selection of followers, you are either greeted or assailed with message types that you are actively seeking or with message types that you aren't actively seeking, kind of like on TV.

I suppose we could consider the now-famous "Motrin Moms"[3] flap an issue of commercial activism. Commercial literally, as the "Motrin Moms" collectively exerted their pressure and caused the maker of Motrin to remove a commercial video which some found objectionable. But in this incident, which has been well-documented (just Google "Motrin Moms" and you'll find all you need on the incident), the moms weren't actively, affirmatively, seeking out information about commercial videos that they might find objectionable. Many of the people who joined into the cause were simply watching their Twitter accounts, and discovered the incident that way. Passively.

So, is online activism always a product of affirmative action? Not if Twitter has anything to say on any subject.

The Future of Activism?

September 15th, 2009

Category: Activism

Here are some results from a survey taken late last year (2008).

I'm not attesting to the validity of this survey, since very little information about its construction is available. But I present the information here only as a point of interest.

On the blog EducationAndClass.com were posted results of a survey addressing the question:

Where's the future of activism?

The largest percentage answer given was for "non-students" (presumably adults) and was designated as "The Marketplace." Meaning that the action area for activism was in the marketplace. Business? Boycotts? Protests? I suppose. The next largest percentage shown for non-students was Congress. Interesting that the commercial arena was chosen over expressing your opinions to your congressperson.

The article notes that the survey may not have been scientific, yet it raises some interesting points for further research, at the very least.

Click here [4] to read their entire article.

Chapter Two - Taking It to the Marketplace
—————— Take-Aways ——————

As you can see, in the first two months of Year One I had only four posts related to this topic of irregular competition and their meme-ing behaviors. One of the reasons for this is, that at that time, I was aggressively pursuing the finish of *Insidious Competition*, so most of my writing energy was going into that work. But no worries, you will see that as Year One progresses the number of essays per chapter will increase.

I originally wrote "Online Activism an 'Affirmative' Action?", the first article in this chapter, to make the point that online activism doesn't need to be something in which people must actively engage. Online activism, and the irregular competition that performs it, can work its magic even when Internet users are only passively engaged, just like television can. Meaning that the Internet, and social media in particular, holds much potential to attract a passive audience and subject that audience to the memes that activists want propagated.

The second article, "The Future of Activism?," drives home my argument about the danger to companies that can exist from this widespread, passive audience attention to online activism. I was astounded when I read that survey respondents believed that the future venue of activism would be in the marketplace, rather than in the political arena. After reading that survey, which remains alarming even if not statistically significant because it shows that even passive participation on the Internet, that growing medium, with all the memes abounding there, could produce activism, I redoubled my work in the research of irregular competition and dedicated myself to learning how this new business threat ticks.

So, now that you have some very basic understanding of irregular competition and how it threatens business from within social media (and please let me emphasize that what I have presented to this point is a *very, very* basic look at what irregular competition means), let's move on to October and take these ideas a bit further.

CHAPTER THREE

Getting Into the Meat

Donated Ad Space for the Social Good?

October 22nd, 2009

Categories: Activism, Threats

In an article in today's Ad Age Digital [5], Allison Mooney discusses the advent of ad networks dedicated to the "social good." She starts off her article by saying:

Now that President Obama has issued a call to arms for activism ...

Well, that's not actually what the president is calling for. What he is calling for is an increase in volunteerism (and he's not the first president to do that, by the way), not activism. Volunteerism and activism are two very different things. But her lead-off sentence does get one's attention.

Allison continues her article and segues this idea into news about the creation of Publishers With a Purpose [6], a consortium dedicated to "encouraging Web site publishers to pledge 5% of their total ad inventory to selected nonprofits and social causes, with the shared goal of simply doing good." Uh-huh. On the surface it seems like it's all good, but let's dig deeper. Let's get past the all warm and fuzzy stuff. There are at least two things about this idea that concern me. In no order of importance:

Selected nonprofits and social causes.

Who selects these non-profit organizations which will be the recipients of the web site publishers' largesse?

The shared goal of simply doing good.

Who says that the selected organizations are "doing good?"

Prior to the creation of such a network, non-profits had to earn "economic votes" in order to have the money to place ads at all. Those economic votes were in the form of donations "democratically" given by a constituency of thousands or tens of thousands. The nonprofits' ideals were therefore vetted by many, many people. But with the creation of such an ad network, the nonprofits now do not need to gain those democratically awarded economic votes. The vetting process is severely impaired. The nonprofits simply have to convince the small constituency of Publishers With a Purpose that the ideals of the nonprofit have merit. Sounds like a concentration of power.

Such power can have negative impact on business.

Not all nonprofits have an idea of social good that everyone would agree with. And, indeed, many ideas that may be listed under the "social good" label, may have negative effects upon business, creating inefficiencies and costing jobs. A loss of jobs can never be considered to be for the "social good."

By giving 5% of ad space to such organizations, business may actually be giving organizations who compete with business more strength, adding to the power of a class of business competitor that I call "irregular," i.e., not your usual garden-variety type of head-to-head competitor. And by awarding that strength, participating publishers may actually help consolidate market and social power within the hands of fewer individuals.

Allison wraps up the article by saying, "sounds like a great way to further corporate social responsibility efforts." Yes. It certainly does. But all corporate social responsibility efforts are not necessarily worth furthering simply because they are labeled as such.

From Market Street to Commune Street

October 26th, 2009

Category: Personal Observations

Just a passing thought. Earlier today I rode down a newly created street in my town. The street is in a newly constructed town business center and is named "Market Street."

Any time a street is named as such, it makes me think of what a great society this is; that people are given the opportunity to make as much of themselves as is within their ability to do so. Yet, as I completed my drive down my local Market Street, I wondered that given all the shifts to the political left that we have recently seen within the United States (and indeed, more of these shifts have been experienced in some states more than in others), how long will it be until we see business district streets named "Commune Street" or "Social Good Avenue?"

Just a passing thought. But is it far-fetched?

Leftists and Big Business ... Strange Bedfellows.

October 27th, 2009

Categories: Activism, Threats, NGOs

Activists and companies used to fight like cats and dogs. Apparently, that cliche can no longer be used as a rule.

Per a recent opinion column [7] on FoxNews.com, groups traditionally seen as left-leaning are getting together with big business and government to hammer out environmental policy.

Hey. What happened to the rights of the voter and the shareholder in determining environmental policy?

According to the Fox News article written by Tom Borelli, the coalition We Can Lead is a broad-based coalition of activist groups and energy and technology companies. Among the companies in the coalition are Hewlett-Packard and Duke Energy. Among the left-wing activist groups, reportedly, are CERES and the Apollo Alliance. The former is reported to be a coalition of investors and labor/environmental organizations that push companies to further environmental policies. The latter is reported to be a coalition of business, environmental, labor, and community leaders. The board members of the Apollo Alliance are, according to the article, members of the United Steelworkers and the Service Employees International Union (SEIU).

In the race to look more "green" than their competitors, companies are throwing in with activists and, as Borelli pointed out in his article, after years and years of fighting the activists, companies have apparently decided to "switch rather than fight," in a take-off of the old Tareyton cigarette commercial.[8]

Okay. Ecology is good. I'm not in favor of wrecking the Earth. But is all this action on behalf of Mother Earth really necessary? And who decides if it is necessary? Who decides if the decisions made and campaigns pursued by We Can Lead are the right way to go? The left, in social media, likes to support the concept of crowd-sourcing, democracy in action via new technologies. But do we see any truly democratic action from groups like We Can Lead on behalf of the people for whom they ostensibly act?

Where do the shareholders, the owners, of Duke Energy and Hewlett-Packard stand on the issues for which We Can Lead advocate? Where do the constituents of the politicians who We Can Lead lobby stand? And who told We Can Lead that they could lead? Yes, they *can* lead. But who told them they *should*? And has anyone given any thought to what the throwing in of the green does to the economic process?

Leftists and big business ... now that's a dangerous combination.

Activists Attack The "Highly" Profitable Health Insurance Industry

October 29th, 2009

Categories: Activism, Anti-Corporatism, NGOs

As we watch the media during this current health care debate, we can see that health care reform activists and progressives are driving the debate with a recurring mantra: high-profit health insurance companies are evil. It's a well-worn, yet still effective tactic, that of activists and NGOs painting the corporate ogre as a greedy, highly-profitable, money-grubbing villain in a drama sure to tantalize. For an example of this type of tactic, let's take a look at a recent AFL-CIO blog post.

On October 7, 2009, the AFL-CIO Now Blog posted "Health Care Action: Union Activists Visit Congress, Deliver Letters from Consumers." [9] In the fifth paragraph of this blog post appears this phrase:

> *... insurance companies that put their profits far, far above the people they are supposed to serve.*

The AFL-CIO blog perpetuates and exploits the drama to which I referred above and in doing so via this phrase they express two opinions: 1) that health insurance company devotion to its customers is lousy; and, 2) that the insurance companies are overly profitable.

For another example of the tactic of painting a money-grubbing ogre, there is also this passage from The Progressive which in an article titled "Health Care Reform on the Homestretch" dated September 13, 2009 said:

Kucinich begins hearings tomorrow in the domestic policy subcommittee entitled 'Between You and Your Doctor: The Bureaucracy of Private Health Insurance' with a witness list that includes the family members of patients denied needed care because the industry needs to maintain its high profit margins. [10]

Again, here they are going for the tactic of painting the health insurance industry as money-grubbers with attention to sacrificing customer service in favor of a buck.

Well, I'm not going to tackle the customer service/attention issue. That one can vary company to company, and certainly service at many companies just plain stinks. But I will tackle the assertion by activists, NGOs, and progressives of a health insurance industry that is "highly" profitable. How will I tackle that? I'll use some facts.

In Fortune Magazine's list of the Global 500 appears a ranking of the 35 most profitable industries. In looking at the rankings for 2008 (the most recent available as of the date of this article), we see the following listing for return on revenues:

1. Mining, Crude-Oil Production 19.8%
2. Pharmaceuticals 19.1%
3. Tobacco 12.3%

Now, those are very good profitability numbers. I wouldn't call them obscenely profitable, but I would call them very good.

But hold on. Where is the health insurance industry? Let's continue farther down the list.

13. Beverages 4.2%
14. Health Care: Insurance and Managed Care 3.7%
15. Metals 3.7%

There it is. The health care insurance industry's profitability is ranked #14 out of 35 industries ranked. I wouldn't call that 3.7% wildly profitable. Even in this relatively stagnant stock market we now experience, the health insurance companies could just exit the market and stick their money in moderately aggressive investments and do at least as well. They could even stick their money in long-term CDs and do much better.

To see other industries that are much more profitable than health insurance (for example, "money grubbing, evil" industries like food products, household products, building materials, and shipping), click here [11] to take a look at the Fortune Magazine industry rankings referenced above.

When activists and progressives characterize as "highly and unfairly profitable" an industry that makes only 3.7%, they just look silly. But to many folks the activists, NGOs, and progressives making these claims would not seem silly because many folks just don't take the time to look at the facts. The folks rely instead on the media-fueled drama which pits David against the overwhelming Goliath. But just remember, Goliath wasn't as overwhelming as he was cracked up to be.

Few things really are what they are cracked up to be, unless of course they are being used in a political campaign.

Chapter Three - Getting Into the Meat
—————— Take-Aways ——————

Here, at this point in *Living on a Meme*, is where we start getting into the "meat" of my arguments.

In "Donated Ad Space for the Social Good?," we see an example of journalist turned activist. How so? Via a meme.

The author, Allison Mooney, builds the premise for her article on a meme that has been flying around since President Obama took office, that the president is calling for all Americans to become activists. Not true, but believed to be true. This equals a meme. Although I neglected to cite my source in my original posting, I will do so here. The president, as have many presidents before him, called for Americans to *volunteer*. That call can be plainly seen at http://change.gov/americaserves/, a White House Web site. Ms. Mooney presents no reference of a presidential call to *activism* and is thereby riding on a meme which was floating around the social web during the time she wrote her article. In her article, she uses that meme to legitimatize what she's going to tell you next, that publishers will be giving free ad space to various non-profit social causes.

Well, as far as the actual distribution of the free ad space goes, I raised my concerns in the article. But there's one further point, one concerning memes and that free ad space, that I'd like to make here. Giving free ad space to social causes, who ride on memes in a manner similar to the way Ms. Mooney did in her article, will only perpetuate the creation and propagation of memes. The ad would bring audience to the social cause Web site or to other offline communications where the memes can continue to pile up, and perhaps award legitimatization to a cause that deserves none. How does that contribute to the social good?

Now, please keep in mind the time during which I wrote that post about the free ad space. Please recall the cultural atmosphere in 2009. Only eight months prior to the time of the writings you see in this chapter, Newsweek published its famous "We Are All Socialists Now" cover (Newsweek, February 26, 2009) and cries of the socialization of the American economy ran rampant on newscasts, both left and right leaning. This socialist thought barrage led me to write my next post "From Market Street to Commune Street" and then straight into "Leftists and Big Business ... Strange Bedfellows."

In "Leftists," I wanted to introduce the idea of left-leaning groups working in tandem with big business, and wanted readers to consider the impact that such associations might have not only on individual company performance, but also what impact these groups might have on the efficiency of the economic system. And right here, right now, is where I want you to start thinking about what those impacts might be when the left-leaning groups, the activists, build their cases and premise their interactions with business on meme. Let's take for example the article " 'Highly Profitable' Health Insurance Industry." My informal review of meme stature tells me that the meme of "fat cat" health insurance companies was one of the biggest, activist-perpetrated memes appearing on the social web during the health care debate of 2009 - 2010. Your own introspective examination can confirm this. Ask yourself this question. How many times in 2009 and early 2010 did you hear the phrase "greedy health insurance companies?" The statistics in the article, from reliable sources, belie that meme. Yet, the meme endured, activists seeking to impact an entire industry prevailed, and the health care reform act was passed, literally in the middle of the night, despite strong public opposition to it. (For health care opinion poll statistics from reliable opinion poll companies, please go to http://www.pollingreport.com/health.htm. These are not memes.)

Are you beginning to get the idea what all of these activist mangled memes can do to business, no less society at large?

Read on.

CHAPTER FOUR

Stand Back.
There Are Memes
to be Exploited.

Free Food is Next on the NGO Agenda

November 3, 2009

Categories: NGOs, Trends

Remember back in the 1990s, when Hillary-Care was being bandied about as a program to provide free medical care for all Americans. During that debate I thought it was only a matter of time until someone went further and started pushing, seriously, for a program advocating free food for all. Perhaps we've reached that point.

Per an article at GlobalGovernanceWatch.org,[12] the Food and Agricultural Organization of the United Nations [13] recently produced a five volume guide entitled the Methodological Toolbox on the Right to Food, [14] the contents of which are very interesting. Let's discuss how the implementation of this publication's call-to-action could lead to free food and, with it, economic instability in the food industry and perhaps social uncertainty.

The article on the Global Governance Watch site states that, since the United Nation's founding in 1948, it has been a goal of the UN that individuals worldwide have the right to an adequate standard of living. In the United States, we call this the "pursuit of happiness." Global Governance Watch (GGW) also says that in 1999, the United Nations clarified this position with General Comment 12 of the UN's International Covenant on Economic, Social and Cultural Rights:

> *... the right to adequate food is realized when every man, woman and child, alone or in community with others, has the physical and economic access at all times to adequate food or means for its procurement.*

As I interpret this quote, its key idea is that governments create an environment where individuals have economic access to food or access to its means of procurement. Very reasonable. In simplified terms, we can call that access a politically-supported environment where those who want a job can have a job so that they can economically access and procure, i.e., buy, food. Again, you have the right to the pursuit of happiness. I support that wholeheartedly.

But GGW reports that in 2005, the game began to change at the United Nations because in that year the General Assembly passed a resolution calling:

… upon States to implement legal and political strategies to ensure that the right to food was not compromised.

Hmm. That's a bit of a shift in thinking, isn't it?

GGW says that for the UN to give "traction" to General Comment 12 and the 2005 resolution, the UN produced the aforementioned Methodological Toolbox on the Right to Food. The Toolbox was recently published (October 23, 2009) and in its website article about the Toolbox, GGW calls specific attention to the first of the five Toolbox volumes. The first volume is entitled "A Guide on Legislating for the Right to Food." [15] In its synopsis of the Guide, GGW interprets the Guide as saying that:

… States must incorporate the right to food into national constitutions … (and) they must establish a "framework" law on the right to food, which sets out obligations for state authorities and private actors and establishes "necessary" institutional mechanisms to enforce right to food legislation and policies.

(The mention of States here is taken to be member states of the United Nations.)

Right now, I'll make a very astute comment, one I'm sure is very often used within academic circles and by political consultants, as well.

"Are you kidding me?"

The United Nations wants to butt into our, the American, constitution to guarantee a right to food? And the UN wants to force the participation of "private actors," let's read that as companies, to participate in that right to food?

What appears to be happening here is that the United Nations wants us to recast that phrase, "the pursuit of happiness," one so engrained in our national consciousness, into a new phrase, something like "the guarantee of happiness."

Let's put the national sovereignty issues aside. I'll leave those to the political scientists to hash out. Right here in this blog, I deal with business issues and how they are affected by social trends and particularly by activists and

NGOs. NGOs like the UN. And one of those business issues is that it should be clear to anyone with at least a basic understanding of economics, capitalist economics that is, that a free food policy could be disastrous.

If food companies are forced to participate in a "right to food" rather than a "right to economic access," serious repercussions will be felt within that industry, compromising the food supply for all. Such actions, although very charitable and humanitarian in their intent, would actually be counterproductive. Here's the scenario.

Let's say there is a legal demand on food companies to make a portion of their production available at no charge. If food companies must provide a significant portion of their output for free, doing so will force prices to rise on the food for which the companies will be remunerated. The result of this scenario would be that there would be less food consumed.

The decrease in food consumption would begin with paying customers on the lower end of the income scale. As food prices rise, to cover production and distribution of the food for which the company receives no compensation, lower income consumers would not be able to absorb the increases. They would buy less food, and indeed most likely join the ranks of individuals receiving the free food, thereby increasing the proportion of the market which receives the free food. This increase in free food recipients would raise food prices further.

Spiraling increases of food prices would occur, with the paying market segment becoming smaller and smaller and, accordingly, profits becoming smaller and smaller or non-existent. At some point the food company would decide to exit the progressively unprofitable market or go bankrupt. The exit of the food company would necessitate other food companies to feed the defunct company's non-paying consumers, for free of course, and the cycle would repeat. Food companies would fall progressively, like dominos.

And as the food companies fall, unless supported by government subsidies which presents different economic problems, "food fights" may begin. Not fights with food. Fights for food.

No. Although this idea the UN has might seem like an altruistically good idea, in practicality the concept of free food, like free health care, only brings negative results and exacerbates the problem it was intended to solve in the first place.

Activism: Harm to the Body Politic?

November 6, 2009

Categories: Activism, Anti-Corporatism, NGOs, Tactics

In their battle against business, one tactic of activists is to challenge the legal parameters within which corporations operate.

In reading about this tactical approach, I came across an article entitled "Paradigm Shift: Challenging Corporate Authority" [16] and written by Paul Cienfuegos. This article appears in a book entitled The Global Activist's Manual, edited by Mike Prokosch and Laura Raymond. On the first page of the article, author Paul discusses how early Americans, unlike modern Americans, understood that a corporation was an artificial entity, one created by law and people. He states that in 1834 the Pennsylvania legislature declared a corporation as a "creature of the law" and that it should be shaped "for any purpose that the Legislature may deem most conducive to the common good."

This position encompasses very astute insights by Paul. He makes the distinction between a corporation and a human. The former being manmade, while the latter being a creation of the Almighty. The corporation being manmade should then be responsible to those who created it, which he equates with the people of the state where the corporation was formed. Excellent point.

Paul continues, "People understood that they had a civic responsibility not to create artificial entities that could harm the body politic, interfere with the mechanisms of self-governance, and assault their sovereignty." Again, all excellent points which I take as Paul saying that the corporation should be responsive to the people who, through their state legislature, created the corporation. Sound reasoning and the basis of a tactic which can be used in the never-ending battle between activists and business corporations.

Activists would adopt this tactic and take it into the legal arena when battling business corporations. The activists' tactic would be to force the legislatures to make business corporations more responsive to the people, who created the corporation in the first place. Yes, again sound reasoning and brilliant thinking.

But brilliance can cut both ways and payback is always a bitch.

Businesses are not the only organizations that are formed under state corporation law. NGO and activist organizations are also formed under the corporate statutes of a state. Can anyone reasonably, semantically, and validly state that NGO and activist corporations do not "harm the body politic" or "interfere with the mechanisms of self-governance" or assault the sovereignty of the people?

Tactics can be turned around.

NGOs and activist corporations benefit from the limited liability protection of state corporation laws. The people of the state have afforded those organizations that privilege. In return the people of a state should expect that their interests should be represented as the "common good." But no one elects NGOs or activists to act in the peoples' interest. NGO and activist corporations decide on their own what the "common good" should be. Through the non-democratic processes under which NGO and activist corporations operate, these organizations by definition "harm the body politic," and "interfere with the mechanisms of self-governance," and assault the sovereignty of the people.

When pursuing or recommending a tactic, perhaps its best to assess how it can be used against one's own position.

Will Too Much Transparency Be Bad for All of Us?

November 11, 2009

Categories: Activism, Anti-Corporatism, NGOs, Strategy

Activist and NGO calls upon companies to act in a more transparent fashion are fine, but only up to a point.

Although I am a business advocate, I'm absolutely not in favor of companies adopting questionable processes, cheating consumers, or raping the land. I am a business advocate to the point of business being necessary and beneficial for the larger society.

So when I hear calls for "transparency," such as is the mantra of many a social media guru, I think that transparency directed at the interested consumer is good, but we can't take those calls too far. As the adage goes, "Too much of anything is not a good thing." Why would I say this? Let's use the following quote as a point of illustration.

In a June 2008 Fast Company article entitled "Buying Local - Isn't it really about Social and Environmental Responsibility?," [17] we see the oft-repeated call-to-action under the topic:

Questions Conscious Consumers should ask:

Transparency and Accountability: is it possible for me to learn where the materials to make the good came from and who made, transported, distributed, and retails the good?

Can I contact anyone of these organizations if I want to learn more?

Before I moved into the area of macro-marketing consulting and analysis of anti-corporate activism, I was a competitive intelligence (CI) analyst. I made my living by examining the strengths and weaknesses of my clients' competitors. One thing that would have simplified my job as a CI analyst would have been more "transparency." When I was a CI analyst, had I known: where my clients' competitors sourced their materials, who transported them, who distributed them, and exactly who retailed them, my analyses would have been absolutely devastating to the competitors my clients were paying me to examine.

With that intelligence, I would have been able to easily zero in on the competitor's cost profile and from there I would have easily been able to back into the competitor's profit margin. Easily. Devastatingly. My clients would have been ecstatic. Good for my clients. Not so good for the competitor. That transparent competitor would have "shot themselves in the foot."

In capitalist markets, and in America we still are a capitalist society at least for the time being, too much transparent information floating around can be bad for the business that releases that info. Excessive transparency can cause reduced competitiveness and with that reduction in competitiveness can go the company itself. "Self-imposed" transparency can cause a company to leave the marketplace, i.e. go out of business, taking the jobs of hundreds or thousands of individuals with it.

And with that company goes competitiveness across the industry. The companies left to compete in that marketplace, companies that are perhaps not as transparent, read that as "stupid," become fewer, consolidating market power. With consolidation of power comes higher prices and fewer jobs through which the work force can finance those higher prices.

In other words, based upon my experiences as a CI consultant, what I can see as a product of too much corporate transparency is a dystopia.

Too much of anything is not a good thing.

Wrap Your Argument in a Principle

November 12, 2009

Categories: Activism, Irregular Competition - Rainforest Action Network, Tactics

Chevron has been embroiled in an environmental case concerning their operations in the Amazon rainforest. The controversy and legal wrangling has been going on for quite a while. Just Google "chevron amazon lawsuit" and you'll see what I mean. Today I'm not commenting on that case per se, but what I am commenting upon is a tactical maneuver by the Rainforest Action Network (RAN).

In a recent article from NGO Watch, [18] it was stated that Chevron said they had been relieved of the liability for the environmental problem via a release from the Ecuadorian government. Per the article, RAN rebutted the claim by Chevron saying:

> *By focusing energy on evading responsibility instead of cleaning up the mess in Ecuador, Chevron is letting children suffer from some of the world's most heinous environmental destruction when they could be doing something about it.*

In the article from NGO Watch, the quote was attributed to Rebecca Tarbotton, Program Director of Rainforest Action Network.

This particular quote caught my attention. It caught my attention because I am currently dealing with the principles of propaganda in researching a new book. In my research, I deal with the principles of propaganda as laid down in the seminal book Propaganda, written by Jacques Ellul.

This 1965 classic deals with the elements of communication and what makes a successful message. One of those elements Jacques discusses is the Fundamental Currents of Society, and within those currents he places the Four Values of Daily Life. One of those four values is youth, or we can interpret that as children. He maintains that bringing into a message any of the four values, and their support thereof, will greatly increase one's argument and make that message more effective.

So very well-played. Bringing the children into the argument. We see this happen periodically and are somewhat accustomed to it. But do we really realize why it works? Why bringing the children into the argument can contribute to the effectiveness of the message?

Jacques Ellul discusses this in-depth. He says, also within the Fundamental Currents of Society and within what he describes as the Four Sociological Suppositions, that the prime objective of humans is to attain happiness. Seems reasonable, yes? And he supports the notion that without youth there can be no progress in society and that without progress humans cannot obtain the happiness.

So, is the argument really about the principle of the protection of children, or is the argument actually about the principle of the attainment of individual human happiness?

To whichever principle you subscribe, the fact remains … wrapping your argument in a principle can be very effective. And the bigger the principle, so much the better.

Personal Charity vs. Charity-By-Law

November 18, 2009

Categories: Activism, NGOs

There are three primary concepts on which society functions: faith, rule of law, and commerce. When these three key functions are allowed to find their optimum, society can really hum along. They act independently, but yet together. There are some overlaps among their functions, naturally. Such as when the ideas of faith form the basis of law, or when the principles of law are used to modify commerce, or when the fruits of commerce are used to support faith or government. Venn diagrams are always interesting and revealing.

The dangers to society though, I think, are when the Venn diagrams of the three primary concepts overlap too much or when one circle overshadows the other. Perhaps we have reached that point of overlap and overshadow.

Over the past few decades I've seen the influence of faith fade in the daily lives around me, with its replacement coming either in the sphere of government or commerce. Faith serves many a purpose. One of which is to support charity, and the caring of individuals unable to do so for themselves. As the influence of faith has receded, so has its ability to offer care to those who need it. And instead of that faith-based care, that which was originally called "charity," the need has been replaced by a faceless societal driver. That driver is from the rule of law, or what we call government.

The Venn diagram of the triad has changed, such that the circle representing faith has gotten smaller, while the circle representing rule of law has grown larger, usurping some of the functions of faith.

When charity was faith-based, the charity was provided by individuals. Charity was then personal. Faith called upon us to be charitable, individually, personally, and offer ourselves to the service of others, on a one-to-one basis. Those in need benefitted as did those who helped. Society was enriched, one helping gesture at a time. We felt good about ourselves.

In an article entitled "Government Usurps Charitable Giving and Nature," [19] author John Atwood explores this idea. He says:

> *An act of charity ennobles the grateful recipient and burnishes the kinder spirit of the giver.*

As the circle of government has grown larger in the Venn diagram of society, as government, aided by NGOs and activists, has increased its influence within society, we are poorer for the lack of good that is created. As John Atwood points out:

> *Government can't bring good to its people, it can only bring force and power and results, numbers, outcomes. The good is within the*

individual and the people. The "good" government does is only defined by the elites who determine those results, outcomes, numbers and forces to exert.

John makes an excellent point. In other words, governments aided through NGOs and activists, have taken the "good" out of charity. They have helped remove the "faith" we used to have in each other. The faith that we would all do right by each other. That faith has been reduced to nothing more than the payment of a tax to a body of law or the payment of a donation to a NGO or activist organization, which is to be distributed by a bureaucrat, and disguised as charity.

And what about that third circle in the Venn diagram of society? That circle representing commerce.

The three concepts of faith, law, and commerce complemented each other. Faith bound us to each other and provided the spiritual needs. Commerce drove the economic engine and provided the earthly needs. And law? Well, law was there to be the arbiter in the inevitable human breakdown of the other two processes.

With the diminution of the faith circle and the enlargement of the law circle, the circle of commerce is left to finance the process of secular charity by law. The circle of commerce becomes the financier of organized, governmental charity. It's a function that commerce was not created to fulfill. Yet, governments, and their assistants in NGOs and activists, call upon commerce to make those contributions, stressing the economic system and pushing it toward dysfunction.

What happens when the circle of commerce ceases to play its new and imposed role in the Venn diagram of society? What happens when governments, with NGOs and activists, push commerce beyond its capability, or willingness to provide? What happens to charity then?

Liberal Access to the Proxy

November 30, 2009

Categories: Activism, Anti-Corporatism, Threats

In a recent Wall Street Journal article, [20] authors Clark Judge and Richard Torrenzano discuss anticipated changes to U.S. Securities and Exchange Commission (SEC) rules which will allow more stockholder freedom of access to the process of corporate resolutions via the annual proxy.

Briefly for those of you unfamiliar with this process, annually corporations have their owners (stockholders) vote on various proposals, foremost of which is the selection of the members of the board of directors.

Per the article, these rule changes would allow various stockholders, or groups of stockholders, to nominate individuals for board seats. That nomination process would be at the expense of the corporation and would, again according to the article, create a campaign and election process much like that of any political election we see staged before us every November. It's forecasted that this process will create more intense debates over various issues before society, offering groups with political agendas such as those of global warming and sustainability, the opportunity to place their candidate of choice on a corporate board. By definition, that candidate of choice would be a candidate who answers to a political constituency, instead of just a constituency of investors, i.e., owners.

A process such as that outlined above would give a clear advantage to activist groups for the placement of their own candidates on a targeted corporate board. This is an advantage which is not currently enjoyed by any activist group. And SEC rule changes such as those proposed above will go a long way to affording more power to activist groups.

But is this just another wrinkle in the everyday ebb and flow of activist vs. corporation? After all, activists and corporations have been wrestling for years. Well, yes, it's possibly a new wrinkle. But I think this wrinkle is more wrinkly than most that have come before it. Why? Well, the article makes the point that, of course, corporations have always had to deal with multiple stakeholders, stakeholders which activists have traditionally claimed to represent. But the article points out something which is the theme of this blog. That theme is that the current environment in which corporations now need to deal with multiple stakeholders, led by activists, is very different. And one of those factors of difference is social media.

Another recent Wall Street Journal article [21] amplifies this point about social media's place in the new corporate activism. For example, in this article by Cari Tuna, it is pointed out that a new social networking site, MoxyVote.com, aggregates "advocates" and individual shareholders so that discussions about various proxy initiatives may be made. The effect of which helps activists to present their position to a group of selected shareholders in a socially-supporting environment.

In her article, Cari Tuna also mentions similar sites which allow advocates and individual investors to engage in political conversation regarding proxy initiatives. One such similar site is TransparentDemocracy.org. This site allows individuals and organizations to post corporate proxy and corporate government election recommendations. Then there is Us.ProxyExchange.org which endeavors to create an exchange via which investors in voting blocs may transfer their proxy to other stockholders. The power of these types of sites for activists is obviously clear.

Such sites enable the activist organization to enter into the corporate proxy process in much the same way that they already enter into the general political process. And the existence of sites such as MoxyVote.com, etc. do much of the organizational work for the activist. Sites such as these present the activist group an audience of previously hard-to-reach individual investors all wrapped up in nice, neat package. And all at no, or virtually no, expense.

Democracy is good, yes. I'm all in favor of individuals becoming more active in their proxy voting process and I have indeed encouraged people to do so in articles I have previously written. Yet, what concerns me in this proposed corporate social media-massaged cyber-democracy is that the interests of the individual stockholders, i.e. the owners, can be substituted for that of stakeholders. This would be very much like that where we have the interests of individual citizen voters replaced by that of one of the two major political parties.

In this proposed model, as Judge and Torrenzano pointed out in their article,[22] the proxy process becomes one that is "about placing people on boards who answer to constituents, not investors." Such procedures have the potential to decrease the importance of capital ownership and reduce it to nothing more than a political process usurped and co-opted by special interests. And don't we have enough of that already?

Chapter Four - Stand Back, There Are Memes to be Exploited
Take-Aways

Carrying over from the previous chapter, the discussion of socialistic advancement in society, touted by many an activist in their battles against business, continues in Chapter Four. In the "Free Food" essay, I suggest how that socialist ideal would manifest in commerce and affect society counterproductively. This seemingly altruistic endeavor of food for all is just that, altruistic. And altruism quickly becomes meme within its own special shield of morality. But when altruism of a specific kind and circumstance is examined under the scope of practicality, and from within the realm of human nature, it doesn't always pass the muster of reason.

The meme of desired transparency in government, in business, in anything, pervades a democratic society. To an extent, yes, of course I think transparency is a good thing. But as I said in that article "Too much of anything is not a good thing." Activists relentlessly exploiting the transparency in business meme can have devastating effects on society, and I painted a very brief picture of what that might look like in "Will Too Much Transparency Be Bad for All of Us?"

In the essay "Wrap Your Argument in a Principle." My research has shown that one of the major strategies of irregular competitors is the exploitation of the meme of protection of the children. The next time you attend to an anti-corporate campaign, just listen. It won't take them long to trot out the idea of whatever it is that their targeted company is doing is ultimately bad for the children. And after a while, through conversation on the social web and elsewhere it can become meme that what those activists are about is "the children," whether or not that is actually true. We'll see later in *Living on a Meme* how that's not consistently true when I begin to break down that meme, showing that the meme is not always *about* the children but sometimes that exploitation of that meme is *through* the children. More on this later.

If wrapped in the meme of protecting children, the effects that anti-corporate activists can have on companies can be significant; devastating if the meme is false. These potential effects must be given more thought when one considers the changes that are, as I write this section of *Living on a Meme*, pending before the United States Securities and Exchange Commission (SEC). New SEC regulations would allow activists to bring their "saving the children" meme to campaigns for the election of corporate directors favored by those activists. The election of men and women under these campaign memes would tug at the souls of shareholders, perhaps enabling the election of individuals who, even though well-intentioned enough, may be singularly meme-focused and not be qualified to take the corporation in the directions it should go.

When selecting the folks who will run our corporations, more than feel-good memes need to be considered. We need to decide who the real heroes are because it is the commercial sector that drives the society.

CHAPTER FIVE

From Hero to Bully

Activist or Corporation. Who's the Hero?

December 4, 2009

Categories: Activism, Anti-Corporatism, NGOs, Strategy

Archetypes. Webster's defines them as a "recurrent symbol in literature, art, or mythology." With reference to psychology Webster's continues by saying that, in regard to Jungian psychology, archetypes are "a primitive mental image inherited from the earliest human ancestors," images which are "supposed to be present in the collective unconscious."

Ah, the collective unconscious. That's the key to what makes us as a society tick.

Everything that happens depends on what makes us tick inside. And those who understand what makes us tick inside, get to control the flow of how things go. But what primitive images, exactly, are they that make us tick and contribute to the control of flow?

I've been reading about these archetypical images in a book by Paul Laudicina entitled *World Out of Balance, Navigating Global Risks to Seize Competitive Advantage.* [23] On page 91 of this book, Paul names some of the archetypes:

> *Hero - implying the spirit of survival.*
> *Outlaw - implying the spirit of rebellion.*
> *Explorer - conveying the idea of the joy of discovery and freedom.*

All positive qualities these are. Certainly, spirits with which most of us would want to be associated. Corporations and advertisers recognized these spirits and their power to influence decades ago. In his book, Paul gives several examples of corporate advertising campaigns which have employed, with great success, these and other archetypes. No wonder we sometimes find the appeals of those "Mad Men" so irresistible. They reach into our souls.

And the reaching into souls, i.e., the employment of the archetype, has not been lost on other types of organizations, some of whom operate at cross-purposes to those who have perfected its usage.

Over the past ten years, since The Battle in Seattle, anti-corporate activists have learned to leverage and co-opt well those principles of the archetype which their opponents had been using, with success, for some decades prior.

In promoting their environmental or labor or economic agendas, activists and their NGO cousins first assumed the role of Outlaw, attracting attention through the leveraging of the spirit of rebellion. They stood out from the rest of society and carved themselves a position outside the normal circle. A position envious to some who occupied the circle of the 9 to 5 grind.

But then, before they went too far outside the normal circle, the NGOs and activists pulled themselves back into the normal social circle by adopting another role, the role of Explorer. They told us they had been outside the circle because they were on a mission of discovery for all of us, and that they were not in it just for themselves. Not withstanding the validity of any of their scientific or economic analyses, NGOs and activist organizations by promoting their agendas with "supporting facts" ventured into issues in the "common interest," making discoveries "affecting everyone" and trumpeting their own freedom to advocate for all.

When they had successfully communicated this message, in doing these things they then almost automatically had the role of Hero cast upon them by the "common interest." The NGOs and activists were then seen as waging a selfless, non-profit battle moving toward survival for us all, against the "faceless," "un-Herolike" for-profit corporation who uses archetypes primarily to portray only their products and services, presumably only for profit. The corporations made the mistake of attaching the archetypes to their products and services, to their profits, rather than to themselves and to what they actually do for society, for the actual common interest.

In such a battle for the archetype, who is likely to win? The Hero. The Outlaw. The Explorer. You think the NGO and activist. But yet, we and the corporation miss the point because the corporation is all of these.

Corporations make a lot of boneheaded mistakes, and since they are not perfect I am not blindly advocating them. (NGOs and activists aren't left out of the boneheaded mistakes category, either.) Yet, who supplies the jobs so that we may feed our children? (Hero.) Who comes up with new products and services that solve our daily problems? (Explorer.) Outlaw? Well, maybe not. But two of three isn't bad, especially the two that contribute so greatly to daily happiness.

But, perhaps just as their opponents used the principles of archetype to turn against them, corporations need to take a page from a playbook they actually wrote and use it to describe themselves, not their products and services, as the heroes and explorers that they actually are.

Activism or Just Keeping Your Mouth Shut?

December 11, 2009

Categories: Activism, Trends

An opinion article [24] about childhood obesity and activism recently appeared in the The Daily Camera, the daily newspaper for Boulder, Colorado.

The article was written by J. Justin Wilson, who is the Senior Research Analyst at the Center for Consumer Freedom, (CCF) a nonprofit coalition supported by restaurants, food companies and consumers to promote personal responsibility and protect consumer choices. Hmmm … could this organization be considered an activist organization themselves? Well, certainly if they are representing the interests of a particular business sector. Although, what I like in that description of the CCF is the promotion of "personal responsibility" as their stated primary goal. More of that sort of "PR" would do us all well.

In the article Justin refers to selected activist initiatives aimed at getting some state legislators to tax certain sugary foods, soft drinks in particular. Many of the usual arguments are made in Justin's article. Such as this one, which for me personally is a bit hard to swallow. (pun intended) He cites no scientific link between soft drinks and childhood obesity. From his article:

> *There is no scientific consensus that sugary drinks are a unique cause of obesity. A scientific review published last year in the American Journal of Clinical Nutrition evaluated the evidence of 12 major studies and found virtually no association between the consumption of sugar-sweetened beverages and children's weight. And an October study found no association between soda consumption and youth weight gain over a 5-year period.*

I suppose the key term in that quote is "unique cause." And you can argue from here to Sunday about whether or not there is a scientific cause underlying this particular issue. Perhaps the children studied don't drink soda, although that idea seems almost as far-fetched as the idea that there is no association between sugar-sweetened soda and weight gain. (If that indeed is true, I going to drink myself silly with Coca-Cola.)

But that's where I think Justin went wrong in his argument. He chose the scientific path as the main basis to support his argument. Science doesn't always a good argument make, and I believe that is especially so when one is representing an activist group, er uh … excuse me, a non-profit coalition of businesses that supports personal responsibility. I feel that Justin's argument would have been better made by hammering home as the central thrust of his article the principle of personal responsibility, because after all that's the declared objective of his organization. Although in the article he did turn briefly to the idea of personal responsibility, his discussion of this form of "PR" was too late in the article and the point was not made nearly powerfully enough. I think he missed his chance here.

Well, hold on, now. Perhaps he didn't make personal responsibility the central theme of the article because that is something kids have very little of. No kid is going to eschew soda for milk if given any opportunity. Or how about some parental responsibility and asking mom and dad to "just say no" when it comes to serving the kiddy bubbly? How about "pounding on" that personal responsibility point a lot more and asking for some shut mouths when it comes to soda consumption?

Oh, just a second. That's right. There's no "unique cause" between weight gain and soft drinks, even though if you "pound down" about five cans of the average soda you will have taken in enough calories for about a third of a pound of fat. [25] (again, puns intended)

Could this be a case of activist vs. activist? With each of them bringing their own scientists into the battle? (You bring your test tube and I'll bring mine.) A case of dueling DIYS (do-it-yourself-science)? Or is this simply an example of a lost opportunity to argue hardily that personal responsibility and keeping your mouth shut in the presence of soda is the best argument made against a trend of activism bent on taxing everything that moves?

You decide.

"Irregular Competition" - The Newest Threat

December 15, 2009

Categories: Anti-Corporatism, Irregular Competition

Competition comes in several classes. Let's discuss.

First of all, you, as a business person, have obviously known about the class of "direct" competitors since you went into business, and probably you have known about this class of competitor as far back as those tender years when you were first able to sit up and recognize for what money was actually used. Direct competitors, of course, are those other companies which sell the same products or services that your own company sells.

Secondly, you've most likely known about the class of "indirect" competitors, also just about as long as you've known for what money is used. When you were a kid with five bucks burning a hole in your pocket, you knew that you could use that moolah to buy a toy or you could use it to buy a movie ticket or you could use it to buy an ice cream cone. None of the companies which produced those goods or that service were direct competitors, but they were indirect competitors vying for that five bucks in your pocket.

The classes of direct and indirect competition are not new. Business people have always taken seriously the impact of direct and even indirect competition, and have planned and altered their business models accordingly. This is well-known.

"Irregular Competition" Introduced

But what perhaps isn't as well-known to you is the class of competition which I have named "irregular competition." That is a term I coin and a concept which I define and introduce to you today.

When your direct and indirect competitors bring their offerings to market, they tell that market just how great are their offerings and how well those offerings can meet the needs and wants of the market targeted. And while making their sales pitch, those direct and indirect competitors play with the image of your company. Your competitors, direct and indirect alike, will take every opportunity to portray your company image in a manner that would not please you and by doing so communicate to your common market how well your products or services do not meet the needs of those consumers that you jointly serve.

Either through comparative advertising, or through innuendo, or via some other communications mechanism, your direct or indirect competition promotes the image of their own company and demotes the image of your company. Again, this is well-known. So if it's well-known, why am I writing about it?

I write about this in order to make a point about competition in general, either direct or indirect, and to tie that point into the less well-known concept of "irregular competition." Competition is not just about promoting competing products or services. It's also about demoting, about tearing down, tearing down the image of the competitor. To tear down the image of a competitor means to battle for what the competitor's company or brand image means, and to achieve an agendized goal in the process.

In the case of your direct and indirect competition, that agendized goal is to sell more products or services than does your company. The irregular competitor is similar in this regard; they have an agenda and a goal. But in the case of the irregular competitor, the nature of their agenda is different. The irregular competitor is not selling products or services. The irregular competitor wants to promote an advocacy agenda at the expense of your company. The irregular competitor wants to promote a program which has as its goal the attainment of some political, social, or cultural change. And one way the irregular competitor achieves its goal is by altering the meaning of your company or brand image in the marketplace.

The irregular competitor which I introduce today is more specifically known as the activist organization, the NGO (non-governmental organization), or the IGO (inter-governmental organization) which pursues an agenda of advocacy for a political, social, or cultural issue and in so doing competes with your company for the meaning of your brand or company image.

Why Would They Do This?

This irregular competition does this because they recognize that by attempting to influence, or even control, what your company or brand image means, the irregular competitor can use the notoriety of that image to achieve publicity and legitimacy for the cause that they pursue.

The irregular competitor is not interested in selling their own products or services that will replace those of your company's in the marketplace. But they are interested in reducing the sale of your products or services, just as are your traditional direct or indirect competitors, in order to pressure your company into helping them achieve their political, social, or cultural goals.

Just As Much a Threat as the Regular Competitor

And because of their agenda and its intent, this irregular competition is no less a threat to your company than the direct or indirect competitor. Indeed, in many ways irregular competition may be more of a threat than the direct and indirect competitor. Therefore, the irregular competitor must be regarded with as much seriousness as the regular competitor.

The irregular competitor is here. They are not going away. They must be dealt with just as any other competitive threat should not be ignored. And it is within this blog, Telofski.com, that we will discuss the ins and outs of dealing with this new competitive threat in your business environment.

Who Says Doing the Right Thing is "Right?"

December 17, 2009

Categories: Activism, Anti-Corporatism

A couple days ago I finished a really great book, Contention and Corporate Social Responsibility by Sarah A. Soule. [26] Although, I purchased this book while wanting to obtain more information about the structure of anti-corporate activism, I bought this book because I also wanted to get additional information on corporate social responsibility (CSR) programs, which are often a knee-jerk response to anti-corporate activist initiatives. Believing that this book was oriented more toward my CSR hunt, and not toward the anti-corporate activism anatomy search, I thought, "Well, I'll buy this one now while I continue to hunt down more works on the anatomy of anti-corporate activism."

After receiving this book and jumping into the first chapter or two, I was pleasantly surprised. This book concerns itself more with the structure and process of anti-corporate activism than it does with the response of CSR. To this point, here is an excerpt from a review I wrote about this book. (The full review appears on both Amazon.com and on my Reading List page in my LinkedIn.com profile at www.LinkedIn.com/in/richardtelofski.)

Although I would have chosen a different title, Sarah Soule turns in a great book here. In this work, Sarah contributes one of the first academic examinations on the structure of anti-corporate activism and its effects on corporate behaviors ... Sarah examines activist initiatives in two time periods: 1960 to 1990 and then from 1990 to present day (2009). Her findings characterize activism, as it affects the corporation, into two different groupings each with historical context, creating a typology by which corporate analysts can categorize activist efforts and devise mechanisms for coping. This typology can be invaluable to corporate analysts attempting to devise various strategies in response to various anti-corporate activist initiatives.

So, in the end, I received that which I sought, but in an indirect manner due to the abstractness of the book's title.

Generally, I liked everything I found in the book such as her approach and her argumentation process, but on page 154 I found a comment with which I must take umbrage.

In the section entitled "The Impact of Anti-Corporate Activism on Corporations," Sarah talks about the key theme of her book being that anti-corporate movements do matter to corporations. As evidence of this assertion, she points to an earlier discussion in the book citing research into the effects of protest on company stock price, as well as other examples of activist influence on corporations as discussed in the book. Of this influence she says:

> *This is good news for activists, of course. But it is also good news for corporations who can find that doing the right thing can actually make good business sense.*

Here comes the umbrage.

The right thing? Who says it's the right thing? This is an attitude that I have found in much anti-corporatist literature, one which automatically assumes that any activist action against a corporation is "right." Right is not always right. To quote Bill Clinton, it would depends on "what the meaning of 'is' is."

"Right," in this sense, is a subjective term, left widely open to interpretation. So, let's go ahead and interpret it."

I have to criticize Sarah here. Throughout the book, I found that she was very objective and didn't appear to lean to one side of the anti-corporate activist argument or the other. That is, until that phrase "doing the right thing" appeared on page 154. Perhaps a more objective way for her to say the same thing would have been "But it is also good news for corporations who can find that doing what the activists suggest can actually make good business sense." Such sentence would have expressed the same thought while preserving her objectivity.

In many cases, yes, a "corporate social responsibility" response to an activist demand can make good business sense. Corporations should not eschew such demands wholesale. But in many cases corporate responses to activist demands do not make good business sense, yet those responses, "right" and "wrong," are positioned under the CSR program, at the expense of the stockholders.

Who says doing the right thing is "right?" Who gets to interpret what is "right" in terms of what activist requests should be folded into the company's CSR program? The answer to that question would turn on who is financing the company. That would be the stockholders. Not the stakeholders.

The stockholders. It's their money which is at risk. And as long as society is still capitalistic, and at least for now in America this is still the case, then I believe that it is up to the stockholders to say whether doing the "right" thing actually makes good business sense. Or not.

The Bully Pulpit of Activism

December 21, 2009

Categories: Activism, Anti-Corporatism, Strategy

By now the controversy of Climate Gate is well-publicized and even starting to simmer down somewhat. Simmer down in the media that is, but perhaps not in the hearts and minds of those deep in the fray and on either side of the issue. Perhaps at this point, the global warming activists are licking their wounds and contemplating a strategic change and a new approach to framing their campaign. And if they aren't, they should be. Here's why.

Back on December 1 (09) there was an interesting article by Debra J. Saunders as posted on the San Francisco Chronicle site (SFGate.com). The article titled "When Scientists Behave Like Bullies" [27] reviewed some of the known faux pas of the Climate Gate gaff - the deep six-ing of the contrary data, the threats of boycotts against scientific journals who printed articles countering the global warming theory, and the alleged threatened punch-out of anti-global warming skeptics. (Somehow I just can't envision scientists getting into a rumble. Can you?) Overall, from her article Debra made a point that:

> *Polls show that Americans are cooling on the notion of man-made global warming. I must credit the bully mentality of activists, whose claims often defy common sense - and at times simple decency.*

Never mind the great opening pun of that paragraph, she makes an excellent point which is …

Nobody likes a bully.

Even before Climate Gate we could see that the global warming movement was suppressing honest discourse on points of view contrary to their own. As activists for a cause, the global warming movement has certainly not been alone in using this strategy. Other activist organizations use bullying as well. But when bullying is recognized by the audience the activist wishes to win, counterproductive results may occur. Audiences are more keen observers than many activists realize. Bully-spotting is easy.

In my new and latest book, *Insidious Competition - The Battle for Meaning and the Corporate Image*, I discuss some strategies that are undertaken by some activists groups and talk about why those strategies, and their supporting tactics, are effective. (Author's Note: When this post was written *Insidious Competition* was then my forthcoming book which was published in June 2010.) *Insidious Competition* is due out in Spring 2010, so I don't want to "reveal the ending." But I can say now that bullying is not one of the strategies that I discuss in the book.

And anticipating the publishing of my new, and fourth book, and to give you a clue as to what those wound-licking global warming activists should now be considering for a new strategic direction, I will say that as a model the wound lickers should look to the Mommy Bloggers.

Certainly not an activist organization per se, Mommy Bloggers still have many of the characteristics of true activist groups. They do many things to create effective messages and to get their points across, but one of the things they do not do is wield the bully pulpit. What strategic position do they take which makes them an effective proponent for almost any issue?

More on this idea as we get closer to publication date. Spring 2010 will be arriving soon.

The Warm and Fuzzy Side of the Anti-Corporate Movement

December 23, 2009

Categories: Humor, Strategy

When you think of the anti-corporate movement usually images of protest and boycott come to mind, with all the rancor, derision, and conflict that come with such things. Think the word "anti-corporate" and our conditioning often leads us into the realm of serious, heavy, and sometimes troubling thoughts.

Well, not today.

Today, think cute. Think warm and fuzzy, literally as well as figuratively. Think yarn.

I recently noticed an article entitled "The Anti-Corporate Gift Guide" [28] on the blog Million Dollar Swim. "Anti-Corporate Gift Guide?" That's a really cute and humorous approach to such a heavy concept. During the holiday season, how could I not read this one? I couldn't. So I did.

This article uses as its theme for anti-corporatism the idea of making gifts to give or the idea of buying handmade articles. This post was written by a woman named Amelia, living in Montreal, and operating a "little yarn shop." Amelia tells us that business was good two weekends ago and that she had many customers rushing into the shop for gift-making materials. I'm glad her shop was busy. I like to see any business do well.

She tells us that to "hold out against consumerism" she will be knitting all the gifts that she is giving this season. (Presumably using materials from her own shop.)

Moving on within this theme of anti-consumerism, Amelia then tells us that if she was to buy gifts this season rather than make them herself, she mentions and pictures about a half-dozen handmade gifts, made by other handcrafters, that she would purchase. You may go to her article here to see those pictures and read those descriptions if so inclined.

I suppose with regard to Amelia's would-be purchase of handmade gifts in lieu of those found at any traditional store, or her preference to make gifts rather than submit to "consumerism," and with regard to her customers who will be using her yarn as handmade "gift raw materials," there will be some lost value-added to the economy, value-added that the Canadian government could have taxed. (Something they really like to do up there in the Great White North.) But, I don't suppose that relatively infinitesimal amount of lost value-added will show up as any negative numbers in any economic report. Unless, of course, this trend continues. But it would seem, at least to my tastes, that such a trend isn't likely to catch fire anytime soon.

Each to his own, as they say. I suppose some folks like this sort of product, but I'll just say that gifts of this type aren't my cup of tea. Perhaps others find them attractive, but I would bet that that segment of the market isn't very large.

And if that segment is actually very small, then big business doesn't have much to worry about from this kind of anti-corporate movement strategy. Yet, I must say that I find this approach to anti-corporatism refreshing, maybe even tongue-in-cheek, and certainly one possessing much more character than the approaches used by pugnacious demonstrators.

Anyway, I wish Amelia the best with her yarn store and hope that her friends and family enjoy their gifts.

I'll be back here on Telofski.com after the first of the year. In the meantime …

Happy Holidays.

Chapter Five - From Hero to Bully
———— Take-Aways ————

In "Who's the Hero," I suggest that the role of hero in our culture has been co-opted by the activist and that corporations have seemingly allowed themselves to be relieved of that role. This, I think, happens because, as I've observed, as activists declare victory after *every* campaign, whether they met their objectives or not (you and I will discuss an example of this later in this book), the meme of activist as hero is perpetuated. Small wonder that more meme is perpetuated. The result of which is that the corporation falls into a "negative meme pit," a pit so deep and one that corporations themselves have for so long dug themselves into, that the road out of that pit will likely be a long, rocky, and precarious one, indeed. Yet, I can see a way for them to get on the road to the "positive meme mountain." They just need a different map.

"Activism or Just Keeping Your Mouth Shut" may provide a strategic clue for the road out of the hole. The route? It's the one marked with the words "personal responsibility." This essay points out a major weakness in the campaign strategy of several adversarial, activist NGOs, particularly the ones who want various food manufacturers to stop making food that the activists allege is making Americans fat. Here's the center of their weakness. The companies do not force their food down the throats of those overweight Americans, yet many activist organizations contend that such is indeed, at least figuratively, the case. And the weakness comes from the implication by those activist organizations that American personal will power is weak. Another meme, and perhaps one that many Americans like to latch onto in an attempt to make themselves feel better about their overeating.

As I pointed out in my essay, the idea of personal responsibility was not used, to my mind, strongly enough as a counterstrategy in the article reviewed and represents not only an opportunity to make Americans feel better about themselves from a position of strength rather than weakness, but also represents an opportunity for corporations to portray Americans as heroes to themselves. No one likes to be thought of as weak. And pointing out this implication, could undermine the meme at the center of this irregularly competitive strategy.

And then we come to the "Irregular Competition" article itself. By mid-December 2009, I had been cogitating on irregular competition long enough to come out with a comprehensive definition of it, putting it into a context that could be understood against that which we normally call "competition." As the concept formed more clearly in my mind, I sought out additional information to augment my idea. Some of that research was reviewed in the article "Who Says Doing the Right Thing is 'Right?' " In writing this article, I was reinforcing a way of thinking, started during the research for *Insidious Competition*, that would carry me on my path of further analysis into what irregular competitors do and how they do it. The way of thinking I'm talking about is semantics.

I discussed semantics extensively in *Insidious Competition*; it is, after all, subtitled *The Battle for Meaning and the Corporate Image*. But at the time of "Right Thing" and "The Bully Pulpit of Activism," I began to more strongly focus my semantical analyses strictly on the activities of activists, some of them bully-like in nature, and how those actions exploit and hoard memes. This is the key, I believe, to "keeping them honest" in their encounters with business, and is very much akin to what they claim to be doing to corporations.

What irregular competitors do is all about semantics; it's all about meaning. That's where one of the nastier battles for business will be in the 21st century, especially given that the global social web is literally at the fingertips of almost every person living in the developed world.

CHAPTER SIX

From Social Entrepreneurism to Extortion

An Activist Strategy to Bank On?

January 5, 2010

Categories: Activism, Strategy

As I mentioned in my last post of last year, "The Warm and Fuzzy Side of the Anti-Corporate Movement," I would be back on Telofski.com after the first of the year. And here I am. You are now reading the "2010 Season Premier."

Happy New Year.

Around the time of my "2009 Season Finale," I caught an article on FoxNews.com about a company called CREDO (credomobile.com). The article, titled "Wireless Company Mixes Liberal Politics with Business,"[29] intrigued me. Author Stephen Clark writes about this wireless phone company who positions itself as "an agent of social change." Stephen says that:

> It (CREDO) pitches its mobile phone services with a vow to fight for 'real' health care reform, free speech, peace and the environment.

Continuing from the article, CREDO has reported that it has raised $63 million for liberal causes such as Doctors Without Borders, Planned Parenthood, ACLU, and Earthjustice. That's a lot of money to be finding its way to various advocacy groups, some of which aren't very business-friendly.

In the article, the main theme is whether or not this type of business strategy is sustainable (no pun intended). Within the article are quoted marketing experts with some saying "yes" while others say "no." The naysayers make their case by stating the obvious strategic view that running a company based on a political agenda will alienate too many potential customers. Additionally, the naysayers cite that a wireless company the size of CREDO, regardless of their positioning strategy, will have a difficult time up against such corporate giants as AT&T or Verizon. While, on the other side, the proponents say that given the level of political rancor and political polarization presently in the country, a "highly partisan" approach could be successful.

The naysayers seem to intimate that CREDO is crazy, in a marketing sense. And yes, I must say that I agree. I think that CREDO might be crazy, but crazy like a fox (again, no pun intended). I'd have to see some marketing research data on this question in order to be sure, but my WAG* on this would be that there is a large enough market segment out there for CREDO to attract, a segment consisting of the political partisanship to which CREDO orients, so that such a marketing strategy may have legs. My WAG is based on my estimate that there are probably at least tens of millions of far-left, or at least left-leaning, adults in the United States, all of which might prefer to send their monthly wireless dollars to a company which will use them to further a political agenda, rather than enrich stockholders.

If you read this blog regularly, you will know that my professional opinion is the opposite; I think companies should enrich stockholders and not causes. But this orientation is not the sort that motivates CREDO, nor the people in the market segment that they target. And it is their motivation, not mine, that is critical within this discussion.

Within the United States, with its current leaning to things liberal, a marketing strategy like that of CREDO might actually work, or work at least well enough so that they can survive while they support various causes. One condition for success in this model is that the company would most certainly need to be privately-held, but I see no indication that CREDO is publicly-held.

Another condition for success is that a strategic operation of this sort would need to leverage social media. CREDO seems to be doing that. With about 38,000 fans on their Facebook page they've made a good start. Although, their Twitter following is around 3500 (about the same as mine, as of the date of this post), with a little effort they could increase that number and use the additional audience to advantage.

No. I have to disagree with the marketing naysayers. This one might have legs. This strategy may contribute to filling the bank accounts of many activist organizations. Conditions in macro-environment, like the aforementioned political situation, line up in their favor. And if this strategy does take off, then it will literally be an example of using a business against the interests of business.

   * Note: WAG is defined as a "wild-assed guess."

Activist Teamwork Scenario

January 7, 2010

Categories: Contrarian, Humor

WARNING: This is a tongue-in-cheek post. Please enjoy it in the facetious spirit in which is was intended.

While relaxing the other day, I was thinking about general activist and NGO strategies. Yes, sorry. Sometimes I think about business even when I'm relaxing. Here's the thought that came to mind.

Often activist or NGOs act at cross-purposes. For example:

A general objective of anti-consumerism groups is that they want people to consume less material goods so that reduced consumption has more positive effects on the environment. Less consumption, less production, less pollution, etc. Let's not talk about the decreased economic development and a reduction in the standard of living. That's a theme for a more serious post.

Let's just contrast this anti-consumerism objective against another popular advocacy group, consumerists.

Consumerist groups want, among other things, for credit card companies to cease "abusive" practices in terms of eliminating excessive interest rates and hidden fees. On this one, you don't get a substantial argument from me, but again further discussion on this issue is better saved for a more serious post.

What I want to point out here today is if these two advocacy movements worked together they could reach mutually satisfactory goals. How? Let's say that consumerist groups left the credit card companies alone, leaving those companies to charge whatever the heck they liked, with excessive fees and hidden charges running rampant. What would happen then, if you follow basic economic theory, is that consumers would curtail their usage of credit cards. With less credit card usage, in the United States at least, there would likely be less consumption, giving the anti-consumerism folks a check mark in their victory column. QED.

But what would the consumerist folks get out of this? After all, if the consumerist folks dropped the credit card company haranguing, a major item on their overall activist agenda, then what would they do each day from 9 to 5? Would there suddenly be massive unemployment in the consumerist activist sector of the economy?

I don't think so.

Such a strategic alliance between anti-consumerism advocates and consumerist advocates would also benefit the overall consumerist agenda. Consumerists aren't solely about nailing credit card companies. Consumerists also seek to achieve better deals for consumers in all product and service areas. And the magic here, in this joint venture proposed, would be that consumers would get those better deals.

Now, of course those better deals wouldn't be from the credit card companies. The consumerists are letting the credit card companies run around like lunatics just busted out of the asylum. Remember? No, those better deals for consumers would be offered from other companies where those credit cards would be used. Like retail stores.

Those better deals in stores, and other credit card accepting businesses, would be because of the decreased consumerism. Business would be flatlining. In the hope of covering costs and just breaking even, stores and other credit card accepting companies would offer out-of-this-world deals just to get customers in door.

Is this a crazy strategy?

Well, its success, of course, is dependent upon consumers' propensity-to-spend, their willingness to use cash as a medium of exchange, the fluctuation of the savings rate, the cost of credit, and about a hundred other factors at play at any given moment within the macro-economy.

But it is something to think about.

Will the Baby Boom Create More Activism?

January 11, 2010

Categories: Activism, Anti-Corporatism, NGOs, Trends

Today I came across an interesting idea in *World Out of Balance* by Paul Laudicina. [30] Yes, I've mentioned this book before. It's been a while since last mentioned and that's because I'm reading it slowly. This one I read while I Nordic Track in the morning, so I might do only about ten pages at a time, and some days I listen to the radio while working out. So progress in this book is slower than normal. But my reading strategy on this book is not because it is not interesting. Quite the contrary. Here's one intriguing thought that came from my reading of this book.

From pages 148 to 149 Paul presents an interesting concept: that there will be an increase in activism because of the Baby Boom. He doesn't say it in quite this way, but he does say that because of the aging of the U.S. population that there will be a decrease in the number of employees working for the American government. Paul hypothesizes, from the perspective of the publication year of 2005, that these retiring employees would likely not be replaced at a rate that would equal the attrition. The reason he gives is that government employment is not as attractive as that in the private sector, and that because of this handicap the attrition rate may exceed the replacement rate.

Of course, that viewpoint was from 2005, before the stuff hit the fan in Fall 2008. Currently, with government being one of the few employment sectors that is expanding its hiring, Paul's theory may not be entirely sound. Yet, analyzing from a current perspective, there are valid take-aways that may be had from this line of reasoning. Paul's theory relates to the quantity of government workers, but he says little to nothing about the quality. Having worked for the federal government at one time, I could say something about the quality of federal workers. But that's material for a different post. For now, let's extend Paul's thinking into present circumstances.

Because the aging U.S. population will cause more and more employees to retire from the ranks of federal employment, there will be progressively fewer experienced workers to carry out the regulatory mandates set down by the feds. Right now, because of government's mania to hire more workers, the issue isn't so much about the quantity as it is about the quality, i.e., the experience factor.

So, my point is that due to the Baby Boom the quality of federal regulatory enforcement may likely decrease because less experienced employees would need to take over for those with decades of experience in regulatory matters. And if there are fewer experienced regulators, then businesses might be less likely to adhere to federal regulations than if the feds were fully staffed with experienced regulators.

How does this problem create more activism? Well, when activists see this situation, and believe me they won't miss this, there would likely be an increase in their efforts. Activists and NGOs would increase their efforts to regulate business because those activists and NGOs would see that the feds weren't staffed to do a "quality" job.

Thus, going forward with Baby Boom retirements which are now in progress, businesses should "gird their loins" and ready themselves for increased actions from advocacy groups.

It's all in the demographics. And those numbers don't lie.

The Marketplace Is Not Stupid

January 14, 2010

Categories: Activism, Irregular Competition - Friends of the Earth - Rainforest Action Network, Trends

From much of my reading, I can see that the power of the NGO (non-governmental organization) is increasing. With regard to how that power affects business, my research shows that over the past decade NGO-influenced corporations are now becoming the norm rather than the exception. And from the projections I've read, it appears that that influence will only become greater over the next decade.

To go along to get along with this trend, multi-national corporations (MNCs) are moving, seemingly together as if in lock step, to establish corporate social responsibility (CSR) programs in order to meet the demands and expectations of NGOs, whether it be on environmental, social, labor, or cultural issues. And to help them craft their CSRs, MNCs now regularly collaborate with NGOs, bringing NGOs to the table as trusted advisors and de facto consultants. And when MNCs do this, which is increasingly often, they seem to do it with a "mea culpa" attitude.

Mea culpa attitudes belong only on the truly guilty. MNCs don't give themselves enough credit. They suffer from a poor self-image. Paraphrasing Jessica Rabbit, "MNCs aren't 'bad.' They're just drawn that way." [31] Their "We're so guilty" attitude is unjustified. MNCs should not sit themselves in a corner.

Yes, it's true that MNCs are guilty of doing some "bad" things. Aren't you? MNCs are operated by humans. Imperfect humans who make mistakes. But I fear their mea culpa is overdone because most, if not all, MNCs indeed do more "good" than "bad." One doesn't need to perform extensive quantitative analysis to realize this.

If the MNCs were not doing more good than bad, then such behavior would be obvious to the marketplace, which is not stupid contrary to the belief of many activists. The marketplace is not stupid. We can use the activist's own thought process to address this issue. Ask any activist how "stupid" the marketplace was in electing Barack Obama to the White House and the majority response will prove this point. So, if the "bad acts" of any MNC outweighed the "good acts" performed to support the economy and society, then the marketplace would know that; the people would "vote" with their dollars, numbering the days of any wayward MNC.

Given this automatic economic voting mechanism, where "election day" for the MNC is every day, is the current and projected level of NGO influence upon MNCs really justified? Which party receives more legitimization?

Yes, MNCs make mistakes. I accentuated the obvious above. MNCs are operated by humans. But so are NGOs. NGOs are run by humans, imperfect humans. NGOs, as well-intentioned as most probably are, are not exempt from making mistakes, and performing "bad acts," whether by accident, or by intention, or by just plain ignorance. But how is the influence of these imperfect organizations counter-balanced? Unlike MNCs, NGOs are not subject to the same automatic regulatory mechanism of the "vote." NGOs are not subject to the same daily "election day" as are the MNCs. The motivations and the acts of the NGO are not examined and evaluated with the same frequency as are those of the MNC. Neither are the acts of the NGO supported with the same number of votes from the public.

For example, according to their IRS Form 990, a publicly-available document filed by all non-profit organizations operating within the United States, for the fiscal year ending in 2008 both the Rainforest Action Network (RAN) and the Friends of the Earth (FOE), two of the most powerful environmental advocacy groups in the world (read that as NGOs), received less than $5 million each in revenue, i.e., fewer than 5 million votes of support. Each. (You may see these documents by going to Guidestar.org and searching on each NGO.) You can plainly see how this vote tally would compare to the annual vote tally of any MNC with which any NGO might collaborate or against which any NGO might compete.

Yet, the MNCs embrace these largely uncontrolled NGOs. NGOs. Organizations who do their best to compete daily for the image of the corporations they target (Note: I deal with this concept of corporate image competition in my newest and forthcoming book, *Insidious Competition - The Battle for Meaning and the Corporate Image.* Due out Spring 2010). (Author's Further Note: When this post was written *Insidious Competition* was my forthcoming book which was published in June 2010.) Organizations who by the number of votes collected possess far less legitimatization than do the MNCs who do their best to incorporate NGO agendas. Organizations who pride themselves on "democratic" principles and acting for the "public good."

Show me the votes. Show me the democracy. Without legitimization, how do these collaborations make sense?

Greenpeace CEO Makes "More" Than Exxon CEO?

January 19, 2010

Categories: Irregular Competition - Greenpeace, Research - Case Studies - Greenpeace, Compensation

Does the Greenpeace CEO make more than the Exxon Mobil CEO?

Well, yes and no. In terms of absolute dollars, no. Not even close. But, in terms of a percentage of their respective organization's revenue, yes. More. Very much more.

In terms of compensation as a percentage of revenue, the Greenpeace CEO pulls in considerably more than does his counterpart at Exxon Mobil.

Recently I performed research addressing this issue. The reason I performed this research was due to activist's and NGO's frequent claims that CEOs of multinational corporations (MNCs) take as compensation an unfair proportion of their companies' overall revenue. After recently hearing this claim again, perhaps for about the 500th time, I wondered, "Who actually makes more in terms of percentage of revenue? Huge multinationals? Or NGOs?" I decided to do some digging, create a comparison, and take a look.

Methodology

Now, to address this question, what I decided to do was just take a "quick and dirty" look. I just wanted to test my theory with some trial research. Therefore, at the outset my intention was not to do an exhaustive study by including a large number of NGOs and MNCs in a representative and statistically controlled sample. When I began this research I decided that I would save that exhaustive study for another occasion should my theory be supported by the results of this "thumbnail" research project.

To commence my pilot research project, I simply selected, very much at random, one NGO and one multinational. The first two of each that came to mind were Greenpeace and Exxon Mobil. These two organizations are often at odds with each other and both are frequently in the news, making them top of mind.

To identify the revenues of Greenpeace I went to Guidestar.org. Guidestar is an organization which aggregates information about non-profit corporations. At their site, you may search for your non-profit of interest and find information you desire, much of it a no charge. One of the pieces of information stored by Guidestar is a non-profit's US IRS Form 990.

The IRS Form 990 is a document that must be filed by all tax-exempt non-profit organizations operating within the United States. This document is much like a tax return and contains some information similar to what you would find in a for-profit corporation's annual report or 10K filing. Among the information shown in a Form 990 is annual revenues and executive compensation. On the Guidestar site, I located Greenpeace's Forms 990.

To obtain the revenue and executive compensation information for Exxon

Mobil, I journeyed to SEC.gov, the site of the Securities and Exchange Commission for the United States. At that site, I accessed Exxon Mobil's Schedule 14A Proxy Statement which contained summary compensation figures for Exxon Mobil executives for the years 2006 - 2008. Also available on that site was the Exxon Mobil 10K, containing the annual revenue figures that I sought. Additional information on Exxon Mobil's revenue was obtained from their 2008 Annual Report available at ExxonMobil.com.

All information for this research comparison was obtained from US Government documents, or from an annual report, and is therefore considered to be highly reliable. The latest information that could be located for both Greenpeace and Exxon Mobil was from 2008. The 2009 figures were not as yet ready as of the date of this post.

Following is a summary of the information that I obtained from the sources.

Findings

	2007 Revenue	2007 Compensation	2008 Revenue	2008 Compensation
Greenpeace, Inc.	$19.5 mil.	$126,573	$26.3 mil.	$103,624
Greenpeace Fund, Inc.	$39.6 mil.	$42,191	$9 mil.	$103,624
SubTotals	$59.1 mil.	$168,764	$35.3 mil.	$207,248
Compensation %age		0.28%		0.59%
Exxon Mobil	$405 bil.	$16.7 mil.	$477 bil.	$22.4 mil.
Compensation %age		0.0041%		0.0047%

Upon visiting Guidestar.org, I found that there are two significant Greenpeace organizations. One is the primary campaign organization, Greenpeace, Inc., and the other is a financial arm, Greenpeace Fund, Inc. When I examined the Forms 990 for both organizations, I found that the same person is the Executive Director for both entities and that that person collects a salary from both organizations. So, that is why in the table above you see two Greenpeace lines.

You can see that for the chief of the Greenpeace corporations his compensation for 2007 totals $168,764 and for 2008 the total is $207,248. You can also see that his total compensation for 2007 represented 0.28% of the joint organizations" total revenue ($168,764/$59.1 million) and that for 2008 that percentage of revenues increased to 0.587% ($207,248/$35.3 million).

In comparison for the chief of Exxon Mobil, although he pulled down a hefty $16.7 million in 2007 and $22.4 million in 2008, his compensation as a percentage of revenue for 2007 and 2008 was 0.00412% ($16.7 million/$405 billion) and 0.00469% ($22.4 million/$477 billion), respectively.

Discussion

Of course, these two chiefs are not in same compensation range, and I have no doubt that because of their different levels of compensation the types of neighborhoods in which they dwell are probably very much different. Yet there are at a minimum two important take-aways to be had from this pilot study.

Take Away One: The first take-away to be noted is consistent with my thesis, that this data indicates that perhaps NGO chiefs take as compensation a higher percentage of their organization's revenue. In this comparison, for 2008 the compensation as a percentage of revenue is about 125 times greater for the Greenpeace chief as compared to his Exxon Mobile counterpart. That's quite a differential.

At least in this case of Greenpeace vs. Exxon Mobil, we can see that my thesis might be true, or at a minimum is well-supported. And yes, this is only one case comparison which as such it is not scientific and may or may not be representative of the greater NGO community, but I noted that research limitation at the top of this post.

However, if the Greenpeace and Exxon Mobil comparison could be used as representative, we would say that NGOs and activist organizations are hypocritical when they accuse MNC chiefs of receiving as compensation an "unfair" proportion of their company's revenues. In order to make that a convincing argument to be applied across the NGO spectrum, more research would be needed in this area. This Greenpeace and Exxon Mobil sample comparison indicates that such research may prove very interesting, indeed.

Take Away Two: Note that for 2008, the Greenpeace chief saw a nice increase of about 23%, during a year when many people saw a decrease of 100% by hitting the ranks of the unemployed. And this 23% increase was during a year when for Greenpeace total revenue declined by about 40%. This Greenpeace compensation increase is, of course, much less than the Exxon Mobil chief's increase of about 34%. But, for 2008, revenue at Exxon Mobil increased by about 17%. For Exxon Mobil, a legitimate argument can be made that the compensation increase is tied to performance. Can Greenpeace make that same argument? How does Greenpeace justify an increase of 23% for their chief when their revenues decreased by 40%?

There are critics who blast the financial industry for rewarding its executives with compensation increases in companies which underperform the previous fiscal year. Doesn't this Greenpeace example speak to the same type of criticism? And if so, why is it that we do not hear in the mainstream media these kinds of disparagements applied to NGOs as well as MNCs?

Conclusion

This pilot research has shown that there is reason to believe that NGOs and other activist organizations do pay their executives a higher percentage of revenues than is paid by the corporations that they combat in the environmental, social, and cultural arenas. The test research performed here indicates that further research should be done in this area.

The outcome of a more statistically reliable enquiry could be used as the basis of counterstrategy against claims by NGOs and activists that executives at MNCs are "greedy" and take more than their "fair share" of revenues. Such a counterstrategy element would perhaps go far in overcoming these corporate image-damaging claims in the eyes of the marketplace.

EXCLUSIVE
Who is Really Behind the Walmart Sustainability Index?

January 21, 2010

Categories: CSR, Irregular Competition - Environmental Defense Fund, Research - Motivation, Strategy

In July 2009, Walmart introduced their initiation, support, and funding of the new Walmart Sustainability Index. [32]

What is the Walmart Sustainability Index (WSI)?

Briefly, the WSI is intended to be a ranking of the ecological efficiency of manufactured products. Factors that go into calculating a product's ecological efficiency are things like the amount of energy used to make the product and how well the product can be recycled after it is used. Walmart wants this ecological ranking to be displayed on each product sold within its stores so that their shoppers can make purchase choices in a "sustainable way." (Source: Walmart Sustainable Product Index: Fact Sheet, a PDF.) [33]

This index is often referred to in the press as the Walmart Sustainability Index, just as I have done at the beginning of this post. But, actually calling it such is a bit of a misnomer. They don't really want the index to be theirs per se. According to the Walmart Fact Sheet, as mentioned above, the WSI is only an initiative created by Walmart. The fact sheet says that the company doesn't intend to "create or own this index," but that instead the company intends to help create "a consortium of universities that will collaborate with suppliers, retailers, NGOs and government to develop a global database of information on the lifecycle of products – from raw materials to disposal." Through their own statement, it is clear that they don't wish to own it; they just wish to initiate it. Yet, since they are the initiators it only seems fair that they should get the credit for it. So, the name Walmart Sustainability Index should stick. And I would think they would want this name to stick, as we shall come to understand later in Part 2 of this post.

Who or what is behind this WSI initiative?

What are the reasons behind wanting to initiate this ecological product ranking? I have two theories as to why Walmart would want to initiate the WSI.

Theory #1

Proposed: Walmart customers are the reason behind the initiation of the WSI.

Premise

All good businesses are customer-centric. As with any good business, and I certainly consider Walmart a good business (otherwise they wouldn't be the world's largest retailer), Walmart must be launching this initiative because this WSI service is something that is desired by their customers. Being a good business and customer-centric, Walmart must be responding to the desires of their customers. Yes, that must be it. The initiation of the WSI must be driven by Walmart customer demand. In fact, Walmart leads us to believe that customer-centricity is indeed the reason behind the WSI.

On Walmart's website, on their Sustainability page, [34] they post the following:

> ... *our customers want products that are more efficient, last longer and perform better. They want to know the product's entire lifecycle. They want to know the materials in the product are safe, that it is made well and is produced in a responsible way.*

Most of what Walmart says here is stating the obvious. All customers want efficiency, durability, and top performance from the products they purchase. All customers want to know that the products they buy are safe and well-made. But, where does it say that their customers want to know about the degree of "sustainability," or ecological efficiency, of the products they purchase? Walmart seemingly makes a big leap here between what their customers say they want and their reasons for the initiation of the WSI. Are you thinking that maybe the sentence "They want to know the product's entire lifecycle," supports that leap? I don't think so because product life cycle means something else and doesn't necessarily relate directly to sustainability issues.

I'd like to see Walmart's research backing up this leap that they make. Short of seeing that research, I just have a difficult time believing that Walmart customers are demanding this type of service. Why? Well, let me explain why by taking a look at the Walmart customer.

Findings

In 2007, according to Supply Chain Digest, [35] Walmart segmented their 200 million customers into the following categories:

- *Brand Aspirationals - People with low incomes who are fixated on brand names like KitchenAid;*
- *Price-Sensitive Affluents - Wealthier shoppers who love deals; and,*

- *Value-Price Shoppers - Those with like low prices who can't afford much more. (I know this sentence is not grammatically correct, but it is a direct quote. I think the "with" should be "who.")*

According to MSN Money, "Walmart customer's average incomes are below the national average." [36]

In 2005, The Washington Post said that the average annual income for the average Walmart customer was $35,000. [37] (Allowing for an inflation rate of 2% per year since then, that brings the average up to only about $38,600 for 2010.)

A Zogby International poll found that in 2004, 76% of weekly Walmart shoppers voted for George Bush and not John Kerry. [38]

Discussion

Hmmmm. My Theory #1, that the WSI initiative is driven by customer demand, doesn't seem to be supported by the facts. The facts seem to point to a customer that is concerned mostly with price and value. The facts don't point to the type of customer that is typically overly concerned with "green" issues. The facts point to a type of customer that wouldn't seem to care one way or the other about the WSI.

The Supply Chain Digest article said that, using Walmart's own customer categorization, Walmart customers were segmented only on the basis of value sought, i.e., they want low prices. On pricing, certainly Walmart is customer-centric. Walmart has a reputation for low prices. In fact, all the Walmart TV commercials I see have price as their selling proposition; in not one of those commercials have I ever seen an allusion to "green" issues. And that customer concern with prices appears to be supported given the data on average Walmart customer income as shown by the Washington Post article and the MSN Money post. People earning below average wages would most probably be more interested in low-prices than in a WSI.

That's the demographic side of the information. Now for some psychographic information.

How do the the political leanings of Walmart customers enter into this argument? Per the Zogby poll info, it seems the average Walmarter in 2004 went for George W. Bush. Well, I could be wrong, but I think it's safe to say that those who voted for Kerry are probably more "green" leaning than those who voted for Dubya.

Theory #1 Conclusion

No. Theory #1 isn't supported by the facts.

I don't think that Walmart customers are the reason behind the initiation of the WSI

The reason for Walmart wanting to initiate the WSI does not appear to be due to customer demand. So the "who" in our question doesn't seem to be the customer.

So, now it's time for an alternate theory.

*   *   *

And you may read that alternate theory in my next post. That post will appear on Tuesday, January 26, 2010. If you are reading this before that date, then please subscribe to the FREE RSS feed so you can receive that article directly. If you are reading this after that date, then simply click here to continue with Part 2 of "Who Is Really Behind the Walmart Sustainability Index?"

There Is Only One Jobs Program Going On Now

January 22, 2010

Categories: Ideas, Personal Observations

This is the first post in my newly created Ideas category.

This category will contain very brief posts addressing random insights that occur to me, well, randomly. I'm jotting them down here because this is a web log, after all. And I'd like to keep track of them for possible incorporation into a future book or article. I'm also posting them here to invite feedback, which would also assist me in putting together future books and articles.

Today's idea is job programs.

Finally, there is a major jobs program being created in Washington, DC.

After last Tuesday's (1/19/2010) Massachusetts special election, which changed the political dynamic in the nation's capital and effectively derailed the health care reform initiative that polls had been telling Washington for months they were ramming through despite the electorate's wishes, the Democrats finally realized that they were at odds with the people's desires.

The majority party is now turning, in a deliberately obvious fashion, toward other "issues of concern," such as the economy and jobs. Yesterday, Mr. Obama announced new, proposed banking regulations and frightened the financial markets. This strategic turn, which is more politically-based than economically-based and (this next clause was added after the market close on Friday, 1/22/10) looks to be nothing more than a temper tantrum from a guy who never even ran a lemonade stand, was made at this point in time in an effort to take the public's attention off the health care reform failure. Today, he doubles down on this new "hissy-fit" strategy and goes to Ohio to give a speech about jobs. All done, I believe, in an effort to convince the electorate that the majority party is addressing the people's main concerns, jobs and the economy. Duh. It took them this long to figure this out? (For now, let's put aside the fact that Mr. Obama's proposed banking changes would actually do more to hurt the economy than help it.)

Yes, these strategic shifts are the leading elements of a new government jobs program.

But this program's primary intent is not necessarily to generate jobs for the general public. The primary intent of this new program, this strategic shift, is to allow the majority party members to keep their jobs after the November 2010 mid-term election.

After last Tuesday's election, the majority party knew that if they continued on the course of ramming health care reform through, against the trend revealed by just about every poll taken on the subject and definitely against the results of the Massachusetts special election, then most of them would be packing their desks come November and hitting the unemployment lines with their constituents.

So, yes. They are now turning to a jobs program. It's just not the kind that you think it is.

The question is, will people see his proposals as an effort to help the economy? And if they misguidedly do, will that save the jobs of the dweebs in Washington? Or will the people recognize it for what it is? A poorly conceived notion. A notion which will actually damage the banks when it's now that we need them the most. If so, then this jobs program is doomed from the start.

EXCLUSIVE
Who Is Really Behind the Walmart Sustainability Index? - Part 2

January 26, 2010

Categories: CSR, Irregular Competition - Environmental Defense Fund, Research - Motivation, Strategy

In my previous post, "Who Is Really Behind the Walmart Sustainability Index? - Part 1," we began looking at the real reason why Walmart would want to initiate the Walmart Sustainability Index (WSI), an ecological product ranking that the company wants attached to products sold in their stores.

In Part 1, I discussed how I had two theories on who or what is sparking Walmart's motivation to initiate the WSI. My first theory was that customer demand was the reason behind Walmart initiating the WSI. But in Part 1 we saw that Theory #1 did not hold together. Regardless of what Walmart says, I don't think it is customer demand that's the driving force behind the WSI. So, now here in Part 2 of "Who Is Really Behind the Walmart Sustainability Index," you and I move onto Theory #2.

Theory #2

Premise

As most people know, over the past decade or so, Walmart has been the victim of negative publicity. That the company has been assailed on a public relations front is not exactly proprietary information.

Issues and accusations over: their influence on small-town mom & pop businesses, health insurance benefits for employees, hourly wages, etc. have been well-documented. [39] Then there was that whole Walmarting Across America blogging gaff, [40] a flap that started over a pro-Walmart blog that appeared on the surface to be organic, but turned out to be at least a little less so. After many years of this sort of treatment in the halls of public opinion, Walmart needed some PR wins. Their image had gotten beaten up. Walmart needed a PR image makeover.

Findings

Per a post from the Harvard Business Review, in October 2005 Walmart announced that it was embarking on a "sustainability strategy" to "dramatically reduce the company's impact on the global environment and thus become 'the most competitive and innovative company in the world.' " [41]

According to an article in the Christian Science Monitor (CSM), Walmart began a collaborative relationship with the Environmental Defense Fund (EDF) in 2005. The article said that EDF's "most intense partnership began in 2005 when Wal-Mart sought out the environmental group for advice on how to craft a better corporate responsibility plan. At the time, the megaretailer was getting lambasted for everything from killing small business to poor personnel management. The relationship grew closer as it shifted to strategy."

Also per the CSM article, in 2007 the EDF opened an office in Bentonville, Arkansas which also is the headquarters city of Walmart. The CSM article also quoted Michele Harvey, the EDF corporate partnerships project manager, in speaking of Walmart as saying, " … we have a greater potential to influence the direction they take." [42]

Discussion

Given the fact that Walmart was being "pasted" regularly in the popular culture, they needed to do something which would allow them to appear as a more "benign" presence within the American landscape. Initiating a sustainability strategy within a larger corporate social responsibility (CSR) program could yield them the softer image that they sought. And "partnering" with a major environmental non-governmental organization (NGO) like the EDF to help implement that sustainability strategy would certainly help Walmart project the image of a large corporate organization that is willing to work with those "defending" the environment, softening the Walmart image. From the PR perspective, the fact that "Environmental Defense" is in the name of that NGO organization was probably not looked upon as a negative when Walmart made their NGO partner selection.

Relative to corporations' entrances into CSR programs, it's been written in the press that many companies undertake CSR programs in order to preclude attacks from NGOs and activist organizations. Indeed in the aforementioned CSM article, Daniel Korschun, a fellow at the Drexel University's Center for Corporate Reputation Management, was quoted as saying "Many companies initially approach nonprofits in order to reduce the risk that the nonprofit will create bad press or organize protests and boycotts."

Could this be the reason that Walmart got involved with EDF in 2005? Perhaps it wasn't because of an altruistic concern that this corporation chose to enter the CSR arena. Perhaps there was a dual objective in Walmart's decision to enter into CSR: to repair the image of the company and to preclude NGO and activist attacks.

Theory #2 Conclusion

Getting back to the central question of this post, "Who Is Really Behind the Walmart Sustainability Index?," perhaps the EDF is really the driving force behind the WSI. Regardless of what Walmart might say about their customer as being the motivation for the WSI, the concept behind the WSI is not consistent with the profile of the average Walmart customer, as we saw in Part 1. But the EDF has the motivation to push this WSI into operation because the concept behind the WSI is consistent with the mission of the EDF.

Maybe the WSI is something that the EDF wants implemented, across all retailing, and not just at Walmart. If this is a goal of the EDF, they have gained a powerful relationship through which to implement that goal. As in the Findings above, the EDF's corporate partnerships manager was quoted as saying, "we have a greater potential to influence the direction they (Walmart) take."

And as goes Walmart, so most certainly will go the rest of the retail world. This perceived influence in this relationship, and thus the perception of the power available to the EDF, is only accentuated by the knowledge that there is an EDF office in Bentonville.

So, what this all comes down to is that there is a strong possibility that the impetus behind Walmart's initiation of the WSI was the influence of the

EDF, and not customer demand as Walmart has indicated. There is no hard evidence of this, but based on the facts that I have located and presented here, the conclusion seems reasonable.

Epilogue

Now, you might be thinking, "Hey Richard, what does it matter who pushed the WSI? What's so bad about the WSI?"

Well, I suppose that, at least on the surface, there would seem to be worse things in business than the WSI. Of course, analyzing its benefit to business and society will take some time, especially considering it isn't even in the marketplace yet.

The WSI is sort of like the nutrition labels that appear on our food products, mandated by the federal government years ago. People can choose to read those labels or ignore them just as they can read or ignore the WSI if they so choose. Yes. Absolutely true. People can ignore the WSI. But the issue that I am raising here is not with the WSI itself. No, the issue I am raising here is one that is more than a label that appears on a product. The issue here is one of process, a process than can affect all companies. That process is one that is built on fear and is one that can insinuate itself into all companies.

When you consider the possibility, a very strong possibility, that it was the EDF who really may have had the goal of the WSI and initiated the WSI through their five-year partnership with Walmart, it doesn't bode well, in general, for a company's control of their own corporation. This loss of control would increase as more and more corporations "partner" with NGOs and activists; "partnerships" that are born in the desire to "preclude" publicity attacks. In so doing, companies may actually overlook the desires of their customers to meet the needs of an outsider. They may do this at the expense of those who actually pay to keep the company's lights on, the customer.

And in this scenario we can see more of the political process insert itself into business as more NGOs become "partners" with fearful companies.

Could Slacktivism Be the Next Big Thing?

January 28, 2010

Categories: Activism, Anti-Corporatism, Irregular Competition - Greenpeace, Trends

In the digital world, most everyone keeps their eye out for what will be the "next big thing." Usually it's a technology, either hardware or software. Lately Google's been hitting it hard and heavy on the forecasted next big thing stage, Google Wave and Droid.

But I've been thinking lately that the next big thing in the online world might be a movement, rather than a technology. And that movement I have in mind is "slacktivism."

What's slacktivism? The word itself is a portmanteau of "slacker" and "activism." Thus, the meaning becomes clear. For further edification, let's take a definition from the UrbanDictionary.com. They define slacktivism as:

> *One of those feel-good internet campaigns that doesn't actually help anybody or has political impact. It's your way of pretending to care while sitting on your butt in front of a computer playing WoW. Also used for people who want to get a million people on their page by before bettering themselves (sic) or the world instead of just doing it.* [43]

Other than the grammar or typo error there in the last sentence, the UrbanDictionary.com is clearly saying that slacktivism is something like what we could call "armchair activism." It's being an "activist" without actually being one, although you could still wear the black tee shirt and/or beret while sitting at your computer.

Slacktivism is a way for people to make themselves feel like they are advocating for a social cause, while actually committing little or no time or money to the effort. It's, for the most part, a feel-good activity. Not only does slacktivism make individuals feel good about themselves when they sign up to be a friend, fan, or follower on the page of a cause's website or social network or Twitter page, but the act of slacktivism impresses others with the individual's "social awareness." That impression, of which the individual is aware, further adds to the individual's ego gratification.

I don't think we need any social psychology references to support these assertions. It's all pretty much backed by common sense acquired from our years of experience with the human condition. So, given the ease of slacktivism as measured against its psychological benefits, it would follow that many people would sign-up online for an activist's cause, and not really add much to the activist effort in the process. To test my theory, let's have an example.

On Tuesday, January 19, 2009 which is the day on which I wrote this post (Yes, I know it's dated January 28th, but thanks to the magic of the Word Press scheduling function such miracles are possible.), I went to the Greenpeace.org/usa site and clicked on the link to their Facebook fan page. When I went to their Facebook fan page, I noticed that, on that date, Greenpeace USA had 41,728 fans. I wanted to see how "active" these individuals might be, so to test my slacktivism theory, I scrolled down to the Greenpeace USA "Causes" box and clicked on "See Greenpeace USA's Total Impact."

For those unfamiliar with Facebook fan pages and causes, following is a brief explanation. Any organization, or company for that matter, may sign-up on Facebook for a "fan page." On the fan page, the organization can gather fans and communicate, interactively, with them through text and pictures. The organization, and individuals can do this on Facebook also, may then sign-up for "Causes" pages, which are pages featuring a particular charitable organization's agenda. On the Cause page, the organization can then accumulate "members," who can be different and/or the same people as on the fan page, and solicit donations for the featured cause.

When I clicked through on Greenpeace USA's "Total Impact" link, I was taken to their page which summarizes the four Greenpeace causes they feature via Facebook: Climate Rescue, Greenpeace Organizing Term, Kleercut, and STOP the Whale Hunt. Clicking through on each cause listed revealed the following activity and support:

- Climate Rescue - 473 members for this cause with $0 contributed.
- Greenpeace Organizing Term - 574 members with $25 contributed.
- Kleercut - 1,202 members with $40 contributed.
- STOP the Whale Hunt - 153,941 members with $23,756 contributed.

Until I got to the Whale Hunt cause, I thought slacktivism was going to make the Greenpeace/Facebook contributions endeavor a total bust. The Whale Hunt cause showed 153,941 members with almost $24,000 in donations.

But that means that on average each Whale Hunt member contributed only about 15 cents.

Perhaps after signing up for the Whale Hunt cause, most of those 153,941 members, feeling good about themselves, went back to playing World of Warcraft (WoW).

Slacktivism? Is it the next big thing?

At least judging by this test case, yes, I think my theory holds.

Chapter Six - From Social Entrepreneurism to Extortion
―――――――――――― Take-Aways ――――――――――

For the first three essays of this chapter, we took a brief break from the discussion of memes and how activists use or exploit them in their work. Sometimes a break from an activity affords us a better perspective and more energy when we resume that activity later on.

In the first of those three, "An Activist Strategy to Bank On?," I highlighted the strategy of using business to fuel activism by telling you about a company that is part company, part activist. That might seen like an unusual combination to you, but in my research I've seen this type of "social entrepreneur" become more common. I wouldn't say that they are becoming a significant part of the commercial landscape, but they might be a harbinger of things to come, mutating a change in the relationship between capitalism and charity. If you are involved in public relations or corporate communications, be on the lookout for an increase in this trend because, if it's successful, it may help fuel anti-corporate activists who make your work day more difficult. In "Activist Teamwork Scenario," I took a humorous and tongue-in-cheek look at a way activist groups could work together (and it's so crazy that it might actually work). When you consider these two somewhat unconventional thoughts about the possible near-future evolution of anti-corporate activism from within the context of the theme of "Will the Baby Boom Create More Activism?," it gives you pause to think. You must take that pause because the demographic shift that might kick activism, and anti-corporate activism in particular, into high-gear could be fueled by the social entrepreneur, sort of a "Capitalism 2.0."

What will the near-future of anti-corporate activism look like? Are companies considering these possibilities? Based on my interactions with companies on these issues, it's doubtful that they're considering them with a whole lot of foresight. I've observed that they are barely keeping up with what anti-corporate activists are doing today, no less thinking about what they will be doing tomorrow. But, in my opinion, just as companies plan future scenarios around more pedestrian business problems, companies need to plan for the problem of the anti-corporate activism of tomorrow. Even the tongue-in-cheek possibilities should be envisioned, "gamed out," and considered in the strategic planning mix.

We departed from the meme examination briefly in those three essays, but then in "The Marketplace Is Not Stupid" we returned to the consideration of the meme's role in the behaviors of adversarial activists. The "mea culpa" attitude that I mentioned in that essay, the one over which I asserted that multi-national corporations (MNCs) flagellate themselves, I feel has become meme, a high meme. No wonder there is self-flagellation in corporate board rooms.

Think about that. Think about that meme. Then think about global oil companies, think about brand name clothing manufacturers, think about the term "multi-national corporation." What do you feel? Could it be because of that meme? But when you dig deeper, to find the essence of that meme, is it really supported? The votes tell the story. Who receives more? My objective in that piece was not only to make the stated point, that of having you move beyond the meme to realize that MNCs are not as guilty as they themselves think they are or as guilty as the adversarial NGOs engaging them want people to think, but also the unstated point which was to get you to think beyond the meme and to suggest at least one method to test the validity of that or any meme affecting a company. And, oh yes, one other point I'd like to make now is regarding that above phrase "as guilty as the adversarial NGOs engaging them want you to think." In the Introduction to this book, I said that for irregular competition "having you 'live on a meme,' is critical to their strategy." The cultural meme of MNC guilt is a strong one for irregular competitors; I talked about the whys and wherefores at length in *Insidious Competition*. NGOs count on its existence and its strength to carry their campaigns to success. Their campaigns cannot succeed without this meme. When MNCs participate in the perpetuation of that guilt meme, MNCs only make it easier for the irregular competitor, e.g., an NGO, to carry out his or her mission.

From these ideas I progressed in my journey of exploring memes and their usage in anti-corporate activism. At this point on the calendar, I was finished with the writing, re-writing, proofing, and editing of *Insidious Competition*, an endeavor that then had gone on for over a year prior. The manuscript was then in the publisher's hands.

As I write *Living on a Meme*, one of the most popular pieces on Telofski.com is "Greenpeace CEO Makes 'More' Than Exxon CEO?" As I said upfront in that essay, as part of my general study into irregular competition, I put that research together in response to general claims that activists often make about MNC executives "taking too much" of their company's revenue as compensation. I expect that you've heard that meme many times. The findings of my research disprove the meme, at least on a one case basis, by demonstrating that there are other organizations, activist organizations at that, which pay their CEOs a much higher percentage of the organizational revenue. Upon reflection, such research gives us pause to think about the memes employed by activists and what it is that they are really trying to "sell" to society.

In "The Marketplace Is Not Stupid," I introduced the idea of how some MNCs collaborate with NGOs to meet the expectations and demands of not only the NGOs with which they collaborate, but, as I implied, also to preclude as much future activist protest as possible. Then in "Who is Really Behind the Walmart Sustainability Index?," I examined this phenomenon of collaboration further with special attention on studying that meme of the "mea culpa." "Walmart Sustainability Index," both parts, concludes that, despite their implication to the contrary, it isn't Walmart's desire to serve their customers better that leads to the creation of the index, which likely would be costly for vendors to implement and possibly increase costs to the customer. But rather it is that MNC's desire to minimize any future impact from that guilt meme floating around our culture. It's this preclusion factor, the one that I implied in "The Marketplace Is Not Stupid" article, that, I think, plays the chief role in the birth of the index. So, as I pointed to in the piece, the danger there is that in corporations' desires to minimize the guilt meme, they may actually relinquish a large amount of control to activist organizations, specialized political groups in reality, and neglect the desires of customers in the process. And if that expectation of satisfying the activist first, and the customer second, is allowed itself to become meme, what does that say for the future of business? What does that say for the future of a democratic society?

Now, so there is no misunderstanding, let me say here what I've said many times before. I am not in favor of allowing MNCs or any other company to junk up the environment, physically or culturally. Although some folks have accused me of being in favor of totally unbridled corporatism, probably the ones who have not read me completely, such a scenario is not what I support. What I do favor is that the customer drives the marketplace, not the activist, and that a company responds to its customers first. If independent groups are needed to suggest operational suggestions to corporations, suggestions which are based in *sound science and economics* and not emotional memes or to inform customers *honestly, objectively, and accurately* on any negative behaviors of corporations, so that those customers may make better purchasing decisions, then I believe that those organizations add a positive value to society. But what I do not favor is when these same groups, these irregular competitors, adopt "name and shame" tactics, exploit memes unfairly, subjectively, and falsely, interpreting those memes to fit their own agenda and not the agenda of the customer. It is that "semantical extortion" or "semantical terrorism" to which I object. And it is in the analysis of those irregularly competitive processes of the distortion of meaning that is the basis of my work.

So, now that I've broached the subject of "extortion" and "terrorism," and perhaps shocked you through their employment, let's move on.

CHAPTER SEVEN

Jumping Into
Anti-Corporatism

NGO & Corporate Collaboration: How Far Does It Go?

February 2, 2010

Categories: Activism, NGOs, Trends

In the field of issues management, some corporations now "partner" with NGOs on various issues of "social concern." That term "social concern" is often one that is defined by the NGO, rather than the corporation, by the way. So now, instead of an NGO and a corporation fighting tooth and nail over an environmental issue, for example, they work together toward a "common goal." Okay. That seems all warm and fuzzy, on the surface. But let's dig a little deeper into the nature of this "partnership."

In a situation like this, what's that "common goal?" For the NGO, the goal would be the achievement of, perhaps, a social agenda objective that they have pursued for years, often via an adversarial relationship with the corporation. For the corporation, what's the goal? What motivates the corporation to take on such a "strange bedfellows" relationship? Well, as a recent article in the Christian Science Monitor commented, corporations often approach NGOs to partner on a common project so that those same NGOs don't turn around in the future and spread bad press about the corporation. [44] A "common goal?" Seems more like a protection racket.

Imagine this scenario. Corporation X is concerned that future bad press could negatively impact their expected future revenues. So, to preclude the threat of negative press, an implicit threat at least, the brass at X dial up their historical foes at NGO Z and play let's make a deal. The brass over at Z aren't going to say, "Hey X, thanks for calling, but no thanks." No. Z's ship just came in. The pressure that the folks at NGO Z have been applying to Corporation X all of these years has just paid off.

Didn't I see a scene something like this in at least one episode of The Sopranos?

Now, when the NGOs and the corporations get together like this, at least according to the previously mentioned Christian Science Monitor article, no money changes hands. The article stated that the NGO doesn't receive any fees from the corporate partner. But isn't there an exchange of value here? Isn't this somewhat like a scene from The Sopranos? Let's look at it this way.

The Sopranos Example - Paulie, grey slicked-back side wings and all, goes into a shop and "tells" the proprietor that the shop could "have some trouble" in the future. This "implicit threat" means that the shopkeeper might lose some of his or her "expected future revenues." But, Paulie and his problem-resolution specialists can "protect" the shop and make that trouble "disappear," for some consideration of course. In this Sopranos example, that consideration is money.

Paulie and his problem-resolution specialists get what they were looking for, i.e., they reach their direct objective. The shopkeeper avoids that "implicit threat" and gets to keep his or her future revenue stream.

The NGO Z/Corporation X Collaboration Example - The presence of NGO Z represents an "implicit threat" to Corporation X, the threat of future negative publicity. NGO Z recognizes that this "trouble" is possible. The presence of this "implicit threat" means that Corporation X might lose some of their "expected future revenues." But, the problem-resolution specialists of Corporation X realize they can "protect" the corporation and make that problem "disappear," for some consideration exchanged of course. In this NGO Z/Corporation X example that consideration is collaborating with NGO Z to allow NGO Z to achieve one of their social agenda objectives.

The Corporation Z problem-resolution specialists get what they were looking for, i.e., they get to keep their future revenue stream. NGO Z gets what they were looking for, i.e., they achieve their direct objective of "social concern," which, of course, is defined by them.

Weird, isn't it?

And once this "partnership" is established, where is the line drawn? How far does this relationship go?

In The Sopranos Example, Paulie keeps returning to the shopkeeper saying there are always "other" troubles on the horizon and that an increased payment is needed to keep those troubles away.

In The NGO Z/Corporation X Collaboration Example, the management of Corporation X realizes that there is always the possibility that NGO Z could spread bad press, regardless of how much or how well they work together on any selected project. What happens after that project is complete? Corporation

X knows that NGO Z will always have "other" future projects of "social concern" on their horizon.

Are these NGO/corporate collaborations a good way to run a company?

How far does it go?

EXCLUSIVE
NGO Social Media: Some Weakness in "Reach"

February 4, 2010

Categories: Irregular Competition - Friends of the Earth - Greenpeace, Research, Strategy

Introduction

Social media is an environment that is seemingly tailor-made for NGOs and activists to exploit. Among other characteristics, social media are accessible to almost everyone in the developed world. Social media are pervasive; more and more people use social media every day. Social media are inexpensive. And social media skew young.

Because of these factors, economically, demographically, and psychographically, social media are perfectly positioned for NGOs to leverage in their campaigns against business. Because of these reasons, and because NGOs are among the chief anti-corporate campaigners out there, companies want to know more about what these atypical competitors, these "irregular competitors," are doing from within social media.

Today, I am going to give those corporations a "mini-heads-up" and give a little bit of insight as to what two NGOs are up to in social media. This heads-up will be limited to the examination of "reach." The NGOs examined will be:

- Greenpeace US
- Friends of the Earth US (FOE)

I've chosen to examine these two NGOs for six reasons.

1. They're both about the same age, and therefore have the same opportunity at notoriety, and reach.
2. They're among the largest of the tens of thousands of NGOs on the planet.
3. Because of their size, these NGOs would tend to have the most potential for influence on the companies they target.
4. These two are among the most active of all NGOs in terms of anti-corporate activism.
5. In an effort to compare "apples to apples," I chose these NGOs because they operate within similar issue arenas, such as the environment; their Venn diagrams of issues coverage overlap, not completely but highly.
6. Again with attention to an "apple to apple" comparison, both NGO operations cover the same geography. Each NGO has an international organization, but in this article I will only be looking at their U.S. operation.

Factors

Reach is significant in social media. Yes, I know that some of my social media colleagues don't regard "reach" as important in social media as it is in traditional media. But I submit that reach is very important, especially so in a medium that is perfectly positioned for NGO goals, as noted above.

One of the elements which produces the social media "reach" of an organization is its size. The bigger the organization then the more well-known will be its brand. And the more well-known its brand, then the more followers, friends, fans, and/or subscribers that brand should have in social media. The more followers, friends, fans, and/or subscribers had by that brand, then the more opportunities for the brand's message there are to be transmitted and discussed and forwarded and discussed again and back and forth and so on. Social media is a medium of discussion and "pass along." So, if the originator of a message, like Greenpeace US or FOE US, has more followers, friends, etc., than a similar organization, well, then there are simply more opportunities for message propagation not only at origin, but also further down the chain of the social web.

So, let's go ahead and do a bit of analysis on the social media reach of these two NGOs.

Findings

Below you'll see a table which details, for each NGO, the number of Facebook fans, the number of Twitter followers, the number of MySpace fans each has, along with similar statistics for each NGO's YouTube presence.

NGO Social Media "Reach" Comparisons

	Facebook	Twitter	MySpace	YouTube Subscribers	YouTube Friends	YouTube Channel Views
Greenpeace	41,582	14,850	123,595	1,851	1,005	66,372
FOE	11,615	3,103	14,676	72	28	3,102

As of January 14, 2010

Discussion

You can see that Greenpeace has FOE beat hands down, across all categories. This could be a function of Greenpeace being a more established organization, with a brand that is a global icon. People like to follow the leader, and they'll do so in social media as in any other aspect of life.

The number that particularly stands out in the table above is that MySpace friends number. Since MySpace is a site heavily trafficked by music lovers, this differential would indicate that Greenpeace has some particular strength with music fans. That's something for corporations in the crosshairs of Greenpeace to keep in mind, i.e., targeting (or not) the music lover segment in future PR battles. But there's a big disconnect between that MySpace fan number and that Twitter number. The Greenpeace twitter number is only a bit over 10% of their MySpace number. I think they're missing something there. Greenpeace could be leveraging that MySpace following into their Twitter effort and using it for effect in various campaigns. And the same idea could be applied to Facebook. With only about a third of the following on Facebook as they have on MySpace, Greenpeace doesn't seem to be doing much in the way of cross-pollination. This lack of cross-pollination should be something kept in mind by targeted corporate communications personnel. Now, let's chat about FOE.

What I find especially disappointing in these FOE numbers is the level of

Twitter followers that FOE has. I have more Twitter followers than that.[45] They simply aren't leveraging their Facebook and MySpace presences to increase their level of Twitter followers which, if FOE had more Twitter followers, could make it easier and more effective for them to spread quick, mini-blog type messages during hot and fluid campaigns. And speaking about their Facebook and MySpace followings, for an organization the size of FOE US, those following levels are terrible. Numbers of that level indicate that FOE isn't doing an adequate job in developing their social media campaigns. Perhaps FOE isn't taking social media seriously? Something else for targeted corporate communications personnel to keep in mind.

What about the FOE YouTube numbers? Well, it seems abundantly clear, about 20 times more clear, that Greenpeace is giving viewers a lot more to look at than is FOE. Perhaps FOE isn't as visually oriented as Greenpeace. Again, you corporate communications managers take note.

So, what can we conclude from all of this?

Conclusion

The take-away, for corporate opponents of these "irregular competitors," is that between Greenpeace US and FOE US, in social media Greenpeace would be a more formidable foe than would FOE itself. In social media, by comparison, FOE isn't much of a foe. With such low numbers, for corporations in a social media PR battle with FOE US, corporations should concentrate very heavily on creating, discussing, and propagating their message in social media. FOE has a relatively underrepresented presence there, and any corporation locking horns with FOE US should take advantage of FOE US's relative absence and comparative disengagement with the medium.

For corporations with high Twitter follower numbers, they should especially concentrate in that mini-blogging venue, both preemptively and reactively. It's apparent that FOE US doesn't realize their weakness there in that social venue. And any corporation that has ever been engaged in a "battle" with FOE US, or anticipates one in the future, should act now to build their following in Twitter, so that FOE may be "out-Twittered" if and when the time comes.

A Journey in Anti-Corporate Thought

February 9, 2010

Categories: Activism, Anti-Corporatism

For those interested in learning about the anti-corporate movement, I recommend a book that I recently completed. *The Rise of the Anti-Corporate Movement* by Evan Osborne is a first-rate work. [46]

Subtitled *Corporations and the People Who Hate Them*, in this book Evan does good work in laying out the history of the corporation, taking us back about four millennia to the origin of what evolved into today's modern corporation. He then moves us forward in time, tracing the development of the corporation from ancient Assyria, up through 18th century Britain, and then to its current form both worldwide and in the United States. At each stop in this journey through corporate time, Evan stops to impress upon the reader the details of corporate myth created at each stage, emphasizing how those myths trickled down into today's collective social conscience, but debunking the myth before continuing the journey.

During the early parts of the journey, he deftly points out that previous forms of the corporation had, by virtue of their legal foundation in significantly less democratic societies, much more power than the corporate form takes in today's America, decrying the claims by anti-corporate activists that modern corporations are omnipotent and all-powerful. He punctuates this illustrative journey of countering the claims of the anti-corporate movement (ACM) with profound insights, based on common sense and everyday observations. One such insight undermines general ACM claims of runaway corporate power by observing the corporate disdain for the corporate income tax and stating that if corporations were truly as all-powerful as the ACM makes them out to be, then indeed there would be no income tax.

About a third of the way through the book, Evan, an economist at Wright State University, takes on the economic assertion often put forth by the ACM, that society is actually poorer because of the existence of the corporation. Over many pages, he does an excellent job explaining how this claim is invalid. His counter-argument is clear, cogent, and convincing. I've read other books making this same argument (For example, *The Role of Business in the Modern World*, by David Henderson. [47]), but they were not nearly as on-point or as substantially sourced as is The Rise.

This is definitely a book that should be read by all engaged in business issues involving activists and NGOs.

It's also a book that could benefit members of the general public, to help dispel some of those corporate myths generated over the past few hundred years. I have no illusions that members of the general public will read this book any time soon. But, the loss is theirs because of the great insights they would miss. I'll close with one of those insights.

Near the end of the book, when Evan invokes the late economist Milton Friedman who stated that the corporation owes no more "social responsibility" than any other member of society, Evan states that it is just as improper for the anti-corporate campaigner to use the law to force a corporation to pursue the campaigner's objectives as it is for a corporation to use the law to force the anti-corporate campaigner to pursue the corporation's objectives. We see many examples of the former and, I'd dare say, none of the latter.

Of course, all the issues found within this book could be debated incessantly in philosophy and business ethics classes. But that's part of what makes this book so interesting, the intellectual challenges found within.

Thanks, Evan for a great book.

One Source Doesn't An Anti-Corporate Environment Make

February 11, 2010

Categories: Anti-Corporatism, Research - Questionable

Wondering how your company can become more competitive in today's "anti-corporate" business environment? (Or at least a business environment that's portrayed as being "anti-corporate.") Hey. Who isn't? Apparently it's "known" that today's company operates in an "anti-corporate" environment. So let's talk about it.

I recently finished reading "Engaging Fringe Stakeholders for Competitive Imagination" by Stuart Hart and Sanjay Sharma.[48] In this 2004 article from the Academy of Management Executive, the authors offer up the theory of engaging with "fringe stakeholders" in order to reach two objectives. The first objective, which is related to anti-corporatism, is about avoiding what the authors call "smart mobs," which they define as the wrath of individuals that can be created and mustered online for the purpose of spreading negative information about the company. The second objective the authors describe is related to efficient product development. The achievement of both of these goals depends upon getting pertinent information from the fringes of the stakeholder sphere which surrounds a company. The article details how companies may go about achieving these goals.

The achievement of the second objective, more efficient product development, is described with various case studies showing how certain corporations have extended their market research operations to the outer fringes of the societies in which those companies do business. From this "fringe information" collected have come new initiatives for products designed to solve problems that the companies had not known existed prior to their journey to the fringe. Thus, the term "competitive imagination" used in this article's title. The insights gained through the fringe market research give those companies who conduct it a competitive leg up on their competition. Very sound reasoning. No objections here at all.

There is a double-edged sword in this approach, one that cuts toward both objectives. The authors maintain that by performing this type of informational outreach, not only may a company discover new consumer insights for application within product development, but the company may also simultaneously engage with fringe stakeholders, or what they describe as "non-salient" stakeholders, who had previously been ignored by the company. As I pointed out earlier, this is the first objective that the authors raised. Hart and Sharma say that through this engagement and interaction with, and from the subsequent input from, these fringe stakeholders, the company may preclude a public relations backlash initiated by these fringe actors, who may manifest as the "smart mob," against future company actions. Again, I have no objections here. Proactive communication can serve as a preemptory tactic, reaping future benefits. But what I do object to is the premise upon which Hart and Sharma base most of their thesis. That premise is found in one pair of statements near the beginning of this article.

On the second page of this article we see the passage,

The power of governments has eroded in the wake of globalization and the growth of transnational corporations with global supply chains that span several continents. Non-governmental organizations (NGOs) and civil society groups have stepped into the breach, assuming the role of monitor and, in some cases, enforcer of social and environmental standards.

The source for these two "statements" is David Korten's *When Corporations Rule the World.* These two statements set up the standard, and progressively tiresome, anti-corporate meme, which is used as a foundation for the balance of the article. The article's foundation of anti-corporatism is vital to the value of the engagement strategies the authors recommend because if there was no anti-corporate sentiment out there, well then, this whole idea of engaging with the fringe would have only one objective, the enhancement of product development. No double-edged sword would be needed. The goal of avoiding the smart mob would not then apply. But since Hart and Sharma say that the power of governments has been usurped by corporations and that NGOs and activists are now our last hope, then the value of the authors' engagement approach is increased. And, as a result, so is the value of their article. No anti-corporate sentiment? Well, then the article is just another take on market research.

I have no idea what the authors, Hart and Sharma, are doing now, but when they wrote this 2004 article they were described as follows. Hart is listed as being the S.C. Johnson Chair of Sustainable Global Enterprise at Cornell University's Johnson School of Management. Hart is also listed as being a professor of strategic management at the University of North Carolina's Kenan-Fagler Business School. Sharma is listed as being a professor of policy at Wilfrid Laurier University in Canada. So, quite frankly, I'm astounded that men with these academic credentials would use only one source upon which to describe a business environment, that tired old meme of the "evil corporation," that supports their thesis. I'm also astounded that the journal editor would let this type of research go to print. And, adding even more to my astonishment, I'm gobsmacked that they would draw that one source from an author who is seen as left-leaning. ("Although Korten speaks from an obviously liberal position … ", see the Library Journal review on Amazon.com. [49]) What the heck happened to academic balance? And what happened to basing your thesis on more than one source?

I agree with the methodology that Hart and Sharma propose in that it can, indeed, be of great value in obtaining "competitive imagination" for use in new product development. And even engaging the "smart mob" preemptively may, under certain circumstances, have value. But as for the overall article,

I just can't get behind their "statement" concerning the supplantation of government by corporation. without some additional and balanced support.

And for that reason, for me, the whole article just falls apart.

The Irregular Competition Threat Index

February 16, 2010

Categories: Irregular Competition - Threat Index

All irregular competitors are not created equal. Nor do they necessarily later all become equal and evolve into threats about which a company should be uniformly concerned. Some irregular competitors have more mojo than others; either because of smarter staff or better funding or both.

When you're a corporate communications or PR person trying to deal with an irregular competitor who is talking trash about your company, it's good to know something about them. (That harks back to what Sun Tzu said.) An understanding of the irregular competitor's strengths and weaknesses will help you: 1) to determine whether you should be responding to them at all; and, 2) if it's determined that you should respond, to have a knowledge of their strengths and weaknesses which can help you choose which strategies and tactics to apply against them.

To assist in this understanding, today I introduce The Irregular Competition Threat Index. This is a scale rating system that I will use in some of the case study posts on this blog. This rating system will rank the irregular competitors discussed in terms of their general strengths and weaknesses in the use of social media. You may select those irregular competitor case studies specifically under the category Irregular Competition or more generally under the category Research - Case Studies.

The ranking of irregular competitors in The Irregular Competition Threat Index will be primarily along factors of their social media and web campaign strategies, but offline strategic factors may also contribute to their rating, and these will be called out in the case study posts.

So, I look forward to presenting some interesting case studies and I also look forward to your feedback.

EXCLUSIVE
Corporatewatch.org Is Not Social?

February 16, 2010

Categories: Anti-Corporatism, Irregular Competition - Corporate Watch - Threat Index, Research - Case Studies

Corporate Watch. [50] Do you know who they are?

Well, Corporate Watch, located in London, UK, is a research organization with the objective:

> *... to examine the oil industry, globalistion, genetic engineering, food, toxic chemicals, privatisation and many other areas, to build up a picture of almost every type of corporate crime and the nature and mechanisms of corporate power, both economic and political. We have worked with and provided information to empower peace campaigners, environmentalists, and trade unionists; large NGOs and small autonomous groups; journalists, MPs, and members of the public.* [51]

Since Corporate Watch keeps an "eye" on corporations, the least I can do is return the favor. So, I keep an "eye" on them. I check their website periodically to catch up on the latest "corporate scandals," much of which is a re-hashing of themes that have been floating around for quite a while. Since I've been visiting their site, I've noticed that CorporateWatch.org is not "social." By "social" I don't mean "socialist," although much of their writing certainly contains that philosophy, and by "social" I don't mean captivating at parties or adept at interaction at a bar. By "social" I mean employing social media in their communications strategy. Such a move would seem to be a logical step for Corporate Watch because, as activists, social media is almost tailor-made for the types of missions that they undertake. Social media is a perfect environment for an organization like Corporate Watch to extend their message. But, no. Apparently, they don't understand that. They don't do that "social thing."

On a recent visit, where I was once again befuddled as to why Corporate Watch doesn't have a social media campaign, it occurred to me that maybe I was missing indicators of their participation in the social web. Upon visits to their site, I've found myself looking for the "obligatory" indicators of a

Twitter, Facebook, MySpace, or other social media account. You know. What I was looking for was those cute buttons hung on websites and attached to social media profiles at Twitter, Facebook, etc. CorporateWatch.org doesn't have those. But that doesn't necessarily mean that they don't participate in social media. Maybe I wasn't looking in the right place. So, I started a hard target search.

In their Nav Bar I noticed "Links" and "Contact & Links" anchor text. I clicked them, with great anticipation I might add. Both links took me to the same place, a portal page filled with links to other anti-corporatist websites. "Interesting. But not what I'm looking for right now," thought I, "Perhaps they just don't want to place those cute little social buttons on their site. Maybe they think those buttons are a little too 'bourgeois.' " So, I moved on. I moved on to Twitter, Facebook, and MySpace to perform a discrete search, to see if I could find a Corporate Watch presence.

Here's what I found.

Twitter: Nothing. No Corporate Watch presence. Tried various spellings. Unless they're hiding it very well (like under a different name), I didn't find a Twitter account for Corporate Watch. I did get search results for a pile of other .org organizations, however. But nothing for Corporate Watch. Yet, while I was there, so it shouldn't be a wasted trip, I updated my own status. Never pass up a good opportunity to tweet, I always say.

Facebook: Again, nothing. No Corporate Watch presence there either. Again, I tried various spellings. The Facebook search gave me some web results for Corporate Watch, but nothing of a social nature, just standard Web 1.0-type website references. I didn't update my Facebook status while I was there, though. My Facebook friends are mostly real friends, friends I've had since junior high, or relatives. Not business associates. I didn't think people I knew in seventh grade and my cousins, whom I've known since Day One, would really care about my CorporateWatch.org hard target search. So, I moved on again. Next stop, MySpace.

MySpace: Ah - hah. Got a hit there. They have a MySpace account at MySpace.com/corporate_watch. There was an Australian Corporate Watch profile there, as well. But I disregarded that, at least for now, because in this post I'm just concentrating on the British version of Corporate Watch.

Let's talk about that MySpace presence.

On the Corporate Watch MySpace profile, the visitor is greeted with the following caption:

> *The Earth is not dying - it is being killed. And those who are killing it have names and addresses.*

Ooooo ... kay. Rather baleful. But let's move past this abstruse warning and the rhetoric and take a look at what's happening on this MySpace profile, or should I say what is not happening on at this profile.

Corporate Watch has only 127 friends on their MySpace account (as of January 27, 2010). I'm not entirely certain how long this profile has been up and trying to gather friends. There is no date indicating creation of this MySpace profile. But the last Corporate Watch administrator login date was shown as June 30, 2008. So, after at most a year and one-half, Corporate Watch has been able to muster only 127 friends. That's not a very impressive following for being in the MySpace game for at least 18 months. Quantitatively, I can say that their MySpace effort is not successful. Now, let's take a qualitative look at those friends.

From a random sampling of their friends list, most of those friends appear to be other activist groups, not individuals. This high proportion of groups as friends indicates that Corporate Watch is having trouble attracting individuals, which I would expect would be extremely important to the success of the anti-corporate campaigns that they undertake. The fact that most of their friends list is comprised of other activist groups indicates that Corporate Watch may be "preaching to the choir." Consistent with their friends list being mostly groups, not surprisingly, many of the comments on their MySpace page are from activist groups, not individuals. This is a strong indication that the Corporate Watch message may have limited reach. To test my theory of limited reach, I took a trip over to Compete.com, a website ranking service. Limited reach, indeed. Compete.com shows that for 2009, CorporateWatch.org attracted between 500 to 3500 visitors per month. Again, not very impressive, is it? [52]

And getting back to those Corporate Watch MySpace friends. They aren't very active commenters. On the date I visited (January 27, 2010), the most recent comment was dated November 18, 2009; the comment immediately prior was dated May 25, 2009. The comment before that? October 1, 2008.

See what I mean? Not a very active MySpace group. The group is limited in interaction, number, and frequency.

So, what does the foregoing mean?

Well, it means that:

1. Corporate Watch is apparently either ignorant of the benefits social media could bring to their campaigns, or is overlooking the benefits that a properly organized social media campaign could have, especially for an activist organization. They either don't understand social media, are afraid to use it, or are oblivious to it. In any case, this is a "plus" for the corporations that Corporate Watch "watches."

2. Due to their relatively limited reach, and seemingly narrowly segmented audience (at least based on the sample seen at their MySpace profile), this "irregular competitor" is not a significant threat against the reputations of the corporations they monitor and on which they report.

All of this is very surprising. For an organization that, by their own declaration on the banner of their website, has been doing "corporate critical research since 1996," one would think that they would have evolved with web technology. That has been a web technology that since 1996 has given birth to new social movements and "legs" to social movements that existed prior to that date. But this activist group, this "irregular competitor," has not kept current with the evolving trends in web communications. Indeed, their website, CorporateWatch.org, looks like something right out of 1996. Click over to their site. See for yourself. The site is of the Web 1.0 variety, static and non-interactive. They don't even offer an RSS feed. In this current configuration, their lack of employment of Web 2.0 technologies and participation on the social web seriously mitigates the degree of efficacy that Corporate Watch can have as an "irregular competitor."

On the "Irregular Competition Threat Index," a scale of 1 to 10 (10 being the highest threat level), I rate CorporateWatch.org as a "3."

EXCLUSIVE
Change.org Is a Formidable Irregular Competitor

February 18, 2010

Categories: Irregular Competition - Change.org - Threat Index, Research - Case Studies

Change.org. [53] That's the focus of this case study in irregular competition. Before we begin, do you need a definition of "irregular competition?" (Author's Note: If so, please refer back to the post "Irregular Competition" - The Newest Threat, which you may read in the December 2009 chapter.)

Introduction

Ready?

Who is Change.org and what do they do? Well, to help define them, let's start with a passage from their own About page (accessed January 28, 2010):

> *Today as citizens of the world, we face a daunting array of social and environmental problems ranging from health care and education to global warming and economic inequality. For each of these issues, whether local or global in scope, there are millions of people who care passionately about working for change but lack the information and opportunities necessary to translate their interest into effective action.*

> *Change.org aims to address this need by serving as the central platform informing and empowering movements for social change around the most important issues of our time.* [54]

Change.org is a site, and an organization, that combines activist editorial with one-stop petition shopping. As a "platform" for social change, their editorial content, both from guest writers and from Change.org staff and rendered in blog format, attracts readers from across the Internet who, once at the site, may participate in the signing of petitions organized for grievance purposes against various targets. The petition initiatives are plainly and prominently featured among the editorial content. Even for the casual reader, not noticing these petition initiatives is almost impossible.

Some of the targets of the petitions are traditional petition recipients, i.e., government entities and legislators. Some of those targets are entities less accustomed to receiving petitions from the general public, i.e., trade coalitions between academe and corporations. And some of those targets are entities even less accustomed to receiving petitions from the public, no less acting on them, i.e., corporations.

The petitions may be started by groups or by individuals. Change.org gives either groups or individuals the platform and the audience to start or augment a social movement.

Since this blog, Telofski.com, is about irregular competition and how it affects business, from here on in this post I will be discussing Change.org from the viewpoint of being an irregular competitor. And as you know from the definition of irregular competition, per the post I mentioned in first paragraph above, irregular competitors are activist organizations and NGOs within the context of their impact on corporations.

At first glance, Change.org would appear to be an activist organization itself, targeting or enabling the targeting of various corporations, and would seem to fit the definition of irregular competition, one aspect of which is that irregular competitors are generally thought to be non-profit. But, after doing some research on Change.org, my findings say that they don't seem to fit this definition completely. And where they don't seem to meet completely the definition of irregular competition is in that non-profit aspect. They don't appear to be a non-profit organization. The reason I say this is due to the findings of my corporate status search for Change.org which I will share with you now.

Findings

Corporate Status

In this corporate status search, I had two objectives. First, to identify the corporate name behind Change.org, and second to determine if that corporation was a non-profit organization.

Identifying the corporate entity behind Change.org wasn't particularly difficult, but it did require some digging, as well as the knowledge of where to dig. The first place I looked for corporate entity information was at the bottom of the Change.org home page. The copyright notice is always a good place to start to look for this type of information and theirs says "© 2010, Change.

org. All Rights Reserved." Hmmm. I thought that it's odd for an organization that describes itself as a "social entrepreneurship venture" not to have the more liberal and permissive Creative Commons [55] copyright notice. This was an indication that they might be a for-profit corporation. A nice clue, but what I was looking for was a corporate name, and the copyright notice didn't give me a corporate name, only the website address. Unless, I thought, the domain name is also the corporate name. I moved on. (Note: This characterization of "social entrepreneurship venture" is also per their About page, same access date as above. Yes, I know that access date is several weeks prior to this post's date. That's because I tend to write ahead and employ the "magic" of Word Press' post pre-scheduling function.)

Thinking that the domain name and the corporate name were the same, I then made a leap of research faith. Presuming Change.org to be a non-profit corporation, I tried searching for Change.org on Guidestar.org which is a database site containing information about non-profit corporations. On the same access date as listed above, Change.org was not listed at Guidestar.org, indicating that they are probably not a non-profit organization. However, there is always the possibility that Change.org was overlooked in the Guidestar.org database input process (even though Change.org lists Guidestar.org as an information "partner." [56]), or that the Change.org organization is registered on Guidestar.org under another company name. I wanted more and better information. I continued my search.

Still in search of that corporate name, to identify it, I tried the old standby, searching the "Whois" Registry at my favorite Internet domain registration website, but that search didn't provide much useful information. I then went back to the Change.org About page. There was a clue there that I had missed before.

The About page said that this social entrepreneurship venture was based in San Francisco, CA. Okay. Now, we're cooking, thought I. So from there I went to the California Secretary of State's website to check for Change.org's corporate filing information. You can see that California corporate filing information, too. Just go to the California Secretary of State's Business Entity search page. [57] Check the "corporation" radio button, then type in "Change. org" in the search box, then click the Search button. After you do that you will see a listing for Change.org, Inc. Click on the company's name and then you will see the following result:

Entity Name:
CHANGE.ORG, INC.

Entity Number:
C2929488

Date Filed:
09/29/2006

Status:
FORFEITED

Jurisdiction:
DELAWARE

Entity Address:
709 DOUGLAS ST

Entity City, State, Zip:
SAN FRANCISCO CA 94114

Agent for Service of Process:
C T CORPORATION SYSTEM

Agent Address:
818 WEST SEVENTH ST

Agent City, State, Zip:
LOS ANGELES CA 90017

Alright, so now I had the corporate name. But, now this search was starting to get very interesting. Yes, Change.org's statement on their About page saying that they were based in San Francisco was confirmed by this state record, although that record was going on four years old at the time I accessed it. But, I wasn't really intrigued by their location. No, an online company being based in San Francisco wasn't a surprise. But, that word "Forfeited" was a surprise. That word intrigued me. So, that I would have a proper definition of "Forfeited," I clicked on the "Field Descriptions and Status Definitions" link provided on the search results page. I looked through the list of definitions [58] and found this:

Suspended or Forfeited: The business entity's powers, rights and privileges were suspended or forfeited in California 1) by the Franchise Tax Board for failure to file a return and/or failure to pay taxes, penalties, or interest; and/or 2) by the Secretary of State for failure to file the required Statement of Information and, if applicable, the required Statement by Common Interest Development Association. Information regarding the type of suspension can be obtained by ordering a status report. For information on ordering a status report, refer to Information Requests.

Researcher's Note: This search of the California records was made on January 28, 2010.

Now, in this particular case study, it didn't matter to me if the corporate status was forfeited for reason #1 or reason #2 as shown in the definition above. Or even if Change.org, Inc. is registered in California or if they even need to be registered in California. Although, it would be interesting to find out these things, I didn't order a status report via the Information Requests link which would have detailed the situation further. If you're interested in further information on these issues, you may always follow that link. No, I had enough of a clue here to reach my second research objective, to determine if this company is a for-profit organization or is of the non-profit variety. That clue was "Delaware."

So, my next stop was at the website of the Department of State: Division of Corporations for the State of Delaware. Delaware, the home of more corporate "headquarters" than any other state.[59] At that site, in the search box you would type in "Change.org," then hit the Search button. From there, click on the result "Change.org, Inc." You will then go to a page entitled "Entity Details" and you will see the following:

Entity Details

THIS IS NOT A STATEMENT OF GOOD STANDING

File Number:
4215439

Incorporation Date / Formation Date:
09/08/2006
(mm/dd/yyyy)

Entity Name:
CHANGE.ORG, INC.

Entity Kind:
CORPORATION

Entity Type:
GENERAL

Residency:
DOMESTIC

State:
DE

REGISTERED AGENT INFORMATION

Name:
THE CORPORATION TRUST COMPANY

Address:
CORPORATION TRUST CENTER 1209 ORANGE STREET

City:
WILMINGTON

County:
NEW CASTLE

State:
DE

Postal Code:
19801

Phone:
(302)658-7581

Additional Information is available for a fee. You can retrieve Status for a fee of $10.00 or more detailed information including current *franchise tax assessment, current filing history and more for a fee of $20.00.*

Yes, it looks like they transferred their corporate status from California to Delaware in September 2006. And I thought that significant, but not pertinent to my research objectives. In the Discussion section of this case study, I will talk about why I think that switch from California to Delaware is significant. That's later. For right now, let's stay on the second objective of determining if this company is non-profit or not.

Now, I believe that that sentence "This is not a statement of good standing" doesn't necessarily mean that the record is a statement of bad standing. I believe this means that to get the official statement of "good standing" you need to pay the record retrieval fee. So, what you see in these preliminary search results would just be an unofficial record. But considering that I was seeking their profit status, I knew I didn't need the official statement. What I needed was right before my eyes. And what answered my profit status question was "Entity Type: General."

If you click on the Entity Type link you will see the definitions:

A - General - Type General refers to a legal entity with no special attributes such as non profit or religious.

R - Non-profit or Religious - This description type refers to a corporation that sets forth in it's certificate of incorporation or subsequent documents that it is a non-profit corporation. The "Religious" literal does not infer that, in every case, the corporation is for Religious purposes only. The intent is to define the corporation as Non-Profit, charitable corporation which maybe formed for Religious purposes. [60]

Researcher's Note: This search of the Delaware records was made on January 28, 2010.

So, according to these Delaware Secretary of State definitions, if Change. org, Inc. was a non-profit corporation, in the Entity Type field it would read "Non-profit or Religious" and not "General."

Therefore, from this research and the evidence found, it appears that Change. org, Inc. is a for-profit corporation. And I will take it that state corporate records are highly reliable.

Why is it important to know whether Change.org, Inc. is a for-profit venture? Well, there are several reasons. And you and I will discuss those reasons when we get to the Discussion section of this case study.

*   *   *

Right now, I'm going to pause this case study by breaking it into two parts. Generally, for readability reasons, I don't like to write over 1500 words in any one post and in this post I've exceeded my own limit by quite a bit. So from here, we will move on to Part 2 of this case study.

Part 2 will be published on Tuesday, February 23, 2010. If you are reading this prior to that date, please click here to subscribe to the free RSS feed so you will be notified when Part 2 publishes. If you are reading this after that date, you may simply click here to be taken to Part 2.

EXCLUSIVE
Change.org Is a Formidable Irregular Competitor - Part 2

February 23, 2010

Categories: Irregular Competition - Change.org - Threat Index, Research - Case Studies

So, here we are in Part 2 of this case study in irregular competition, a case study that focuses on Change.org. If you haven't read Part 1 and you wish to do so before proceeding on with this second part, then please click here to go to "Change.org Is a Formidable Irregular Competitor - Part 1." (Or, if reading the book version, simply turn back to the previous article.)

In Part 1, we left off with the Findings, Corporate Status. In today's post we'll pick up with the research findings and take a look at some of the web traffic factors of Change.org.

Findings

Traffic

Change.org is no slouch when it comes to attracting traffic on the Internet. Let's see what Alexa.com, one of the major Internet traffic trackers and a unit of Amazon.com, says about Change.org.

Alexa.com

Per Alexa.com, accessed on January 29, 2010, based on traffic Change.org was ranked as the 16,464th most popular site on the Internet. You can check their ranking today by clicking here.[61] Now, this ranking of 16,464 might not seem very impressive at first blush. But, I can tell you that this level of traffic ranking is very impressive. Here's why.

Alexa.com tracks approximately 20 million websites. Number 20 million would be the least trafficked website that Alexa.com tracks, while number 1 would be the most popular. (On the date that I checked this, Google.com was the number 1 site.) This ranking of 16,464th is a global ranking. Alexa.com showed that the ranking for United States traffic is 4,350. This is especially important since most of the social issues with which Change.org deals are American issues. With Change.org being the 4,350th most popular website in the United States, it's plain to see that many Americans are receiving the Change.org message.

Okay, traffic rankings are fine. But what do these rankings translate to in terms of the numbers of visitors that actually go to the site? Alexa.com doesn't provide much in terms of identifying actual numbers, but Compete.com does. So, let's go over there.

Compete.com

On the same date as shown above, I went over to Compete.com to learn about Change.org's traffic level. You can take a look at the current Change.org status by clicking here. [62] On the date that I examined it, Compete.com showed that in 2009 Change.org averaged around 300,000 unique visitors per month. That means that every month well over a quarter of a million people are seeing the social change, and anti-corporate, messages that are being sent via Change.org.

Where's all this traffic coming from? Well, Alexa.com says that Change.org has 2,321 sites linking in. Compete.com, on the date I visited, showed that approximately 28% of Change.org's referrals were from Facebook.com. This is a considerable percentage of their referral traffic, and may account for much of those 2,321 inbound links reported by Alexa. com. So, it would appear that the social media program of Change.org contributes heavily to their activist efforts. Let's take a look at that social media program. (Author's Note: The previous two paragraphs were edited slightly from the original post.)

Social Media Program

Here we're going to take a focused look at Change.org's social media program. You and I are going to concentrate today only on their Facebook and Twitter efforts. They do have other areas of the social web in which they are active and I may come back to those areas in a future post. But because Change.org's social media effort is so extensive, for now, I would just like to concentrate on their Facebook and Twitter initiatives.

On the date examined, January 29, 2010, the Change.org Facebook main fan page contained about 4,000 fans.[63] This is a respectable amount, but it is not overly impressive when you consider the amount of traffic that they have going to the Change.org site every month. Yet, the Change.org Facebook blog effort more than makes up for any seeming deficiency in fan levels on the main Facebook page. Let's take a look at the fan blogs they have on Facebook and also at their individual Facebook blog fan numbers.[64] (See table on next page.)

A number of over 27,000 Facebook blog participants, as of January 29, 2010, is quite impressive and most likely contributes to those heavy unique visitor numbers we saw above. Of course, it could be that some of the 4,000 Facebook primary page fans participate in more than one blog, making the blog fan numbers appear larger. Yet, it is clear that with a blog fan number of over 27,000, the Change.org message has great "legs" and propagation potential.

A random sampling of the fans that I observed in the blog pages, and on the main fan page, shows than most are individuals and not groups. So, this means that Change.org is not necessarily "preaching to the choir." A high proportion of fans being other groups, similar in agenda to that of the social causes that Change.org promotes, would certainly indicate that their audience characteristics are limited. But with individuals comprising most of the audience, we cannot say that the audience is necessarily skewed.

Name of Facebook Blog	Number of fans
Global Warming	981
Criminal Justice	773
Animal Rights	5,819
Gay Rights	6,700
Education	326
Women\'s Rights	3,202
End Homelessness	1,427
Social Entrepreneurship	1,848
Universal Health Care	1,321
Humanitarian Relief	228
Immigrant Rights	564
End Human Trafficking	1,443
Global Health	225
Poverty in America	275
Sustainable Food	1,995
Job for Change	258
Total Number of Blog Fans	27,385

And with a "Take Action" tab prominently displayed on their Facebook fan pages, any of the many blog participants can make an easy trip to that "Take Action" [65] area where they will find at least three choices for petition participation. Change.org has many more than three petitions active on their main website at any given time. So, on their Facebook Take Action page, they have displayed a convenient link which when clicked will take the Facebook user to the Take Action area of the Change.org website. [66] There the user will be greeted with a full menu of petitions. The visitor merely needs to enter in some identification info and press submit. There are many other features that Change.org deftly employs on their Facebook fan page, almost all of which will further their activist campaigns, but I'm rapidly approaching my self-imposed 1500 word limitation for blog posts. I've more to say in other areas, so we will need to move on. Let's move to Change.org's Twitter use.

Their Twitter main profile page shows, on January 29, 2010, a Twitter following of almost 10,500. [67] This number is nothing to be "sneezed at." There is a lot of controversy on the level of Twitter followers. The arguments revolve around quality or quantity of followers. Of course, just accumulating followers for the sake of inflating your Twitter following number may not increase the power of your message. But a high Twitter number certainly doesn't decrease the power either. Although this Twitter following is not considered extremely high, it is a decent level and indicates that the following of Change.org on Twitter can help increase the efficacy of Change.org's message. This number of 10,500 may also help contribute to their petition effort. As new petitions are launched on the main Change.org site, tweets may be launched, automatically, driving traffic to the site for petition participation, signature, and completion.

As I alluded to above, there is so much that can be said about Change.org's social media program. I've barely scratched the surface. I could probably write a book about how this particular irregular competitor exerts force against various business efforts. Perhaps I will. But right now, because I'm approaching my own words per post limitation, I'm going to wrap up this case study and move on to the Discussion and Conclusion section.

Discussion and Conclusion

Overall, this is one very high-powered irregular competitor. They are a very adept activist organization and they make use of their digital tools, as we saw above, in an effective manner.

If indeed Change.org is a for-profit corporation, which they certainly seem to be as shown by the evidence in Part 1 of this case study, it certainly makes one wonder why they use the dot org upper level domain name in both their corporate name and in their URL. There is no prohibition in for-profit companies using the dot org upper domain level name. It's just that it's not customary for this to be done. The dot org designation is usually reserved for the non-profit organization. Of course, I have my own theory as to why they use the dot org upper level domain name. A theory about which I will leave you to ponder. You may have your own theory as well.

Their presumed status as a for-profit company, as explored in Part 1 of this case study, if true, is quite unusual for an activist group. This would make Change.org a new breed of activist. They are a new breed of activist not only for their ability to combine editorial content with activist initiatives, but they would also be classified as a new breed of activist because of their apparent for-profit status. And this presumed status combined with Change.org's excellent use of digital technology, as we have seen here in Part 2, makes them a formidable irregular competitor.

In Part 1, I said I would discuss why their for-profit status would be important. Here it is.

The fact that they are a Delaware corporation (remember from Part 1 that they switched to become a Delaware corporation in 2006), and if they are indeed a for-profit company, affords them certain state income tax advantages not available to corporations domiciled in other states. This tax advantage gives Delaware corporations comparatively more net income with which to work. Perhaps that's why they made the corporate registration switch from California to Delaware in 2006? And in the case of Change.org, such a status would simply give them relatively more resources with which to communicate activist, and sometimes anti-corporate, messages; perhaps some of which are aimed at your employer. Ironic, isn't it?

You may be thinking that since non-profit 501 (c) 3 organizations don't pay any taxes at all, wouldn't a better organizational strategy be to simply form under that tax-exempt, non-profit status, and have even more resources with which to operate? Not necessarily. I have two theories for which they may be organizing their corporation in this for-profit manner.

The first theory is that for-profit companies can do more in terms of backing political candidates, as we have seen, at least in part, from the recent U.S. Supreme Court decision in Citizens United vs. FEC. Non-profit corporations, i.e., 501 (c) 3 - tax-exempt organizations, because they do not pay taxes and in effect operate partially on implicit tax payer dollars, have many, many, restrictions on the backing of political candidates. Thus, for-profit activist groups can have a far greater impact on the political process, and by extension a greater effect on corporations, than can their non-profit activist group cousins, with all the anti-corporate effects that implies.

The second theory is that for-profit companies can raise funds in the private money market. Venture capitalists are often looking for new tech companies to invest in. And a tech-based company such as Change.org would represent a new vanguard of company, one with a differential advantage. This might increase their overall ability to attract funding, and make them not have to rely on the capriciousness of donations as would a non-profit corporation. Thereby, the possibility exists that this type of activist organization could be better financed than the non-profit variety.

Of course, these are all theories. If Change.org is not a for-profit corporation, I would certainly like to see them correct their "Entity Type" status on their

Delaware corporate filing, as shown in the Part 1 post, so as to avoid further confusion.

What all this comes down to is, based on the evidence shown in both Parts 1 and 2, Change.org is a very formidable irregular competitor.

So, on the "Irregular Competition Threat Index," a scale of 1 to 10 (10 being the highest threat level), I rate Change.org as a "9." If this organization has your corporation in its activist sights, well then, you may need some help.

FOE Plays Anti-Corporate Card

February 25, 2010

Categories: Anti-Corporatism, Irregular Competition - Friends of the Earth, Truth

While recently reviewing the Friends of the Earth US (FOE) website, I saw that they introduced a new genetic engineering policy campaigner named Eric Hoffman. [68] Congratulations to Mr. Hoffman. Perhaps at a future time, he and I can have some interesting discussions on issues of mutual concern. But I hope that those future discussions would be based upon better writing than that which I found in connection with Mr. Hoffman's employment announcement.

As part of the FOE US [69] introduction of Mr. Hoffman, FOE used the following lead-in passage:

> *Friends of the Earth is a fierce advocate of scientific progress, but corporations often seek profit from scientific developments with little regard for human health. We must take precaution (sic) to ensure new technologies don't do more harm than good.*

Now, I'll put aside the minor spelling error in their second sentence. I'll also put aside the fact that there was no date on this post, which is really just a "bush league" error when it comes to Web site writing and management. Instead of those small errors, I'll just concentrate on the meaning of the passage itself.

This approach of playing the "anti-corporate card" gets a bit wearisome, and is plainly just bad argumentation. The anti-corporate card to which I refer is the phrase, "corporations often seek profit from scientific development with little regard for human health." Let's take this phrase apart to see how it represents poor argumentation on the part of FOE and only weakens any argument that they are trying to make.

"Corporations often seek profit." Yes. Okay, I can go along with that part. That is the function of a corporation, to seek a profit in its activities, many of which are directed at scientific developments. Thankfully they do that. Without profits, no one would ever get a merit raise in pay. And without scientific developments, people would be dropping dead from what are now, as compared to the past, "easily-cured" illnesses or from complications arising out of minor injuries. Now, let's move on to the next part of the phrase and talk about "with little regard for human health."

This part of the phrase conjures up a picture of research & development departments operated by zany, madcap scientists who indiscriminately toss new products out the door without adequately testing them, or at least without testing them to the satisfaction of government regulators within the jurisdictions in which their corporations do business. In my career, I've known many R&D personnel, and have found them to be painfully cautious and responsible personalities, almost to the point, perhaps, of being too cautious. I've yet to meet one who I would consider as either a businessperson or scientist with "little regard for human health." If, indeed, these individuals, and the corporations for which they worked, "often" acted as portrayed by this phrase, their mad scientist-like lack of "regard for human health" would produce deadly products quickly killing thousands, drawing the ire of the marketplace, causing the corporation to lose revenue quickly, putting the company out of business in short order. And if the marketplace didn't do this, government regulators surely could and, I would hope, would.

Using unsupported phrases such as "corporations often seek profit from scientific developments with little regard for human health" is plainly unfair and irresponsible. Had they sourced that passage, I might not be writing this post. Phrasing of the sort used in this FOE example plays upon people's tendency to believe whatever it is they read, just as long as it's in black and white, and not vet what it is that they read, especially on the Web. (How can I make a statement such as that one? With support. For more on this human tendency to believe without question what's written on the Web, please see: "Making the Call on Web 'Facts'." The Christian Science Monitor. October

11, 2009, [70] and Universal Mc Cann's study entitled "When Did We Start Trusting Strangers?" [71]

In using this type of phrasing, it appears that FOE and perhaps many other NGO and activist organizations base their media tactics on this knowledge that people won't question what they see in writing. And in making such unsupported, anti-corporate statements, it seems that organizations making such statements will count on their audience to call upon the NGO or activist organization to "right the wrong" as defined by the self-appointed "expert" group. (Don't forget the second sentence in the passage: "We must take precaution (sic) to ensure new technologies don't do more harm than good.")

No. For me, at least, unsupported, "anti-corporate card" plays of this sort only make this organization appear weaker, as if they can't find enough examples to support what they contend. And I would think that an organization of FOE's stature would be able to find examples through which to set up a better argument.

Chapter Seven - Jumping Into Anti-Corporatism
——————— Take-Aways ———————

The idea about NGOs and activists extorting companies over their reputation is not one that I originated. Though, I wish that I had because it's a very astute observation. I've read about this idea in other articles but I don't think that their explanations of the concept were as clear as mine. The piece "NGO & Corporate Collaboration: How Far Does It Go?" illustrates this idea of extortion more colorfully than others who have written about it and it makes the point, I hope, more strongly than others I've read. Using the "Paulie" example really puts things into context. Keeping this idea of how NGOs and activists extort corporations in our heads while reading the next article, "NGO Social Media: Some Weakness in 'Reach'," is important because after reading this article we can come to realize that not every NGO or activist can be a big corporate name extortion threat.

In "Some Weakness," I looked at the social media strategic strengths and weaknesses of two of the world's most influential environmental NGOs, Greenpeace US and Friends of the Earth US (ironically abbreviated as FOE). I performed this short analysis in an effort to determine which NGO could be successfully more "Paulie-like" in their use of social media. The answer to the analysis was that Greenpeace US was much better equipped to use social media, a medium which can be an especially effective meme and reality bender due to its anonymity factor. Such a tool can be invaluable when it comes to extorting a corporate image. NGOs get a reality-bending boost from social media when they are in the process of propagating the memes that they use to extort a corporate image. And they also get a lift from a general meme that permeates society both online and offline, that of *anti-corporatism*. The next three articles delve into this subject of anti-corporatism.

Do you like large, red-tape based organizations?

See what I mean?

In "A Journey in Anti-Corporate Thought," "One Source Doesn't An Anti-Corporate Environment Make," and "FOE Plays Anti-Corporate Card," I take a look at the anti-corporate meme that so many people pass around society without really thinking about it. Corporations are "evil." Don't you know that? And "FOE Plays" gives a prime example of this sort of "meme mangling" as it manifests in social media. Through my travels across the social web, or sometimes what I would call the "anti-social web," I've observed that the manner in which meme mangling is commonly done within social media is by making unsupported statements. People do this every day in conversation, and now such communicational laxity has extended itself onto the social web. This happens because such an action is easy and easy actions are likely to be undertaken by non-professional writers, with which social media abounds. But the impact of the social web is so much greater than just a conversation among a few people. The reasons why are obvious. Although in the case of "FOE Plays," I would hope that an organization would have more responsibility in its Web statements, but, after all, this is FOE. Expecting such semantical responsibility would be naive and performing it would be counter-productive to their meme and reality bending, activist agenda.

In "Journey," I touched on information that would counter the meme of anti-corporatism, demonstrating that corporations are not as "evil" as the meme might have you believe. And in that article I took the semantical responsibility and cited some reliable sources of that information. However, as I mentioned in "Journey," it's a shame that those sources may not be helpful in countering the meme because of their nature. They are mostly of the "dry" academic variety, a genre of literature to which most people just don't gravitate naturally. This problem not withstanding, the anti-corporate meme, which helps support so much of the work of the irregular competitor, is further reinforced when writers use only one source to "support" the existence of that anti-corporate meme. Such was the type of approach highlighted in the "One Source" article. And if that anti-corporate meme is supported via a one source reference in an academic paper, what hope do we have that that anti-corporate meme, so integral to the irregular competitor's strategy, will be dispelled on the social web any time soon?

After the exploration of these philosophical themes, I shifted gears a bit and got into the more practical. With "The Irregular Competition Threat Index" article, I established a ranking process which I would apply in subsequent pieces; the better with which to see and evaluate potential "meme manglers." I then embarked on a three-essay journey in which I applied the criteria of the Irregular Competition Threat Index (ICTI). By creating such an index, it's my hope that "victims" of irregular competition could use these analyses to classify and categorize those NGOs and activists with whom they must deal on a daily basis. By having a ranking of "Paulies," corporations would know which irregular competitors have more "meme mangling mojo" than others, and thereby prioritize and strategize responses accordingly.

CHAPTER EIGHT

The Meme
Marches On

Think Global, Act Local on Childhood Obesity

March 1, 2010

Category: Ideas

"Think Global(ly), Act Local(ly)" is the mantra of many NGOs and activist groups. Aside from yet another two adverbs taking it on the chin, this is a central theme to many of their strategies.

Recently the White House announced the signing of an executive order establishing a task force to fight childhood obesity. [72] The executive order calls for the assistance of NGOs, as well as corporations, in fighting this problem. A worthy pursuit. But what about the mantra? The mantra states the solution.

Acting locally on childhood obesity, very locally, could be the solution to the problem if that local action was parents encouraging, and requiring, their children to exercise regularly (We used to call this "playtime.") and discouraging (read that as "prohibiting") their children from eating "garbage." Discipline is not a word with which parents should be unfamiliar.

Perhaps if there was more very local, "household-local," common-sensical, parental attention to the problem, people wouldn't need yet another expensive government/NGO/corporate task force to tell them what they should already know.

You Could Say That This Post Serves as My Annotated Resume

March 2, 1010

Category: Personal Observations

Recently, I've received some enquiries regarding my expertise in anti-corporate activism analysis, in competitive intelligence, and in the analysis of online media. Since this is an unusual profession, I can certainly understand the curiosity. I appreciate all of your questions and hope that I have responded satisfactorily. Knowing that FAQs are popular on many sites, I am today writing an FAQ of sorts.

Today, I write this post to help future enquirers and to give you some background on my previous experiences. In this post, you will learn about my credentials and the experiences I have had which have built my expertise in anti-corporate activism analysis, in general, and in digital anti-corporate activism analysis, in particular. You could say that this post serves as my "annotated resume."

Educational Background

My specific experience for my profession began just before I received my MBA in Marketing from Rider University. While completing that degree, I worked as a Research Assistant for the Marketing Department. In that capacity, I extended what I learned from the classroom into the real world. Having learned much about performing objective research, with special attention paid toward the reliability and integrity of sourcing, I performed many market research studies across different product and service areas. Upon completing my MBA, I served several years as a faculty member at Monmouth University and at Georgian Court University. Between both of those schools I taught international economics, finance, and marketing courses.

Out-of-the-Ivory-Tower

After several years as an educator, I received an offer from a consulting unit of the New Jersey Economic Development Authority. This consulting unit was the Trade Adjustment Assistance Center (TAAC) which was a U.S. Department of Commerce program administered by the NJEDA. In my role there as a Senior Project Officer, my responsibility was to work with New Jersey manufacturers who were getting "hammered" by foreign competition. Specifically, I was tasked with the duty of analyzing the strengths and weaknesses of those manufacturers with the intention of creating strategic plans to accentuate their positives and eliminate their negatives.

It was at NJEDA that I first formally became involved with competitive intelligence. When writing the strategic plan (or the "adjustment plan" as it was called there), it was necessary for me not only to analyze my client's strengths and weaknesses, but it was imperative for me to analyze those of the competitor, as well. Please note that those competitors were, of course, foreign. This was during the late 1980s, before the Internet became the research avenue it is today, and gaining critical, public-domain, information even on American companies was difficult. So, you can probably imagine that obtaining information on foreign companies was even more difficult.

However, from my experience as an academic researcher, I knew how to dig and from my training as an MBA, I knew for what to dig. So I dug. And from my efforts I was able to uncover much information that went into my analyses and the creation of effective strategic plans for my TAAC clients.

My Own Shop

In 1991, after having good success with the foreign competitive intelligence function at the NJEDA, I decided to open up my own shop, a competitive intelligence consultancy. At that time, competitive intelligence as a business discipline was just coming into its own and it looked like a great business opportunity. It was.

The Becker Research Company, Inc. was one of the original competitive intelligence companies in the United States. During the company's tenure, it was a market leader. At Becker Research, my staff and I worked on hundreds of competitive intelligence projects for Fortune 100 type clients. We met the demand for competitive information and strategic recommendations concerning the competitors, foreign and domestic, of many of America's top companies. Becker Research was involved in and delivered critical competitive intelligence for several major due diligence projects, many competitive manufacturing benchmarking studies, and almost countless competitive product introduction forecasts.

By the late 1990s, the Internet was in full bloom and that network was changing the way business was done. This was one of those historic transformations that I got to experience up close and personally. The opportunities offered by this transformation were unprecedented. Realizing another good potential business, I opened a second consulting practice, eBusiness Analysts, which offered competitive analysis services and strategic counseling in the area of e-business and e-commerce. My understanding of the Internet's power in business gelled in that period of time and it was then that I wrote my first two books, *Fast Food for eBusiness Marketers* (High Street Press: 1998, currently out-of-print) and *Dangerous Competition* (iUniverse: 2001). eBusiness Analysts performed well but ultimately became a victim of the dot bomb crash of 2000.

A Transitional Time

At that point in my career, even though Internet fever had risen and fallen, I knew that the Internet was not going away and that it's impact on business would not fade. We weren't going back to business without an Internet. I could foresee that a tool such as this, one which networked human communication so easily, would have effects on business more profound than most could ever realize. So, I decided to continue to do business in Internet related areas. Some who were licking their dot com bomb wounds then called this masochism. I looked at it as a prudent strategic decision. My foresight proved correct.

So in 2001, after eBusiness Analysts and after selling the assets of The Becker Research Company, Inc., I opened The Kahuna Content Company, Inc. In its early days, Kahuna Content was an independent supplier of Internet content, both text and images. Although, Internet "fever" had burst, the "illness" was still there. Many sites were upgrading their strategies and in doing so were seeking solid, quality content. The number of content suppliers at that time was low. Kahuna Content helped fill the void. During those first years of Kahuna Content, I increased my knowledge on how the Internet worked, how business could benefit from it, what people wanted from it, why they wanted what they did, and how people could use the Internet as a social tool. One of my tasks during those early Kahuna Content years was to supply images. To do so, I called upon my photography skills which I had been developing on the side (pun intended) since high school, becoming even better at that art which some call a science. In addition to web articles, Kahuna Content also supplied various photography and imaging services. As a sideline, I dabbled in art photography, participating in many group shows, winning national awards, and securing four solo gallery exhibitions. And during that time I authored my third book, "*Conehenge - The Story of a Jersey Schlub,*" which I did to poke a little fun at how business is conducted in New Jersey.

What Happens Next?

So far in this post, you have read a condensed version of some of my experiences leading up to the analysis of anti-corporate digital activism. But, there is more. What happens next? Well, I will be happy to tell you. But, because I prefer to keep blog posts no longer than about 1500 words (one of the many lessons I learned in Kahuna Content's early days), and because I am rapidly approaching that limit, I will break here, thank you for reading thus far, and pick up this story in my next post, "You Could Say That This Post Serves as My Annotated Resume - Part 2." In that next post, you'll learn how I built my current profession upon the sum of my experiences and knowledge in competitive intelligence as well as upon my activities in Internet related businesses.

*   *   *

Part 2 of this post, "You Could Say That This Post Serves as My Annotated Resume," will be published on Tuesday, March 2, 2010. If you are reading this before that date, please subscribe to the FREE RSS feed so that you will be notified when the post publishes. To subscribe to the feed, just click here. If you are reading this after that date, simply click here to go to "You Could Say That This Post Serves as My Annotated Resume - Part 2."

You Could Say That This Post Serves as My Annotated Resume - Part 2

March 4, 2010

Category: Personal Observations

This post picks up the story of how I became an analyst of "irregular competition" which we know here on Telofski.com to be anti-corporate activists and NGOs.

In the previous post, "You Could Say That This Post Serves as My Annotated Resume," I discussed my foundational experiences and knowledge that support my current expertise in the analysis of anti-corporate digital activism. If you haven't yet read that post, you may do so by clicking here.

Now, here in Part 2, I pick up the story where I left off. Here in Part 2, I describe how The Kahuna Content Company, Inc. and I evolved from an Internet content supplier to that of anti-corporate digital activism analysis.

Web 2.0 Appears

Through 2001 I had acquired quite a bit of experience in competitive intelligence analysis as well as an expertise in online business. In Kahuna Content's early days as an independent supplier of online content, I learned about what people wanted from their online experiences. During that period of time the web was a relatively static communicator of information; there was little "interaction" due to the technologies that existed then. However, around 2005, as the web started to evolve into the more interactive environment that I knew it could and would ultimately become, I began to learn about and experience what later became known as "Web 2.0." At that time the Internet was truly becoming an "environment," a social one. Because of technology shifts, it was then that people began to convert the Internet into an "environment," one which affected them and one which they affected back in return.

It was at that time, in that "2.0" shift in the Internet, that Kahuna Content, and I, began to change focus. As the wave of what later came to be known as "user-generated content" rose, I saw that the need for independently supplied online content would fade. So, Kahuna Content made a gradual move away from content supply. Watching the rise of the "social web," I saw that with the tools that were starting then to become available, people could and would transfer their human "conversational jones" for interaction from the real to the virtual, taking it global and making it a 24/7 activity. I saw that people would start talking about every thing under the sun, and out in public. Going back to my roots as a competitive intelligence analyst, this shift told me that people, everyday people, could become "competitors" to the very companies from which they bought their goods and services.

The Insidious Competitor Threatens

Now, I wasn't really the first person to realize this. The Cluetrain Manifesto had forecasted this change about a half dozen years prior. But at this point in the story, I realized that individuals could actually do what the Cluetrain had predicted. When Cluetrain was written, the "social media" tools that could enable markets to "laugh" at the companies who supplied them weren't fully configured enough for that to be much of an actual business threat. But by around 2006 to 2007, my competitive intelligence/threat analysis personality was screaming at me, saying that the Cluetrain threat was truly here. In overdrive. Social media was going to develop fully and companies needed to be aware of what those "insidious competitors" (i.e., people of all shapes and sizes) were saying about them. Here was a problem, and I knew how to solve it. Web monitoring and analysis.

So in 2007 after gradually moving toward this new business of web monitoring and social media initiative analysis, Kahuna Content changed its business focus entirely to that, which I positioned as "competitive intelligence from social media." We offered social web monitoring and analysis of online "conversations" related to a client's products/services/markets, with an eye on discovering what customers and consumers were saying about the companies they patronized. This was an exploding area, and there was quite a bit of interest in our services. Offering this service called upon the threat analysis skills that I had first learned back there at the New Jersey Economic Development Authority, when I first became involved in foreign competitive intelligence, and later perfected in my own competitive intelligence company, The Becker Research Company, Inc. And this "competitive intelligence from social media" service was also built upon the online and digital environment expertise that I had built at both eBusiness Analysts and perfected in the early days of Kahuna Content. My skills, expertise, experience, and knowledge had coalesced here in the enhanced version of Kahuna Content, perhaps more accurately phrased as "Kahuna Content 2.0."

The Irregular Competitor Appears

Around 2008, as social media usage increased tremendously, it began to be employed by not only individuals, but also by corporations, both of the profit and non-profit variety, as well as by an American presidential campaign which reached its objective, largely via social media usage. Each type of organization, the profit and non-profit, started to use the medium to speak to their publics. I saw that these online media, being relatively inexpensive, were perfectly positioned for employment by non-profit activist groups as well as their non-governmental organization (NGO) cousins. These are organizations who, because of their financial structure, are always "desperate" for less expensive ways to communicate their agendas and gather support. During this year, as a by-product of my social web monitoring work, I saw that more and more activists and NGOs were taking their messages online where they were gathering support for their organizations. Their success with this medium at that time was likely spurred, and supported, by the online social activity generated from that aforementioned presidential campaign. Many of those activist and NGO messages were "anti-corporate," some directed at specific companies while other of them were simply directed against capitalism in general. This new type of commercial competition, this "irregular competition," is what you and I discuss here on Telofski.com.

Anti-corporate activists and NGOs have been picking up speed and supporters, in the offline world, since the early 1990s. During that decade, they had increasingly become a "competitive" threat to businesses. Then, in 2008, near the end of the first decade of the 21st century (can't we just agree to call that decade the "Ones"?), they were enhancing that competitive threat through usage of the tools of social media. I knew how to analyze competitive business threats and I knew how to analyze online media. I had much experience and expertise in both. And I enjoy both.

A Return to Home Plate

My circle was complete. I had returned to my "knitting." But this time, it was of the 21st century variety.

In 2009, I transitioned Kahuna Content from consumer-type web monitoring toward the area of anti-corporate digital activism analysis. And it is during this time that I have written my fourth and latest book, "Insidious Competition - The Battle for Meaning and the Corporate Image." (Author's Note: *Insidious Competition* was published in June 2010. You can find more information about the book at www.InsidiousCompetition.com.)

As you can see, from Parts 1 and 2 of this post, my background is well-suited to the analysis of anti-corporate digital activism. This endeavor is one that I find interesting and enlightening, as well as one which is now absolutely necessary to business.

I hope that you have enjoyed reading my annotated resume. If you have any questions, please feel free to contact me.

EXCLUSIVE
How Does RAN Rank As An Irregular Competitor?

March 9, 2010

Categories: Irregular Competition - Rainforest Action Network - Threat Index, Research - Case Studies - Rainforest Action Network

Today, you and I will begin a case study analysis of the Rainforest Action Network as an irregular competitor. Not sure what an "irregular competitor"[73] is? Check the definition here then. [74]

Okay. Ready?

Let's Start with Twitter

In this post, the first in a series about the Rainforest Action Network as an irregular competitor, we'll begin our case study by taking a look at the Twitter strategy employed by this organization.

One of the benefits behind social media is that one can use it to be, well, social. Being social means engaging others in conversation, talking with them, not at them. This is not a new idea, especially in social media circles.

Recently, I visited the Twitter page [75] for the Rainforest Action Network (RAN). I do so periodically to keep current on what they, as well as other NGO and activist groups, are doing on the social web. I must say that I was not impressed by their Twitter strategy.

I looked at a random sample of 93 of their most recent tweets. Then I reviewed each of those to determine which were "shouts" and which were attempts at engaging their following. Only 12 of the 93 tweets, or about 13%, were attempts at engagement. The other 81 tweets, or about 87%, were just "shouts." From this summary analysis, it would appear that RAN has difficulty, on Twitter at least, in engaging their audience in a worthwhile conversation. Apparently, RAN has not yet learned the conversational value of Twitter. And this perceived lack of value is plainly reflected in their Twitter statistics.

On the date I checked, Tuesday, February 23, 2010, RAN showed only 1,426 followers. Similarly, on that same date their Twitter page showed that RAN followed only 1,104. With regard to the total Twitterverse, and considering that the Twitterverse is likely "teeming" with the RAN primary demographic, these follower and following numbers are very, very low. What am I saying? These numbers, for this type of organization, in this type of social media environment, are extremely low. And it's entirely possible that these numbers are low because potential followers don't see any conversational value coming out of the RAN tweets. If you don't have anything to discuss, people just won't follow you on Twitter.

What does this mean for the corporate opponents that RAN has targeted. Well, for companies like Chevron, JP Morgan Chase, General Mills, and others I saw mentioned in RAN's "broadcast-like" tweets, it means that, at least, from the tool of Twitter, these corporate opponents of RAN have little to worry about. My analysis indicates that RAN has a very difficult time in establishing a conversation in the Twitter environment. They are not using this social web tool to its fullest advantage. And by not using this tool to its fullest advantage, they handicap their other social media efforts.

So, due to RAN's employment of Twitter, I would rate them very low on the Irregular Competition Threat Index, probably about a "2" on a scale of 1 to

10, 10 being the most threatening. But this "2" is only a preliminary rating because Twitter is only a part of the total social media effort of RAN. As we go through subsequent posts, it's likely that you and I will see this preliminary rating change.

*   *   *

Part 2 of "How Does RAN Rank As An Irregular Competitor?" will be posted on Thursday, March 11, 2010. If you are reading this before that date, please subscribe to the FREE RSS feed so that you will be notified when the article posts. Click here to subscribe. Or, if you are reading this after that date, please click here to be taken to "How Does RAN Rank As An Irregular Competitor? - Part 2."

Activist Stockholders Gain Strength

March 10, 2010

Categories: Activism, Tactics, Threats

My fourth and latest book, *Insidious Competition - The Battle for Meaning and the Corporate Image*, is scheduled to be published in June 2010. For more information about my new book, please click here [76] to go to the book's Web site.

In the book, I discuss nine different types of insidious competitors present in social media. One of those types of competitors is NGOs and Activists, the "irregular" competitors that are the basis of our discussions here at Telofski.com. In fact, it was from the research on Insidious Competition that the concept of irregular competition evolved.

Well, putting aside irregular competition for a moment, I'd just like to mention that one of the insidious competitor types I discuss in my book is Activist Stockholders, cousins of the irregular competitors NGOs and Activists. In reviewing my news feeds recently I discovered the article "Divided SEC Proposes Investor Access Plan" [77] which talks about how Activist Stockholders may be gaining more strength in their struggles against corporate management.

This article is quite interesting and updates an issue which I have been following for a while. The issue pertains directly to the discussion of Activist Stockholders as it appears in the book. Summarizing, the article discusses relaxation of U.S. Securities and Exchange Commission (SEC) regulations for shareholder balloting in annual public corporation elections. You know. The annual "proxy fight." The proposed rule changes would make it simpler for various stockholder groups to gain access to the corporate board and thereby control certain corporate decisions.

In my new book's discussion of this type of insidious competitor, I mentioned that there is a pending rule change. I also mentioned that that change may take place as soon as early 2010. From what this article says, it looks like I was right. When this regulation change is combined with the force and power of social media, as I pointed out in the book, the influence of the Activist Stockholder will increase tremendously. And because of this potential shift in power, it should be incumbent on all C-suite executives and corporate communications personnel to learn how to deal with this impending threat to corporate operations.

Insidious Competition - The Battle for Meaning and the Corporate Image discusses these "how-to's" in detail.

I'll keep you updated on the publication of the book.

EXCLUSIVE
How Does RAN Rank As An Irregular Competitor? - Part 2

March 11, 2010

Categories: Irregular Competition - Rainforest Action Network - Threat Index, Research - Case Studies - Rainforest Action Network

In the first part of this case study on the social media strategy of the Rainforest Action Network (RAN), you and I discussed how RAN uses Twitter. In that first part, we saw that RAN doesn't use Twitter very well at all. If you have not as yet read Part 1, you may do so by clicking here.

As well as RAN doesn't use Twitter, they make up for it in their employment of Facebook. And that's what you and I are going to discuss today. Let's make a short assessment of their Facebook strategy.

Face the Facebook

The first thing that hit me when I looked at RAN's Facebook page was their number of fans. On Tuesday, February 23, 2010 (the same day I wrote about their Twitter strategy), RAN had 11,249 fans. This is almost eight times as many Facebook fans as the 1,426 Twitter followers on that same date. (See Part 1.) The question "Why?" popped into my mind as it might be right this moment popping into yours. Why this big difference between the level of Facebook fans and the level of Twitter followers. I see this a lot. This type of difference serves to reiterate the point I made in Part 1, that RAN does not realize the value of a good Twitter relationship and seemingly makes little to no effort to develop those relationships. So a Facebook fan level of 11,249 by comparison is very good, but yet it would seem that an organization with RAN's focus and stature could attract a lot more Facebook fans. Yet, although their fan level may not be quantitatively outstanding, a qualitative assessment of the RAN Facebook effort says that they do a good job.

The nature of their posts on Facebook are essentially the same as those on Twitter. The posts announce actions that RAN is taking or are calls to their Facebook fans to participate in RAN sponsored actions. As on Twitter, many of those actions and calls concerned companies such as Chevron, General Mills, and JP Morgan Chase. But unlike on Twitter, fan conversation can be seen quite easily the Facebook page. No hashtags to search in order to see the level of fan/follower conversation. Facebook makes that engagement quite plain to see, as well as the number of fans voting "thumbs up." That sort of visibility and approval can breed further conversation and even more fan approval.

Social Media Day of Action

In a direct action against JP Morgan Chase, RAN announced on Facebook an event they titled "Put Chase On the Run: Social Media Day of Action." On Facebook, they announced this February 18, 2010 event beginning about February 12. Good decision on timing. Enough lead time for fans to be aware, but not so much that fans will forget in the meantime. The details of the event were spelled out on a Facebook event page. Here is part of those details:

This Thursday morning (February 18, 2010) at 9am EST,

DirtyMoney.org will reveal a list of simple actions people can take online, letting Chase know that America is aware of the bank's involvement in destroying the Appalachian Mountains. Participants will have a choice of actions to take on a variety of social networks, including Twitter, Facebook, Flickr and the new collaborative video platform, Citizen Global.

DirtyMoney.org is a domain name that when clicked redirects the browser to a Chase direct action page on the main RAN site. On February 24, which is the date I wrote this section that you are now reading, when I went to that domain name, I was taken to the Chase direct action page, but there was no "choice of actions" menu to be seen. Since my arrival there was almost a week after the event, I did not find this unusual. However, near the bottom of the page there were links related to this event.

One of those links went to a related story on the RAN site, and described some of the RAN Social Media Day suggested actions:

Some ways to take action:

1. *Update your facebook status with this message: "Chase is bankrolling the destruction of American mountains for coal. End mountaintop removal and PUT CHASE ON THE RUN. Take action today at DirtyMoney.org.*
2. *Upload this Chase brand jam image to your Facebook picture (image to the left)" [Richard's Note: I have not included that image in this post.]*
3. *Brand jam Chase's Facebook page "Chase Community Giving." (follow this link) [Richard's Note: I have not included that link in this post.]*
4. *Tweet this message: #Chase is bankrolling the destruction of American mountains. Take action at DirtyMoney.org. #coal #mtr #RAN Please RT.*
5. *Upload the Chase brand jam image to Flickr (image to the left) [Richard's Note: I have not included that image in this post.]*
6. *Blog the social media day of action*

Another of the links near the bottom of the Chase direct action page went to a page on the RAN site with an article describing the results that were generated from the Social Media Day of Action. That list of results was as follows:

- *RAN and allies Tweeted to over 330,000 people*
- *RAN and allies touched 180,000 people on Facebook*

- *had over 30 unique blogs posted, including posts on Huffington Post, Treehugger and Grist*
- *had 3,000 people "defriend" the Chase Community Giving Facebook fan page*
- *reports of dozens of people cancelling their Chase credit cards and bank accounts.*
- *one Appalachian activist started a "Boycott Chase" Facebook group.*

You and I will take a critical look at those results in the next post in this series about RAN. For now, we're going to wrap up this particular post with a few thoughts.

Wrap-Up

Overall, I would say that RAN employs Facebook generally well. There are areas for improvement of course, but for the most part they seem to understand how to use this tool. Yet, although they appear to understand this tool fairly well, it remains to be seen how effective its usage is.

Regarding the Social Media Day of Action, the Facebook event page (on February 24, 2010) showed only 843 confirmed attendees and only 586 listed as "maybe attending." Now, remember. The RAN Facebook page has at least 11,000 fans. A combined figure of 1,429 fans as either confirmed or possible event attendees is not a very impressive display of the Facebook fans involvement in a direct action. These numbers go to the issue of effective usage as raised above. A conversion rate of fans to event attendees in the range of 13% is low. This might be a sign of "slacktivism," a natural human trait which plagues all online activist efforts.

So, for now I am going to raise the Irregular Competition Threat Index rating for RAN from the "2" which we saw in the previous post. Right now, I am going to raise it to a "7" based upon their overall employment of Facebook. But in the next post, you and I will discuss those Social Media Day of Action results as shown above, to get closer to the answer of just how "effective" RAN's Facebook, and overall social media strategy, really is.

*   *   *

Part 3 of "How Does RAN Rank As An Irregular Competitor?" will be posted on Tuesday, March 16, 2010. If you are reading this before that date, please subscribe to the FREE RSS feed so that you will be notified when the article posts. Click here to subscribe. Or, if you are reading this after that date, please click here to be taken to "How Does RAN Rank As An Irregular Competitor? - Part 3."

EXCLUSIVE
How Does RAN Rank As An Irregular Competitor? - Part 3

March 16, 2010

Categories: Irregular Competition - Rainforest Action Network - Threat Index, Protests in Social Media - Social Media Day of Action, Research - Case Studies - Rainforest Action Network- Social Media Campaign Analysis

In Part 1 of "How Does RAN Rank As An Irregular Competitor?," you and I took a peek at the Rainforest Action Network's (RAN) Twitter strategy and found that it was somewhat lacking. In Part 2 of this post series, we examined the Facebook strategy of RAN and found that it was quite a bit better than their Twitter approach, but that their Facebook initiative wasn't perfect. If you haven't yet read either, or both, of those posts, and you would like to do so prior to reading this post, then just click here for Part 1 and here for Part 2.

Let's Analyze the "Social Media Day of Action"

Today you and I will discuss the RAN Social Media Day of Action (Thursday, February 18, 2010) which was discovered during the research described in Part 2. We saw in Part 2 that the Social Media Day of Action was an online direct action against JP Morgan Chase and that RAN encouraged their fans to make various forms of protest via the social web.

As shown in Part 2, some of those forms of protest as suggested by RAN, on a page at their main website, were:

1. *Update your facebook status with this message: "Chase is bankrolling the destruction of American mountains for coal. End mountaintop removal and PUT CHASE ON THE RUN. Take action today at DirtyMoney.org.*

2. *Upload this Chase brand jam image to your Facebook picture (image to the left)" [Richard's Note: I have not included that image in this post.]*

3. *Brand jam Chase's Facebook page "Chase Community Giving." (follow this link) [Richard's Note: I have not included that link in this post.]*

4. *Tweet this message: #Chase is bankrolling the destruction of American mountains. Take action at DirtyMoney.org. #coal #mtr #RAN Please RT.*

5. *Upload the Chase brand jam image to Flickr (image to the left) [Richard's Note: I have not included that image in this post.]*

6. *Blog the social media day of action*

Also as discussed in Part 2, RAN posted some of the results of these actions:

- *RAN and allies Tweeted to over 330,000 people*
- *RAN and allies touched 180,000 people on Facebook*
- *had over 30 unique blogs posted, including posts on Huffington Post, Treehugger and Grist*
- *had 3,000 people "defriend" the Chase Community Giving Facebook fan page*
- *reports of dozens of people cancelling their Chase credit cards and bank accounts.*
- *one Appalachian activist started a "Boycott Chase" Facebook group.*

What you and I are going to talk about now is the results of the six suggested forms of protest, as shown above, and we are also going to check, where possible, the veracity of their result claims.

Facebook Status Updates

Shown above as #1 in the forms of protest list, RAN asked supporters to update their Facebook status with the phrase "Chase is bankrolling the destruction of American mountains for coal, etc." A simple Google search of that passage, performed on February 23, 2010, returned 26 results. Most of those results were updates from Facebook fan pages. The fan pages were those belonging, primarily, to organizations similar to RAN (e.g., the Waterkeeper Alliance, Greenpeace, TreeHugger.) Now, please be aware that, generally, Facebook is a closed system to search engines. Personal Facebook page updates don't appear in Google search results. But fan pages are not part of the Facebook closed system. So, Facebook fan pages will appear in search engine results.

Finding, at most, 26 fan page updates containing the passage RAN requested to be updated in Facebook isn't very impressive, and it doesn't lend a lot of credence to RAN's claim, as shown above in their results list, "RAN and allies touched 180,000 people on Facebook." Yes, Google won't show the personal Facebook pages of those "touched" 180,000 people. But the sample of only 26 fan pages seems to stretch the credulity of the 180,000 claim. And anyway, what does "touched" mean?

Does "touched" mean that 180,000 Facebookers posted that passage as requested? Does "touched" mean that 180,000 Facebookers saw status updates from their Facebook friends which contained the passage? And if so, did those 180,000 Facebookers read the passage? Comment on it? "Like" it? The RAN claim is vague and unverifiable. Therefore, it's veracity is questionable.

Similarly with their second suggestion, #2 in the forms of protest list, to upload the Chase brand jam to the Facebooker's image profile, the verification problem is the same as that noted for the status updating of the passage. So, I won't be able to examine action #2, continuing to place the veracity of their 180,000 result claim in question.

Brand Jamming and Defriending

RAN's third suggestion, #3 in the forms of protest list, to brand jam the "Chase Community Giving" Facebook fan page, [78] can be analyzed. Presumably, RAN meant for its RAN fans to become a fan of the Chase Community Giving page and then send a brand jammed logo image to the wall of that fan page. I assume that this brand jammed image would also be the one referred to in suggested action #5, as shown in the forms of protest list above. I won't be showing that brand jammed image here in this post, but if you like you may view it by clicking through on this link. (That image was viewable via that link as of February 24, 2010. If the image is no longer on that page, you may wish to try this link.) So, now let's go to the Chase Community Giving fan page to see what we find.

First, I must make a comment here regarding the appropriateness of this tactic. Perhaps you feel the same way. The Chase Community Giving fan page is a place on Facebook where interested parties would cast a vote for their favorite charity to receive a share of $5 million that JP Morgan Chase will donate. Brand jamming such a philanthropic effort, regardless of what anyone may think of any financing of mountaintop removal, is a highly inappropriate approach to protest. The Chase Community Giving initiative is not the financing arm of the company, and defacing that fan page would be an act of very low character. But even if someone was inclined to do so, I am not so sure that they could have.

On February 24, 2010, when I visited the Chase Community Giving fan page on Facebook, I found no indication of any brand jamming on the Facebook Wall of that fan page. Neither did I find any indication of brand jamming anywhere else on that Facebook fan page site. It could be that Chase may have set the fan page so that no fan posting could occur. But when I visited the fan page wall, the most recent posting from Chase was dated January 27. And that January 27 posting indicated that the charitable voting had concluded, that the funds had been awarded to the charities, and that the functionality of the fan page had been closed. This was three weeks before the Social Media Day of Action. How could anyone, even if they were so inclined, brand jam the fan page when it was essentially closed three weeks prior? Didn't RAN know this?

As for the RAN claim of 3,000 fans "defriending" the Chase Community Giving page, when I visited the page there were approximately 2 million fans shown. If only 3,000 people "defriended" or "defanned" the page, that change would represent an attrition rate of only about 15/100ths of one percent. This is a change that is probably statistically insignificant and would seem to be an action that is largely meaningless. What could JP Morgan Chase, or any other observer, interpret from this level of attrition? Likely, not much.

Tweeting, Flickr, & Blogging

Let's turn now to a brief analysis of RAN's suggested forms of protest in numbers 4, 5, and 6, as shown above.

Regarding #4, the re-tweet of the message "#Chase is bankrolling the destruction of American mountains. Take action at DirtyMoney.org. #coal #mtr #RAN Please RT.," I searched at search.twitter.com for the phrase "Chase is bankrolling the destruction of American mountains." I selected the advanced search tab and chose the "all of these words" option. The results given were 8 pages of 50 re-tweet search results on each page, meaning that there was a total of 400 re-tweets. The oldest of those results were from February 18, meaning that these re-tweets did not commence before the Social Media Day of Action, February 18.

This number of 400 re-tweets might seem small on the surface, but of course network effects are in play here. RAN's claim of they and their "allies" tweeting to over 330,000 people, as shown in the claim list above, is plausible. To reach this number of 330,000, each of the re-tweeters would need an average of only 825 followers. A follower level of 800, or more, is common among many Twitters in the Twitterverse.

With regard to protest form #5, on February 25, 2010, I searched Flickr.com. Following are the search terms I used to find the Chase brand jams, suggested by RAN as shown in the forms of protest list from above, and the results for each search string:

- "Chase brand jam" - 0
- "Chase blows up mountains." - 0
- "Dirtymoney.org" - 1,256 results, but none contained the Chase brand jam
- "mountain top removal" - 3 of 653 results contained the Chase brand jam
- "mountaintop removal" - 12 of 1,666 results contained the Chase brand jam
- "mtr" - 13 of 155 results contained the Chase brand jam (I limited this search by date.)

So, by using search terms that were commonly associated with the Chase brand jam request, as per RAN's own Social Media Day of Action page, only 28 Chase brand jams were found on Flickr.com. Not very impressive.

We now come to protest form #6, blogging. A quick search at blogsearch.google.com resulted in 135 references for the term "Social Media Day of Action." That search was set for "all dates." Based on these findings, the RAN result claim of "over 30 unique blogs posted" is likely accurate, but with such a low number it remains unimpressive.

Miscellaneous

Regarding RAN's last two claims of "dozens of people cancelling their Chase credit cards and bank accounts" and "one Appalachian activist started a 'Boycott Chase' Facebook group," these actions were not requested by RAN in their forms of protest list as shown above. Although these actions are direct, their effects would appear to be limited.

Conclusion

As mentioned above, RAN's Facebook effort for the Social Media Day of Action is largely unverifiable, leaving their claimed results questionable. So on this tactic, I can't really award many, or any, points to them toward their Irregular Competitor Threat Index ranking. However, I will subtract some points based on the effort to deface the Facebook fan page of a charitable undertaking. Such tactics are "bush league" and are potentially counterproductive for the party undertaking them.

Concerning the tweeting, I'll say that it's likely that they did achieve what they claimed, and a reach of over 300,000 isn't bad. But where they really failed to shine was in their Flickr and blogging efforts as we just discussed a few paragraphs ago.

Taking into consideration everything you and I discussed in all three parts of this article, I will set the overall Irregular Competitor Threat Index ranking for RAN at "5."

Insidious Competition Nears Completion

March 22, 2010

Category: Insidious Competition

You thought this blog was about "irregular competition," correct? Well, then what is "insidious competition?"

Well, it's actually "Insidious Competition" because it's the name of my fourth and latest book, Insidious Competition - The Battle for Meaning and the Corporate Image.

So what is insidious competition and how does it differ from irregular competition? Simply put, what I refer to as irregular competition is a subset of insidious competition. Insidious competition contains those non-traditional, atypical, and irregular competitors of NGOs and activists that you and I discuss here at Telofski.com. But the term insidious competition applies to many more competitors than just NGOs and activists. The label insidious competition covers competitors such as Tagging Terrorists, Mommy Bloggers, Foreign Governments, Consumers, Employees, Activist Stockholders, Labor Unions, and Culture Jammers. You can learn more about them in the book.

Indeed, the work I do on irregular competition, here on Telofski.com, is a direct outgrowth of the research I conducted for my book Insidious Competition.

The book Insidious Competition deals with the nature and characteristics of all these types of competitors that I mentioned above. The book deals with how they compete with your company's corporate image from within social media, why they attack your company's good corporate name, how they mount their attacks, what tools they use to mount those attacks, how they are organized, and, perhaps most importantly, what you can do to become an insidious competition warrior and decrease the effectiveness of their attacks.

Over the past two years I have been writing and editing Insidious Competition. During the winter, my copyeditor and I put the finishing touches on the work. I have recently completed all the manuscript reviews and have submitted all the copyedited and proofed files to my publisher. Whew. It was a lot of work. But, now the book has now moved on to the production stage. The publisher and I will be moving over the next few months toward the publication of this new book. And, as of right now, it looks like the book is right on schedule and set to debut during June of this year.

If you'd like to stay apprised of the production and publication process, you may subscribe to the free RSS feed by clicking on the icon in the right column of this blog.

Would you like to learn more about Insidious Competition - The Battle for Meaning and the Corporate Image? Perhaps get a look at the Table of Contents or the back cover copy? Then please click here to go to the book site.

Thanks. And if any questions on the book, please feel free to contact me.

Two Sides to the Coin of Corporate Power

March 23, 2010

Categories: Ideas, NGOs

A quick idea for today.

Currently I am reading *When Corporations Rule the World* by David Korten. Among anti-corporate thinkers, this book is touted as one of the leading works in modern anti-corporate theory. I'm only up to page 65 so far, but I must say that, although overall I don't agree with David's point of view, in this book David has raised some interesting issues. A few of his arguments have been well-made and well-sourced, while some others ... well ... not so much. Today's idea concerns one of those arguments that could have been made more soundly.

On page 59 of the paperback edition, near the beginning of Chapter Four - Rise of Corporate Power in America, when discussing the significance of the corporation as an institution, David states:

> On the negative side, it (the corporation) allows one or more individuals to leverage massive economic and political resources behind narrowly focused private agendas while protecting themselves from legal liability for the public consequences.

Yes. This is true. Business corporations do do this.

And the corporation, at least the type to which he refers, pays taxes in return.

Yet, there is a type of corporation which fits David's description and that does not pay taxes. Not one cent. In fact, the type of corporation of which I am thinking, in essence, does its business at the expense of taxpayers. Let's consider David's description from the perspective of the modern non-governmental organization (NGO).

Modern NGOs are corporate entities which permit one or more individuals to leverage and apply their economic and political resources on narrowly focused privately-defined agendas while they and their employees enjoy the liability protection of the corporate form. And let's add to this description of NGOs that they do so while receiving a tax-exempt status, so that, in essence, taxpayers are implicitly paying for the actions of the NGOs and the common resources that those NGOs consume at taxpayer expense.

This corporate format has worked out very well for businesses, yes. But it has also worked out well for NGOs. Remember. There are always two sides to every coin. Were it not for the corporate form, NGOs would probably not enjoy much of the power that they currently exercise.

The coin of corporate power cuts both ways, but when making an argument it should be incumbent upon the advocate to consider both sides of any coin.

Who is Really Responsible for Corporate Power?

March 24, 2010

Category: Anti-Corporatism

Yesterday I posted about David Korten's book, *When Corporations Rule the World*. This author is one of the leading thinkers in the area of anti-corporatism, and has published extensively on the subject. Although I don't agree with much of what he writes, I do like reading him and others to keep abreast of anti-corporate thinking, both current and historic.

When I read much of the anti-corporate literature, I keep coming back to the thought of "who is really responsible for the corporate power" that we see today? Of course, "corporate power," and its degrees, is a relatively defined term and is the subject for many, many other posts. But for today and the purposes of this discussion, let's just go with the overarching theme of "corporate power" as it is often referred to in anti-corporate literature.

Throughout *When Corporations Rule the World*, David "points the finger" of the genesis of corporate power at the corporations themselves. I suppose that would seem logical, but to me it seems logical only in a superficial way. For example, on page 64 of my edition, David talks about how corporate power in America coalesced after the Civil War.

The huge profits pouring in from military procurement contracts allowed industrial interests to take advantage of the disorder and rampant political corruption to virtually buy legislation that gave them massive grants of money and land to expand the Western railway system. The greater its profits, the tighter the emergent industrial class was able to solidify its hold on government to obtain further benefits.

Let's look more deeply at the logic. (Perhaps you already realize where I'm going with this.) I didn't check David's reference for this statement, but, for the sake of this discussion, let's just assume that he is reporting accurately. I'll repeat the question which is the title of this post.

Who is Really Responsible for Corporate Power?

In the quoted example David gave, how about placing at least some of the blame on the folks in government? Talk about personal responsibility.

One of the themes of anti-corporate thinkers is that they maintain that the corporate form, and the legal protections it affords, abdicates the personal responsibility of the people that run the corporation. From my readings of anti-corporate thinkers and writers, this neglect of personal responsibility appears to be anathema and is one of their "pet peeves." So, then, in anti-corporate thinking, why isn't the idea of personal responsibility applied back against government? In my readings of anti-corporate literature, I rarely see the idea of lack of personal responsibility thrown back into the face of politicians.

Corruption is a two-way street. The corruption to which David alludes in the quote above could not have taken place had the government officials had a sufficient level of personal responsibility and integrity.

So, again, who is really responsible for corporate power?

It takes two to tango.

How About Some Facts to Support Some Facts?

March 25, 2010

Categories: Anti-Corporatism, Truth

In a recent Guardian article entitled "The Trouble with Trusting Complex Science," an apparently self-avowed anti-corporatist writer ("despite my iconoclastic, anti-corporate instincts …" (a quote from the 10th paragraph of the article cited)) George Monbiot, discusses the frustration of dealing in facts when debating the climate change controversy. [79] He describes how efforts to convince climate change disbelievers are often frustrated in spite of the facts presented. As a fan of facts, I can feel George's frustration, although he and I may be on opposite sides of the climate change issue.

But the issue of climate change aside, what I want to comment on is his belief in truth and facts to make an argument. He and I are in sync on that and if you read this blog regularly you will understand what I mean.

From the theme of his article, it appears that George is very interested in the proper portrayal of reality, but yet he lets that reality take a bit of a walk in the third paragraph of an article that discusses journalistic integrity. In referring to journalistic castigations of climate scientists as an "attack on climate scientists" and as a "widening to an all-out war on science," <u>George</u> makes a bit of an attack himself. Not on climate scientists, mind you, but he makes an attack on reality.

He says in the third paragraph:

> *Views like this can be explained partly as the revenge of the humanities students. There is scarcely an editor or executive in any major media company – and precious few journalists – with a science degree, yet everyone knows that the anoraks are taking over the world.*

Just so you know and I understand, I had to look up "anoraks." We here in the U.S. would call that a parka. But that, of course, isn't what troubles me.

What troubles me is that for an apparent champion of the truth, George makes a blanket, unsupported statement about the paucity of science degrees held by journalists and does so without reference to a source. He pins his argument, that climate change science is being "poo-pooed" by unqualified persons, on a statement that is itself unqualified, and without demonstrating that those opponents themselves are unqualified. And this is a key point in his overall argument. Sure, if it was just a passing comment, I would understand the passage not being sourced. But it's not a passing comment. His article turns on this passage.

How do I know? How do I know if there is or isn't a paucity of science degrees in major media companies and/or in their news rooms? Is the reader to take as true, and on trust, what George says about the lack of science degrees in the news room?

The proliferation of science degrees in the news room isn't what's important here in this post. What's important is the proper representation of reality and the integrity of a valid argument. As a reader, if you want me to take credence from your argument, then please present me some facts, especially on key points.

EXCLUSIVE
The Kit Kat Incident and an Abuse of Power

March 26, 2010

Categories: Irregular Competition - Greenpeace, NGOs, Protests in Social Media - The Kit Kat Incident, Research - Case Studies - Greenpeace Studies - Social Media Campaign Analysis, Strategy

On February 4, 2010, I wrote a post on this blog about how well-resourced Greenpeace US was in the social media arena. In that article I mentioned that Greenpeace US would be a formidable irregular competitor for any corporation that woefully fell into their sights.

Well, I was correct. Recently, on March 17, 2010, Greenpeace took on Nestlé regarding its alleged participation in palm oil farming/deforestation in Indonesia. Although, technically, this protest action was initiated by Greenpeace International and not Greenpeace US, what I am calling "The Kit Kat Incident" demonstrates that Greenpeace, as a worldwide NGO, represents an organization that is a formidable irregular competitor.

A Direct Action Begins

Briefly, here is some background on The Kit Kat Incident. This protest arises as the next step in direct actions that Greenpeace has been applying against Nestlé for several years. These direct actions have been asking the food maker to reduce or eliminate its use of palm oil in its products. Greenpeace's contention has been that farmers, particularly in Indonesia, clear-cut rain forests so that palms may be planted for later harvesting and supply to companies like Nestlé. In addition to their claims about deforestation and how that may impact climate change, Greenpeace also contends that such deforestation destroys the habit of the orangutan.

The battle over palm oil reached a decisive turn on Wednesday, March 17, 2010 when Greenpeace International released a report titled "Caught Red-Handed: How Nestlé's Use of Palm Oil is Having a Devastating Impact on Rainforest, The Climate and Orang-utans." [80] The report's release was simultaneously supported by a social media protest campaign, initiated by Greenpeace [81] and aimed at a popular Nestlé brand, Kit Kat. (Note: This strategy, of targeting a brand rather than the corporation at-large, is standard procedure for an anti-corporate direct action. Please note also that the Greenpeace campaign has been centered on the Kit Kat brand internationally and not in the United States where Hershey is the licensee and manufacturer.) That social media campaign is currently being touted in the mainstream press as one which ignited a "firestorm" on the social web. As this social media campaign has been already well-documented in the press, I won't describe it here. However, if you would like more detail on this campaign, I direct you to a chronology of that firestorm which can be reviewed by visiting this link to Social Media Influence. [81] When viewing that chronology, though, please note that it focuses on the related social media events only and not on broader issues within the campaign, like power and its abuse which I will address below.

The Action as Firestorm

A social web firestorm it has been, indeed. On Wednesday, March 24, 2010, a week after the campaign began, I reviewed the Nestlé Facebook fan page,[82] which was the primary battle space of attack as requested by Greenpeace, and found that the page was still being heavily attacked, receiving negative posts at the rate of about one every ninety seconds. Though, a similar review I did on Thursday, March 25, 2010 showed that the frequency had slowed to one negative post about every five minutes.

Hot was this firestorm, but perhaps Greenpeace could have picked an even better primary battle space. Instead of targeting the corporate Nestlé Facebook fan page with, at this writing, about 94,000 fans, Greenpeace could have more wisely chosen the Kit Kat Facebook fan page [83] with, at this writing, about 463,000 fans. The Kit Kat Facebook fan page has an audience that is almost five times the size of that for the corporate Nestlé Facebook fan page. It's puzzling why Greenpeace did not select the Kit Kat fan page as the primary battle space, especially since Greenpeace focused the campaign's attention on the Kit Kat brand instead of the corporation at-large.

Nevertheless, the Greenpeace social media campaign was well-executed, but it probably would not have spread as quickly or as far had Nestlé not "shot themselves in the foot" with some inept tactical decisions made by the company's Facebook fan page administrator. Perhaps the company would have been able to preclude some of the damage had their corporate Facebook fan page administrator handled the initial attack on March 17 & March 18 in a more appropriate fashion. As their mismanagement of this corporate communications challenge has also been well-documented I won't rehash it here, but if you would like to learn more about it I will refer you to CEC Insider for a good synopsis of that problem.[84]

Broader Issues

As I mentioned three paragraphs ago, I want to discuss some broader issues, and not just the social media tactical events. These broader issues are not widely discussed in much of the press on this incident. So, since I believe that those issues are important, I will discuss them here and hopefully add more to the overall discussion and learning about The Kit Kat Incident. These broader issues concern "bullying" and the power that supports bullying.

Books such as Cluetrain [85] (which was mentioned several times in some of the anti-Nestlé posts on the Nestlé Facebook fan page), Future Shock, and Powershift (both before Cluetrain), talked about the shift in power from corporations to the "masses." Well, this paradigm flip has certainly been well-recorded over recent years, and its occurrence is no longer news. An application of this power flip is precisely what we are seeing in The Kit Kat Incident; the exercise of crowd power, realized and orchestrated by a savvy irregular competitor. But what I want to point out in this post is that this isn't just a mere flip of power. My main point is that this situation demonstrates an abuse of power. And abused power is for what Greenpeace, and other NGOs, have so long denigrated the very corporations that they have targeted. Let me explain how they have abused their "Cluetrain" power. Let's start with the Greenpeace demands.

The Demands

On Wednesday, March 17, 2010, Greenpeace issued the "Caught Red-Handed" report. If you go to page 12 of that report (page 9 on the PDF version), [86] you will see the "Greenpeace Demands" listed. Those demands are:

> *To protect Indonesia's last remaining forests, and to live up to its own commitments, Nestlé must immediately:*
>
> *1. STOP THE PROBLEM: NO MORE TRADE WITH THE SINAR MAS GROUP*
> *Stop trading with companies within the Sinar Mas group. This includes Golden Agri Resources and its subsidiaries, as well as Sinar Mas Forestry and Asia Pulp & Paper (APP).*
> *Stop buying Sinar Mas palm oil and pulp products from third-party suppliers.*

2. START THE SOLUTION : SUPPORT ZERO DEFORESTATION
Engage with the Indonesian government and industry to deliver a moratorium on forest clearance and peatland protection.

(A background note is needed here. It was Greenpeace's contention that Sinar Mas, a palm oil supplier, conducted improper farming procedures (e.g. clear-cutting) which contribute to the central Greenpeace issue, that of climate change and the destruction of the orangutan habitat.)

Let me say before you and I discuss these issues any further, that I have no financial interest in this battle between Greenpeace and Nestlé. Neither party is a client of mine. I don't own any Nestlé stock. And, quite frankly, I don't really care which party "wins" this particular battle. So then why am I writing about The Kit Kat Incident? I write about this incident as an interested observer of activist organizations and their behaviors in media. I offer this post as an educational article, and as a different perspective, toward greater understanding of what activists do right and what they do wrong. My interest here is not financial, but I do have an interest in this incident, an intellectual interest.

Generally speaking, I offer this post because I have an intellectual interest in the proper representation of truth and the accountability of activists and NGOs to that truth. Not only should activists and NGOs behave with integrity toward truth, but corporations should also do the same. Specifically speaking, I offer this post about The Kit Kat Incident because I believe that if Nestlé, or any other company, or Greenpeace, or any other advocate organization, is doing anything "improper," then they must "correct" that behavior. And apparently, in The Kit Kat Incident, Nestlé has done just that.

The Acquiescent Result

On Wednesday, March 17, 2010, the same date that the "Red-Handed" report was issued and the same date that the Greenpeace social web campaign was initiated, Nestlé issued the following statement: [87] (Updated Note, May 26, 2010: Nestlé has updated this statement, at the Web addressed linked to, from that originally shown on March 17, 2010. The original March 17 statement no longer appears on their Web site. However, to support my March 17 dating of this statement, I refer you to another blog which picked up the statement on the referenced date. Their date stamp appears on the post. You may visit that blog here. [88] You may also view other sites which picked up that statement with the March 17, 2010 date by clicking here.[89])

Specifically, Nestlé has replaced the Indonesian company Sinar Mas as a supplier of palm oil with another supplier for further shipments. We confirm that Nestlé has only bought from Sinar Mas for manufacturing in Indonesia, and no palm oil bought from Sinar Mas has been used by Nestlé for manufacturing in any other country.

Regarding our sourcing of paper and packaging products, we confirm that we do not buy any materials from Asia Pulp & Paper (APP).

We have also joined other major purchasers of palm oil in making sure that companies, such as Cargill, understand our demands for palm oil which is not sourced from suppliers which destroy rainforests. At this point in time our suppliers of palm oil say they can't currently guarantee that one particular company is excluded, due to the mingling of palm oil in a very complex supply chain. We will continue to pressure our suppliers to eliminate any sources of palm oil which are related to rainforest destruction and to provide valid guarantees of traceability as quickly as possible. We will not portray palm oil as free of such oils unless such guarantees are clear and reliable.

Although they did not mention the Golden Agri Resources demand, it appears that Nestlé met the first demand, and *on the same day as the report's issuance and the start of the social media campaign.*

The next day, March 18, 2010, Nestlé issued another statement, [90] in a Q&A format, which addresses the second demand:

Is Nestlé part of the "Roundtable on Sustainable Palm Oil" (RSPO) and what certification methods does it offer?

Yes, Nestlé has been closely associated with the Round Table on Sustainable Palm Oil (RSPO) through the Sustainable Agriculture Initiative Platform since its inception and the company has now full corporate membership. This was established in 2004 to promote the growth and use of sustainable palm oil. Today it has over 300 members. RSPO have developed Principles and Criteria for Sustainable Palm Oil Production.

Although this second statement doesn't address the second Greenpeace demand directly, it appears to do so indirectly and is addressed to the larger issue of how to go forward in a responsible manner.

The Bullying Sets In

But, the time after these two Nestlé statements were issued was the time when the Greenpeace social media campaign was hitting high-gear. Yet during this time period, I have observed that a high percentage of the Nestlé Facebook fan page posts asked the company to stop buying palm oil from sources that threatened deforestation. The company had already agreed to do that before these posts went up. However, during that time I observed no Facebook communication from Greenpeace claiming victory, asking its followers to stop, or even asking their followers to redirect their efforts to the second demand which was, as I noted above, not as clearly addressed. Instead, Greenpeace issued this statement from their Web site: [91]

> Sometimes a company can issue a reactive statement – like Nestlé did upon the launch of our Kit Kat campaign – that appears to wrap up everything for which they are being criticised in a neat little package, when in reality nothing changes. In this case Nestlé's neat little package definitely stinks – and nobody's buying it.
>
> Nestlé announced it would cancel contracts with Sinar Mas, the largest palm oil producer in Indonesia, after we released a report exposing Sinar Mas' involvement in illegal rainforest and peatland destruction to make way for their palm oil plantations. The report was released the same day as our 'Have a break?' video. The statement Nestlé made in reaction was not only nothing new – it won't be anywhere near enough to protect Indonesia's rainforests, orang-utans or peatlands. But they're acting as if they've done enough - and luckily they don't seem to be fooling anyone.

Well, perhaps they're "fooling" me, because Nestlé was quite clear in its acquiescence to the Greenpeace demands, especially the first demand, saying not, as portrayed by Greenpeace as shown above, that they "would cancel contracts with Sinar Mas," but rather saying that they "replaced the Indonesian company Sinar Mas as a supplier of palm oil with another supplier." How much more clear could Nestlé have been? If there is any fooling going on here, it could be on the part of Greenpeace. The battle is pretty much over. Greenpeace just won't declare victory.

Yes, I know that those who disagree with what I am saying here will use the comeback that it isn't Greenpeace that is doing the bullying, but rather they will say that it is Nestlé that is bullying the rain forest and the orangutans. Yet, we have seen that Nestlé is "down" and has "cried uncle" while Greenpeace still continues to pound them with "Cluetrain" power. What this type of behavior reminds me of is street fights I witnessed as a kid, when one fighter (usually the neighborhood bully) was sitting atop the other unmercifully, and needlessly, pummeling the loser's face into a pulp.

Conclusion

This type of bullying puts Greenpeace in a poor light. Greenpeace got what they demanded. Representing the outcome as anything else is an abuse of their "Cluetrain" power, a power that is granted to Greenpeace by the people. Asking their followers to continue, or rather not disengaging them, on an objective that has already been met not only abuses the time, and the trust, of their digital supporters, but doing so lowers the status of Greenpeace as a "reputable" advocate. In my opinion, this type of behavior just makes them look "small-minded" and only self-interested which are characteristics for which they denigrate their corporate opponents.

Collateral Damage in The Kit Kat Incident?

March 26, 2010

Categories: Irregular Competition - Greenpeace, NGOs, Protests in Social Media - The Kit Kat Incident, Threats, Social Media Campaign Analysis

Here is another thought regarding The Kit Kat Incident, about which I blogged earlier today. So far in the blogosphere, or in the mainstream media, I haven't seen this concern raised as yet.

Greenpeace's argument over palm oil and image attack on Nestlé has been tactically oriented toward the Kit Kat bar. (Please see my previous post, "The Kit Kat Incident and an Abuse of Power," for a synopsis of this direct action/PR event.) Nestlé produces the Kit Kat bar internationally, but Nestlé does not produce the Kit Kat bar in the United States. In America, the Kit Kat bar is produced by Hershey [92] who, at least at the time of this writing, is not being targeted by Greenpeace.

Greenpeace has not made this distinction abundantly clear. Yes, they did note this difference on their initial call-to-action page. [93] But their notation was extremely tiny, brief, and at the bottom of the page. And in subsequent Greenpeace Web sites posts and actions in social media, I am hard-pressed to find further references to this distinction between Nestlé and Hershey as it relates to the production of the Kit Kat bar. Clearly, this situation represents a business threat to Hershey.

So, this situation begs four questions:

1. Concerning Hershey, is this a responsible way to conduct an anti-corporate direct action?
2. In the form of lost sales, will there be "collateral damage" against Hershey, who at this point in the protest appears to be an innocent by-stander?
3. If there is collateral damage, will it form a basis of legal action against Greenpeace?
4. And if a legal basis is formed, will Hershey pursue it?

It will be interesting to see how this plays out.

Living on a Meme

March 30, 2010

Categories: Anti-Corporatism, Truth

A few weeks ago, I was attracted to an article turned up by one of my Google Alerts. This article link has been sitting in my "Things to Write About" folder. That is until today.

On March 8, 2010, the San Francisco Chronicle posted an article titled "Anti-corporate vs. Anti-government Anger: Who to Trust?," written by Dr. Jim Taylor, a psychologist and author. The first line of this article reads: "This post is not a partisan polemic intended to attack those who hold different views than I." I smiled when I read that line because when someone prefaces an article in this manner, a polemic is often what that article turns out to be. Polemic it is. And Dr. Jim puts forth his opinion. That's fine. I don't happen to agree with his opinion, to which he is most certainly entitled. But his opinion is not to what I object. What I object to in this particular article is the way he constructs the argument and presents the information that expresses his opinion. He constructs his argument and presents information in a way that not only contradicts his own views, but also in a way that generates and propagates unsupported meme, which can damage the "reality" that we must all share. Let me explain.

On the article, under the author's name, was listed a link to the author's Web site. Once clicked, I was taken to Dr. Jim's site where I noticed there was listed a blog article entitled "Technology: How Social Media Can Ruin Lives." [94] Being involved with social media, I clicked on this post. I found that the article deals with the issue of how Internet media has the potential to spread innuendo and rumor and how that process can ruin people's lives. (Yes, no kidding. This is part of what I study in my consulting practice.) In this story about how social media can ruin lives, from a psychologist's perspective, Dr. Jim cites an anecdotal "case" of a young man who had, per the story, been maligned via social media. Dr. Jim refers to this tale by saying that:

> *His* (the young man's) *story illustrates the dark side of information in the 21st century and confirms our need to ensure that, in our real-time, instant-access world, the information that is spread through cyberspace is both timely and accurate.*

You will get no argument from me on this issue. In my work, I spend much time in studying how "inaccurate" information incorrectly changes meaning and alters our perceptions of reality. Now, if you are a regular reader of my blog, you probably already know where I'm going with this quote from Dr. Jim. But if you aren't a regular reader, please stay with me because it's going to be well worth the trip.

Put into other words, in this article about how social media can ruin lives, Dr. Jim addressed the problem of how memes can get started and then how, taken as "truth," those memes can put into play a sequence of events, with negative consequences occurring. Paraphrasing Dr. Jim from the article, he believes that information spread via the Internet must be accurate. Now let's flip back to that "anti" article that Dr. Jim posted on the San Francisco Chronicle.

Apparently he didn't remember his thoughts about the need for "accurate" information on the Internet when he wrote the article on anti-corporate vs. anti-government, which, by the way, really didn't have much discussion of the anti-government position. This anti-corporate vs. anti-government article amounts to a long polemic, the integrity of which is dependent almost entirely upon anti-corporate meme. Let me demonstrate how this is so by showing you a sample passage from that article:

> *It's easy to understand the anti-corporate anger felt by so many Americans these days. Big Business reaps massive profits through often-times reckless dealings and cost cutting. Plus, after causing the Great Recession, it gets a bailout because it is 'too big to fail.'*

Sure. It's easy to understand anti-corporate anger that's based on unsupported meme. It's easy to whip up fervor by repeating things, negative memes, that aren't necessarily true. But repeating memes doesn't make something true. And living on an unsupported meme can result in severe damage to your perception of reality. However, Dr. Jim simply rolls with the standard anti-corporate meme and makes his statements with no support. Would you please show us the support, Dr. Jim? Show us the money … in numbers. Where are the massive profits? Where are the reckless dealings? Who caused the "Great Recession?" Rather than meme, let's see some "proof."

Let's talk about that meme of "massive profits." And not from an emotional meme perspective, either. Because they're such a "whipping boy" for political purposes, and because of the health care debate currently raging (even though the bill is now law), I'll use the health care industry as an example. I've discussed this one before on this blog, so you can refer to my October 2009 post on this subject, "Activists Attack The 'Highly' Profitable Health Insurance Industry," or simply look at the information I'll show below. The information below is taken from my recent comment on a PR blog, Credible Context. In that writing, I wasn't defending health care insurance companies, per se; I've had my hassles with them just like many other people, and I'm not one of their fans. But in that writing I was defending truth and the idea of putting business arguments into a context that present a credible position. In other words, I was being a fan of accurately representing information and arguing **against** memes.

Per Fortune Magazine:

Health Care: Insurance & Managed Care
Industry Profit as a Percent of Revenues
- *2006 - 5.8%, ranking 33rd of 50 industries ranked - http://cnnmoneycontrol.com/magazines/fortune/fortune500/2007/performers/industries/return_on_revenues/index.html*

- *2007 - 6.2%, ranking 28th of 50 industries ranked - http://money.cnn. com/magazines/fortune/fortune500/2008/performers/industries/profits/*
- *2008 - 2.2%, ranking 35th of 50 industries ranked - http://money.cnn. com/magazines/fortune/fortune500/2009/performers/industries/profits/*
- *Comprehensive industry stats for 2009 are not as yet in.*

Please keep in mind that the above figures are just for the for-profit companies. These stats don't include results for the non-profit health care insurance companies such as Blue Cross/Blue Shield or Kaiser Permanente, which by definition are not "profitable."

Note: You may see the entire post and my comment by going to "Business innovation initiative suffers in context." http://crediblecontext. com/?p=459#comments (accessed March 30, 2010)

Here's an industry, health care insurance, that via meme is consistently accused of reaping "massive" profits. My statement here isn't just a meme. For proof, turn on any cable news broadcast and you probably won't need to wait too long until you hear that meme. Or go to this Google search (click here) to understand how widespread this meme is. "Massive" profits they are often accused of having. Yet, profit margins of about six percent or less can't be considered "massive." And when folks insist on spreading that meme about "massive" profits, against the facts they just make themselves look foolish.

Information that is "accurate," as Dr. Jim said in his post about the dangers of social media, is what the Internet needs. Well, the Internet has it. I used the Internet to obtain the above information about industry profitability. But apparently some people, including Dr. Jim in his "anti" article, would just rather live on a meme. In the short run, I suppose living on a meme makes life easier. You don't need to take the time to vet information and seek out those "pesky" facts. But, in the long run, living on a meme actually makes life more difficult. Living on a meme can distort one's perception of reality, perhaps even "ruining" your life, as Dr. Jim alluded to in his own story on social media.

But "meme-ing" business isn't where Dr. Jim stops in the "anti" article. From that article, let's move on to another "meme-d" subject that Dr. Jim "tackles," that of income taxes.

What I find so odd is that the anti-government populists don't even want the wealthy to be taxed. You'd think that they would at least want the rich, who got massive tax cuts under the Bush administration and who have been the cause of so many recent problems, to suffer for their sins.

Well, I'm not going to tackle the definition of exactly what a "massive tax cut" is. (Seems that Dr. Jim likes to use that word "massive.") You and I already addressed the problem of meme generation/propagation by using such words. What I want to address now is meme generation/propagation via two issues that are in the above quote from Dr. Jim. Those two issues are represented by the terms: 1) "the cause of so many recent problems;" and, 2) "to suffer for their sins."

But because I like to keep my post length under 1500 words, and because I'm rapidly approaching that limit, and because the discussion of these next two issues, with their attendant "pesky" facts, is going to take a while, I will pause here and continue this post on Thursday, April 1, 2010. (And the post won't even be an "April Fool.")

If you are reading this before April 1, 2010, you may simply subscribe to the FREE RSS feed so that you will receive that next post automatically. Just click here to subscribe. Or if you are reading this after April 1, 2010, you may click here to proceed to Part 2 of "Living on a Meme."

Is Greenpeace Research Reliable?

March 31, 2010

Categories: Irregular Competition - Greenpeace, NGOs, Protests in Social Media - The Kit Kat Incident, Research - Questionable - Social Media Campaign Analysis

Two weeks ago Greenpeace launched their "Caught Red-Handed" campaign with a report of the same name. The issuance of the report was supported by a simultaneous social media campaign against Nestlé. [95] These events were well-documented in the blogosphere and in the mainstream media. I summarized the situation in my blog post titled "The Kit Kat Incident and an Abuse of Power," and you may go to that article for a synopsis if you are unfamiliar with this incident.

The subject of today's post is the report itself, "Caught Red-Handed," [96] or rather the research integrity thereof. If you go to the report, which you may do by clicking here, [97] and turn to page 13 (page 8 on the PDF version) you will see Greenpeace's "Sources of Evidence" page. Or, as it would be more commonly called, the Bibliography. On this page of listed sources, Greenpeace shows a total of 73 sources. If you read through those sources, you will find that fully 22 of those sources are from Greenpeace documents or files. This means that 30% of the total sources used in this report were internal, and not of a diversified and external nature.

When I attended graduate school, I was instructed that, in performing research, a researcher should not use their own work as references in a research paper. And if doing so was absolutely, positively necessary, then reference to that researcher's own work should be employed very, very sparingly. The reasons against a researcher not using their own research in subsequent papers is obvious. The more diversified research sourcing is, the stronger is the research argument. "In-bred" references only weaken a case.

Is 30% a "sparing" employment of internal sourcing? Does 30% internal sourcing in "Caught Red-Handed" weaken the study's argument? I suppose that depends on your point of view. My view is that 30% internal sourcing is highly excessive, and seeing that high of a percentage in this Greenpeace report makes me call into question the integrity of their research and, consequently, the validity of the Greenpeace argument presented in "Caught Red-Handed."

Is this a case of being "caught red-handed" in an issue of reliable and fair research?

You know my opinion; you're certainly entitled to yours.

Chapter Eight - The Meme Marches On
—————— Take-Aways ——————

At the start of this chapter, I gave you a little peek into how I came to undertake this work in which I am currently engaged. The two pieces titled "You Could Say That This Post Serves as My Annotated Resume" explain how my skills match this quest for showing how memes, false memes specifically, are often taken for truth, a "truth" that those who foster perhaps believe will become "true" if it is repeated often enough.

I demonstrated one irregular competitor's tactics toward this goal, of making meme truth, a truth on which they would like you to base your view of reality. The three part essay series, "How Does RAN Rank As An Irregular Competitor?," gave an overview of how Rainforest Action Network (RAN) uses social media venues to put forth one of their desired memes, that is their level of success in using social media in their campaign against corporations. In those three pieces, my analysis showed that the RAN claims of social media success, a meme, must be viewed with skepticism.

A general meme on which, I think, irregular competition would like people to base their lives is that of anti-corporatism. Of this one, people need to be highly skeptical. "Two Sides to the Coin of Corporate Power" and "Who is Really Responsible for Corporate Power?" look more deeply than the meme meisters might want people to look into the nature of the anti-corporate meme. If the anti-corporate meme was not alive and well, none of the other memes on which irregular competition would like people to base their realities would be very effective. These two posts give some food for thought on the validity of that anti-corporate thought. And to that idea of validity I partially, at least, allude in "How About Some Facts to Support Some Facts?" In "Facts," I discuss how a fan of facts deserted facts in order to "make" an argument about climate science. The facts he chose to abandon would seemingly be easily accessible in the public domain, yet he took a short-cut in his argumentation which just yielded more meme making. We then moved onto a more in-depth examination of how irregular competitors play with meme and truth.

In "The Kit Kat Incident and an Abuse of Power," I point out how a meme was perpetrated by one of the best meme meisters in the irregular competition business, Greenpeace. Through supported facts, I point out how Greenpeace was not truthful when they claimed Nestlé did not meet their demands, and used that meme-d "truth" of their own making to propagate further damage on the image of the food manufacturer. Then, in "Collateral Damage in The Kit Kat Incident?," I suggested how the meme made by Greenpeace, the meme of rainforest destruction as demonstrated in "Abuse of Power," might damage an innocent business bystander, Hershey. Damage from memes is not always restricted to the target in the reality play of the irregular competitor. When realities are mangled, others can suffer.

Then in "Living on a Meme," the post whose title inspired this book, I discuss in much more detail my point about meme meistering when I demonstrate how even those who think that there should be truth on the Internet succumb to the disease of an alternate reality via a meme. "Be careful of what you read" are the watch words here, and those words are particularly relevant to the type of "research" that was found and discussed in the chapter concluding essay "Is Greenpeace Research Reliable?" When dealing with irregular competition, an examination of their sources is always recommended.

CHAPTER NINE
_____

The Meme Marches
On ... And On

Living on a Meme - Part 2

April 1, 2010

Categories: Anti-Corporatism, Truth

In my previous post, "Living on a Meme," I discussed a San Francisco Chronicle article entitled "Anti-corporate vs. Anti-government Anger: Who to Trust?" [98] Written by psychologist Dr. Jim Taylor, the article discusses many reasons why he thinks people are angry at large corporations. What does he say about the anti-government reasons? Well, there aren't as many of those given. If you haven't read my Part 1 of Living on a Meme, you may do so by clicking here. Or if you would like to read the article by Dr. Jim, you may click here. [99]

What you and I are discussing here in "Living on a Meme" is, specifically, how Dr. Jim, as an example of a meme writer in the "anti" article, not only contradicts his own views in that article, but also uses unsubstantiated claims, claims that just keep floating around in the popular culture, to put forth his "argument." And, generally, what you and I are discussing here is how articles, like Dr. Jim's "anti" article that is based on meme, can further generate and propagate misinformation, damaging the common "reality" that we must all share.

To illustrate these problems, I am using Dr. Jim's "anti" article as an example, and am refuting his meme with "pesky" facts. And I am illustrating these problems while pointing out that, conceptually, Dr. Jim agrees with me. He agrees with me, in principle, that information should be "accurate." Yet, he didn't seem to practice this in the "anti" article. In Part 1 I pointed out that, in a post about social media dangers and how those dangers can ruin lives, Dr. Jim maintained that Internet information should be "accurate." Yet, unfortunately in the "anti" article he relies on meme, and the inherent inaccuracies that lie within meme, to make his case for anti-corporate anger.

When we left off in Part 1, you and I were about to discuss meme generation/propagation via two issues: 1) "the cause of so many recent problems;" and, 2) "to suffer for their sins," that were in the following Dr. Jim passage from the "anti" article mentioned above.

> *What I find so odd is that the anti-government populists don't even want the wealthy to be taxed. You'd think that they would at least*

want the rich, who got massive tax cuts under the Bush administration and who have been the cause of so many recent problems, to suffer for their sins.

First, let's tackle "the cause of so many recent problems" meme. What problems, Dr. Jim? To make a credible argument, not dependent upon meme, you shouldn't accuse a group of people of causing a problem without demonstrating what the problem is. Meme is divisive and serves no purpose other than that of its own unfounded propagation. And using meme in this manner is discriminatory. This type of unsupported meme is that which keeps fanning the flames of social fragmentation and divisiveness, doing nothing to support a cohesive society. This is surprising to see from a writer who said in his social media post [100] that Internet information should be "accurate."

Second, let's tackle the "to suffer for their sins" meme. What sins are those? Would that be the sin of paying most of the personal income taxes in this country and then being denigrated for paying not only their "fair share," but the "fair share" of about 20 other people, as well? Lest you think that claim meme, let's have a look at some "pesky" facts.

U.S. Federal Personal Income Tax Burden

Year	Tax Percentile Ranked by AGI	AGI for Percentiles	Percent of Federal Personal Income Tax Paid
2004	Top 10%	$99,112	68.19%
2005	Top 10%	103,912	70.30%
2006	Top 10%	108,904	70.79%
2007	Top 10%	113,018	71.22%

Note: The source for the above statistics is the National Taxpayers Union (NTU). AGI means Adjusted Gross Income. NTU's source is listed as the Internal Revenue Service. Click here to go to the NTU site for further details. [101]

For purposes of illustration and discussion, let's refer to the "top 10%" of wage earners in this country as the "meme-d rich" to whom Dr. Jim refers. The fact is that the "rich" pay 70% or more of the personal income tax in the United States. Is that a sin? In some ways, yes, but not in the way that Dr. Jim is "meme-ing." And that tax cut meme? Please note, Dr. Jim, that during the period of 2004 through 2007, when the Bush tax cuts were in effect, the "rich" top 10% paid an increasing percentage, by three points, of the total federal personal income tax. So, how is that a "massive" Bush tax cut?

*   *   *

I could go on refuting the memes that appear in Dr. Jim's "anti" article. That article is a very rich "meme target environment." However, doing so would become tedious and probably boring for you, the reader. I believe I've made my point. So, I'll wrap this up now.

Living on a meme, using unsupported information, is just lazy writing. And the type of writing Dr. Jim used in the "anti" article is disappointing. He is surely capable of better writing, like the type I saw constructed in his article on the dangers of social media.[102] Lazy writing of the type I've discussed here does much to contribute to the damage of the reality that we must all share.

Passing on memes, even in just a matter of fact way, simply perpetrates inaccuracies and causes all who experience them to obtain a false sense of reality. A society built on false realities helps no one, and only creates a world with more problems.

EXCLUSIVE
Greenpeace Chooses Wrong Success Indicator

April 2, 2010

Categories: Irregular Competition - Greenpeace, NGOs, Protests in Social Media - The Kit Kat Incident, Research - Case Studies - Greenpeace Studies - Social Media Campaign Analysis, Truth

Last week I wrote about The Kit Kat Incident, a Greenpeace International direct action, staged in the social web, targeting Nestlé, and their Kit Kat brand, over palm oil ingredient sustainability issues. If you are unfamiliar with this protest, which grew into a somewhat unintentionally "target-amplified" PR debacle for Nestlé, you may read my post "The Kit Kat Incident and an Abuse of Power" by clicking here. Please note, also, that I have no financial interest in this battle between Greenpeace and Nestlé, neither is a client, and I own no Nestlé stock.

The subject of today's post is about how Greenpeace International attempted to claim a financial impact in The Kit Kat Incident, but chose the wrong measurement device by which to claim their effects. Let me explain.

Their Claim

In a Greenpeace Web site announcement [103] made after their social media campaign began, which was on Wednesday, March 17, 2010, the NGO stated:

> … *see how Nestle's stock has fallen in the last day* …

and they linked that phrase to a Nestlé stock quote page on the financial Web site, Market Watch. [104] (Greenpeace International did not date this Web site announcement, but based on the comment dates and other information on the page, I estimate that this Web site announcement was made on Thursday, March 18, 2010.) That link went to the page for the stock symbol NSRGY, which is a Nestlé stock issue traded on the "pink sheets" in the American OTC (over-the-counter) market. Nestlé has several different issues of common stock. If you go to a financial site, such as Yahoo Finance,[105] and type in "nestle," you may see the several different issues. Here I am going to talk about only two of those stock issues, the two pertinent to The Kit Kat Incident. Let's discuss NSRGY and another Nestlé stock issue designated as NESN.

There *Is* a Difference

NESN is the stock symbol that represents the company's corporate stock. Because Nestlé is a Swiss-based company, NESN is based, or traded, on the Swiss Stock Exchange (SIX). NESN is primarily traded in countries other than the United States. What Nestlé stock is traded inside the United States? I'm glad you asked.

NSRGY is the stock symbol that trades the American version of NESN. NSRGY is bought and sold on the American OTC market, and is technically known as an "ADR," which means an "American drawing right." [106] If you are in the United States and want to trade Nestlé stock easily, you would simply buy or sell the ADR version, NSRGY. If you are outside the United States and want to trade Nestlé stock easily, you would buy or sell NESN, and not NSRGY.

Now, please understand that either stock represents the entire international corporation. NSRGY does not represent just the American operations of Nestlé; NSRGY represents the international operations of the company. But even though both stock issues represent the entire corporation, NSRGY and NESN prices do not track exactly. You may go to any financial site, such as the aforementioned Yahoo Finance, and check their movements. Their prices are not the same. Their variations are not the same. There are variations in each of their prices from day to day due to the number of shares in each issue, foreign currency fluctuations, and other idiosyncrasies of the financial markets such as how each market views the company and the business issues it must face. One of those business issues would be how each market, U.S. and international, would view the threat potential of the Greenpeace International direct action. Let me emphasize that this idea of each international market's view of Nestlé is key to our discussion in this post.

Different Markets, Different Views

This idea is key because when their social media campaign began on March 17, Greenpeace International stated on their call-to-campaign page [107] that the Kit Kat bar, the central Nestlé brand targeted in the direct action, was made by Nestlé internationally everywhere except the United States. Technically speaking, Greenpeace International did briefly state this fact in small font at the bottom of their call-to-campaign page. (Although practically speaking, I took issue with this tactic in my previous post, "Collateral Damage in The Kit Kat Incident?") Please note that in the United States, Kit Kat is licensed and manufactured by Hershey and that Greenpeace International did not target Hershey in this particular direct action.

Since this was a direct action aimed by Greenpeace International (and not Greenpeace US), at least technically as mentioned above, at Nestlé Kit Kat customers in markets outside the United States, investors outside the U.S. would be more sensitive to the effects of the direct action. Those international investors would be the intended recipients of the Greenpeace International message, rather than U.S. investors. So, Greenpeace International would logically want to assess their protest action internationally, and not in U.S. markets. But Greenpeace did not do that.

Jump back six paragraphs to the Greenpeace International quote, from their own Web site, referencing how "Nestlé's stock has fallen in the last day." You may go to that Greenpeace International page by clicking here [108] and, if you like, search for the quoted phrase, click on their link, and see how it is connected to a financial page for the stock symbol NSRGY. (That is, of course, if they haven't changed the link after reading this article.)

Conclusion

So, what can be concluded from the above information?

What can be concluded from the above information is that when it came to tracking the financial impact of their direct action against a Nestlé brand not sold in the United States, Greenpeace International chose to measure the ups and downs of NSRGY, the American drawing rights stock, a stock traded in the United States. Clearly, if Greenpeace International wanted to measure any impact of their direct action on the stock of Nestlé then, since this was an action directed at markets other than the United States, Greenpeace International should have chosen the NESN stock issue for analysis. Here is a clear strategic error in an attempt to claim an impact. Greenpeace International sought protest action outside of the United States and chose to measure their success by evaluating an American stock.

How does this make sense?

On the surface, it doesn't make sense from a business or financial analysis standpoint. On the surface, the selection of NSRGY over NESN would appear to be an error of carelessness or even ignorance. But, let's dig below the surface.

In my next post, entitled "Greenpeace Did Not Influence Stock Price in The Kit Kat Incident," which will publish on Tuesday, April 6, 2010, I will present my theory that the Greenpeace International selection of NSRGY over NESN was not an error, but rather a conscious strategic decision.

If your are reading this prior to April 6, 2010, you may subscribe to the FREE RSS feed so that you will receive that next post automatically. Or, if you are reading this after April 6, you may simply click here to go to "Greenpeace Did Not Influence Stock Price in The Kit Kat Incident."

EXCLUSIVE
Greenpeace Did Not Influence Stock
Price in The Kit Kat Incident

April 6, 2010

Categories: Irregular Competition - Greenpeace, NGOs, Protests in Social Media
- The Kit Kat Incident, Research - Case Studies - Greenpeace Studies - Social
Media Campaign Analysis

In previous posts, I have discussed The Kit Kat Incident which was a Greenpeace
International direct action against Nestlé concerning the latter's involvement
with palm oil supplies, and a dispute over the sustainability thereof.

If you aren't familiar with The Kit Kat Incident, you may click through to my
posts, as shown in the links in the first sentence of this post, to learn about
the event.

Please note, also, that I have no financial interest in this battle between
Greenpeace and Nestlé, neither is a client, and I own no Nestlé stock.

The Claim

Today, almost three weeks after the commencement of that Greenpeace
initiative, which was based in social media by the way, we have a little more
perspective from which to analyze a Greenpeace claim made during the fracas.
That claim was one of an effect on the company's stock price.

On a Greenpeace International Web site page, [109] which appears to have been
created around March 18, 2010, the day after their social media campaign
against Nestlé began, Greenpeace International claimed:

> *... Nestle's stock has fallen in the last day ...*

and they linked that phrase to a Nestlé stock quotation page. [110] As I discussed
in my previous post, "Greenpeace Chooses Wrong Success Indicator,"
Greenpeace International chose an incorrect measure of impact on the
targeted company's stock price. Per my article, Greenpeace International
conducted a campaign aimed outside the United States, but when they chose
to demonstrate their financial impact on the company, through the claim

of falling stock, Greenpeace International referenced a stock that is traded within the United States.

In my "Wrong Success Indicator" post, I said that on the surface, this selection of an incorrect indicator appears to be an error of carelessness. But I also said that I would dig below the surface of the appearance of error, and discuss my theory that the selection of the incorrect indicator was a calculated strategic decision.

That's what you and I will discuss today. If you haven't yet read my article, "Greenpeace Chooses Wrong Success Indicator," you might find it helpful to do so before reading the rest of this post.

NSRGY vs. NESN

By way of quick review, in "Wrong Success Indicator," I discussed two Nestlé stock issues, NSRGY and NESN. To demonstrate the effects of their social media campaign, the stock issue chosen by Greenpeace International was NSRGY. This choice was incorrect. For the reasons discussed in my previous post, for financial impact demonstration purposes (no pun intended), the correct stock issue that Greenpeace should have chosen is NESN. But, after an examination of the stock prices of both issues, I've concluded that this "mis-selection" was not an error. Let me explain why by taking a look at the numbers.

	NSRGY Closing Price	NESN Closing Price
Mar 17, 2010	51.40	54.15
Mar 18, 2010	51.18	54.10
Mar 19, 2010	50.36	53.15
Mar 22, 2010	50.97	53.90
Mar 23, 2010	50.90	53.90
Mar 24, 2010	50.04	53.85
Mar 25, 2010	50.19	54.10
Mar 26, 2010	50.23	53.75
Mar 29, 2010	50.55	53.85
Mar 30, 2010	50.57	54.00

Source: Yahoo Finance.

Nice numbers, but what do they mean? We'll look at these numbers with four issues in mind:

1.   Can a direct action, such as the one we are discussing, be determined to impact stock prices?
2.   Per my theory that the selection of the incorrect indicator was not an "error" but instead a calculated strategic decision, we'll look at why Greenpeace International chose NSRGY instead of NESN;
3.   Per their claim shown four paragraphs ago, we'll look at how Greenpeace International got the "backing" for their claim that their direct actions caused the stock to decrease in one day; and,
4.   We'll look at whether the Greenpeace International direct action had any effect on the movement of the stock price over the two week period shown.

The Analysis & Discussion

Issue #1: Let's tackle the first issue, whether or not a direct action such as this can be determined to impact a stock's price. As all the statisticians out there would say, "Most likely, not." The reason? The reason is that there are so many variables impacting a stock's price on any given day that, unless you can hold constant all the variables except the one you are measuring, it is very difficult to determine the effect the measured variable has on the stock price. Yes, statisticians can attempt this, but the results of the work are almost always arguable. However, for purposes of discussion, we are going to disregard this general rule, and say that we can determine this. So, now let's go on to the second issue to show why Greenpeace chose NSRGY instead of the more correctly applied NESN.

To show the reason why Greenpeace made this choice, we'll need to take a look at another table of numbers.

	NSRGY	NESN
Slope - March 17 through March 30, 2010	-0.0953	0.002
Percent Change - March 17 vs. March 18, 2010	-0.42	-0.09
Percent Change - March 17 vs. March 30, 2010	-1.614	-0.27

Issues #2 & #3: The second row in the above table shows that the percentage change for NSRGY, during the first two days of the social media campaign, was greater than the percentage change for NESN. Both in a negative direction, yes, but NESN only minimally so, almost imperceptibly so, while NSRGY's negative movement was about 4.6 times greater than that of NESN. Is there any wonder why Greenpeace International chose NSRGY instead of NESN? Yes, NESN would have been the more appropriately selected stock for the reasons laid out in my previous post, "Wrong Success Indicator." But it appears apparent that Greenpeace chose NSRGY to say, "Nestle's stock has fallen in the last day," because NSRGY had the greater loss. And a loss of less than one half-percent isn't really considered a "loss." A movement of such small size can be considered a fairly normal stock price fluctuation for a 24-hour period.

No. I think that here Greenpeace International was just being opportunistic and selected the bigger percentage change that would help them make their argument. (Research procedures of this sort were the subject of another previous post on this blog, "Is Greenpeace Research Reliable?")

Issue #4: As I mentioned above, trying to determine if a particular market variable affects the price of a stock is a statistically "sticky" question, especially if you are trying to do so over the course of only one day. Statistically it is more valid to seek changes over a longer period of time. So, again for the sake of discussion and disregarding completely the larger rule, instead of looking at just one day's change, let's try to make the analysis a bit more broad and see if any there were any longer term "effects" on the Nestlé stock. That's what the top and bottom lines in the second table, above, are about.

The top line shows the statistically calculated "slopes" of the "lines" that are represented by the data in first table on this page. The slope means the average "rate of change" that takes place in those series of numbers. To keep this discussion as simple as possible, and understandable by the widest possible audience, let's not address the value that those slope numbers represent. Let's just look at the slopes in terms of their direction (positive or negative) and their relative values.

NSRGY shows a negative slope of 0.09 while NESN shows a positive slope of 0.002, yet a slope of 0.002 is almost imperceptible and therefore virtually meaningless. Statistically this means that the NSRGY series of stock prices decreases while the NESN series of stock prices increases, albeit infinitesimally, and, as shown by their relative slope values, NSRGY decreases more rapidly than NESN increases. These slopes are somewhat consistent, in terms of magnitude, with the percentage change data that is listed in the other two rows. All indicating that NSRGY is the bigger "loser" of the two stocks shown.

The bottom line of the table shows that for the comparison dates of March 17 and March 30, 2010, both NSRGY and NESN decreased percentage-wise, but NESN (the more likely stock to be affected by Greenpeace's campaign) showed a much smaller decrease than did NSRGY. In fact, the NSRGY decrease was over 6 times greater than was the NESN decrease for the same period. Please note that, as pointed out in my previous article "Wrong Success Indicator," NSRGY represents a stock traded in a regional market where the Greenpeace International direct action was not aimed.

Based on what we have discussed so far in this post, I would not be surprised if, any day now, Greenpeace popped up and opportunistically claimed the credit for the decrease in the March 17 to March 30 NSRGY, even though NSRGY is traded in a national market where the Greenpeace direct action was not aimed.

Conclusion

What does all the foregoing tell us? Well, in addition to the discoveries I mentioned in my previous post, "Is Greenpeace Research Reliable?," the foregoing tells us that we should not take Greenpeace claims or research at face value, and that we should dig a bit deeper.

Stay Calm and Assertive

April 8, 2010

Categories: Activism, Tactics, Greenpeace

Over the past couple of years, I've seen several companies get "rattled" when they are attacked by activists, advocates, or NGOs via the social web. Two examples stand out in particular: The Motrin Incident (November 2008) [111] and The Kit Kat Incident (March 2010). In The Motrin Incident, the makers of Motrin, Johnson & Johnson, were unsettled by a swarm of Mommy Bloggers who objected to the nature of an online ad for Motrin. In The Kit Kat Incident, Greenpeace attacked Nestlé, the makers (except in the United States) of the Kit Kat bar, as another salvo in their ongoing battle over the meaning of "sustainable" palm oil.

Each incident had different types of players, with different types of characteristics, operating under different conditions. But there is one element which is common to both of these incidents; neither of the attack victims remained calm and assertive.

The term, "stay calm and assertive," is largely attributed to Cesar Millan, the Dog Whisperer. If you watch the show, the Dog Whisperer, on the National Geographic Channel on Friday nights, you will know of whom I write. Briefly, Cesar Millan is a "dog psychologist." Now, don't think that he sits dogs down and shows them Rorschach drawings or asks them about their deepest feelings concerning their parents. (Imagine if it was the latter, certainly the patient would always call their mother a "bitch." :-)) What Cesar does is, as he says at the beginning of each Dog Whisperer episode, that he rehabilitates dogs and trains people. From his 20+ years of observing canine behavior, Cesar achieves his amazing rehabilitations by adopting a positive mental attitude and then communicating that attitude by "speaking" to each dog via a body language that is based on the core of the animal's pack instincts. In essence, via body language, Cesar says to the dog that he, Cesar, is the "pack leader" and not the dog.

I've watched this show for several years and, even though the disclaimer at the beginning of each show says not to use Cesar's techniques without first consulting a professional, I have done it anyway and have had success in using his techniques. Now, I don't have a dog myself, but I have tried some of his techniques on neighborhood dogs as I take my daily constitutional. The results are amazing. Calm assertiveness wins every time.

What's this have to do with companies being attacked by online activists?

In business, I have applied some of these Cesar techniques. In meetings, in presentations, in private discussions with clients and colleagues, the same body language techniques work almost as well with humans. When I met Cesar at a booksigning at my local Barnes & Noble, after signing my book I told him about how I've applied his techniques, with success, in business. He seemed a bit surprised and asked me if I also did the "Tsssssst!" (The "Tsssssst" is a sound Cesar makes to get a dog's attention and to distract the animal from unwanted behaviors.) I replied that I hadn't gone quite that far, but was holding the option in reserve. My comeback received a chuckle and a hardy handshake. What a friendly guy.

In The Motrin Incident and The Kit Kat Incident, neither of the parties under siege was both calm and assertive. At the beginning of The Kit Kat Incident, the Nestlé Facebook fan page administrator was "assertive," but not calmly so. His excited missteps early in that fray just made the overall engagement all the more "bloody." As the battle widened, the administrator retreated, and relinquished the battle space to the attackers. Assertiveness was deserted. And in The Motrin Incident, the makers of Motrin displayed "calm," but not assertiveness. In fact, J&J was so "calm" that they completely faded away early in the battle, and over the days that followed left the social media hordes to define J&J's place and character in the incident rather than the other way around.

In both incidents, the companies became "rattled." Neither appeared to adopt the "positive" attitude that Cesar recommends. By not doing so, they could not approach the attack calmly and assert their position in positive manner. Please understand that "assertive" does not mean aggressive, it simply means standing up for your position with confidence and communicating that position with certitude.

Now, granted, you can't use body language in social media in order to communicate your calm assertiveness. But you can communicate these qualities through the demeanor of your writing. In his shows, Cesar regularly points out that you "get what you give." In other words, he means that the attitude you project is the attitude, and the behavior, you receive in return.

Seems like these are words to live by, not only when engaged in an online activist battle, but also for life in general.

Greenpeace Rates as an Irregular Competitor

April 13, 2010

Categories: Irregular Competition - Greenpeace - Threat Index

That Greenpeace is an "irregular competitor," certainly should be news to no one. No one, that is, who knows what irregular competition is. (Author's Note: Irregular competition was defined in Chapter Five's "Irregular Competition - The Newest Threat.")

Given Greenpeace's recent direct action against Nestlé, an action which I labeled as "The Kit Kat Incident," I must award that NGO at least a "7.5" on the "Irregular Competition Threat Index;" that's a scale of 1 to 10 (10 being the highest threat level). Greenpeace would have rated higher, except for their mistakes and competitive weaknesses which I pointed out in my five article series about The Kit Kat Incident.

Another reason that they lose points is due to their own hypocritical action when a social media campaign turns against them. And you and I will talk more about that action in my next post, "Greenpeace Hypocritical in Social Media Action," which posts on Thursday, April 15, 2010.

Greenpeace Hypocritical in Social Web Action

April 15, 2010

Categories: Hypocrisy, Irregular Competition - Greenpeace, NGOs, Threats

In the recent Greenpeace direct action against Nestlé, which I have labeled as The Kit Kat Incident, early in the fray the NGO accused Nestlé, the target of the Greenpeace social media campaign, of censorship [112] when Nestlé asked YouTube to delete a Greenpeace culture jamming protest video from the YouTube site. If you are unfamiliar with The Kit Kat Incident, you may catch up on the details by going to this Wall Street Journal article. [113]

Accusations of censorship can cut both ways.

At about the time that The Kit Kat Incident was simmering down, according to British newspaper, The Guardian, [114] Greenpeace India's communications director, Gene Hashmi, posted this entry on the Greenpeace blog:

> *If you're one of those who have spent their lives undermining progressive climate legislation, bankrolling junk science, fuelling (sic) spurious debates around false solutions and cattle-prodding democratically-elected governments into submission, then hear this: We know who you are. We know where you live. We know where you work. And we be many, but you be few.*

Now, per the Guardian story, this entry was posted on Thursday, April 1, 2010. Was it an "April Fool?" No article that I have read about this somewhat, at least, threatening post has indicated that it was an April Fool. The Guardian reports that hours after this Greenpeace blog post, the blogosphere was alight with conversation regarding these Greenpeace words "as nothing less than an incitement to intimidation."

The Guardian's story further reports that over the days that followed, Greenpeace Web staff tried their best at damage control, posting explanations as to the "real" nature of the post (i.e., in PR parlance, this is called "walking it back"), but then finally elected to remove the questionable post on Tuesday, April 6, 2010.

Censorship? Yes.

Hypocritical? Especially when compared to their own censorship accusation[115] against Nestlé about two weeks previous? Definitely.

This example of Greenpeace not being able to "bear the heat of the kitchen" points out another weakness in Greenpeace's media strategy, particularly as it concerns the social web. And it also goes toward demonstrating the attitude of Greenpeace toward the ideas of "openness" and "transparency" upon which the social web is presumed to be built.

What was it that George Orwell said in Animal Farm? About "all pigs being equal?"

The Kit Kat Incident as a Harbinger

April 16, 2010

Categories: Activism, Irregular Competition - Greenpeace, Protests in Social Media - The Kit Kat Incident

Just when you thought it was dying down, you find that it isn't.

Yesterday, Greenpeace continued their direct action against Nestlé over the usage of palm oil as an ingredient in Nestlé products. This Greenpeace campaign, which has been going on for years, heated up a month ago when Greenpeace initiated a social media protest against the food manufacturer. For background on this protest action, which I have labeled as The Kit Kat Incident, you may click here. [116]

The continuation of The Kit Kat Incident hit another sour note for Nestlé yesterday at their annual shareholders meeting held in Lausanne, Switzerland. Although not widely reported, Greenpeace, in addition to the employment of common street theater tactics and building on their breach of security at, and the scaling of, the Canadian parliament building last December, [117] managed to break through the ceiling of the building where the Nestlé annual shareholders meeting was held. Activists rappelled down through the opening, showering leaflets over the crowd and displayed a protest banner.

As I mentioned above, reports of this incident are difficult to find in the mainstream press. However, I've assembled this information from, although not objective, fairly reliable sources. One source is a YouTube video.[118] Even though the video appears to be shot by a Greenpeace supporter, it does appear to be an accurate visual record of the event as I've summarized here and as was reported by a "green" news site, Mongabay.com. [119] The video visually corroborates the Mongabay story.

When I learned of this event yesterday, the first thing that went through my mind was "Where was Nestlé corporate security?" The second thing that went through my mind was "Will the director of Nestlé corporate security be able to keep his or her job?" They should have seen this brewing.

Given the recent social media action against Nestlé (i.e., The Kit Kat Incident), given the aforementioned Greenpeace-engineered security breach of the Canadian parliament building, and given that Greenpeace mounted a similar action last July at Mount Rushmore, [120] how is it that Nestlé corporate security didn't see this one coming? Of course, there wouldn't be much corporate security could do about the street theater demonstrations taking place at the shareholder meeting. But the scaling of the building? The penetration of the ceiling from the exterior? The activist entering the building through the ceiling and the rappelling?

It's as plain as the nose on anyone's face. In today's business environment, social media protest actions need to be considered as harbingers to direct actions occurring in the non-virtual world.

Don't Bother Inviting Greenpeace

April 19, 2010

Categories: Activism, Irregular Competition - Greenpeace, The Kit Kat Incident

On Tuesday, April 13, 2010, the Chairman of the Board of Nestlé, Peter Brabeck-Letmathe, sent an open letter to Greenpeace executives. The letter was sent in response to an April 8, 2010 Greenpeace letter to Nestlé, the subject of which was deforestation and its relationship to the supply of palm oil, a raw material used by Nestlé and other companies. The April 13 letter from Mr. Brabeck-Letmathe can be seen by clicking here. [121] (Author's Note: This letter exchange represents another chapter in the running battle between the two parties over the harvesting of palm oil and claims of deforestation effects. This battle recently heated up in a social media protest action which I labeled as The Kit Kat Incident.)

Summarizing, in the April 13 letter [122] Mr. Brabeck-Letmathe states the Nestlé position concerning palm oil and acknowledges what the company has done to reduce any rainforest deforestation impact that may be related to the harvesting of that crop. Concerning a related issue, Mr. Brabeck-Letmathe also addresses the previously expressed concern of Greenpeace regarding Nestlé's use of pulp, for paper packaging, which may be related to the deforestation process. Mr. Brabeck-Letmathe says:

> ... we are committed to finding solutions, and as first step (sic) to eliminating packaging which can be traced to paper pulp derived from rainforest destruction, we invite you and other organizations committed to ending deforestation to examine with us analyses of paper supply chains and work with us in a collective effort to eliminate packaging which uses paper made with pulp resulting from destruction of rainforests.

I don't think Greenpeace will be interested in any invitations toward collaborative efforts.

Why do I think that?

Because Greenpeace is a "dark green" movement.

"Dark green?"

Yes. In an article titled "Shades of Green," by Andrew Hoffman and published by the Stanford Social Innovation Review (Spring 2009) of the Stanford Graduate School of Business, [123] Greenpeace is characterized as a "dark green" environmental NGO (ENGO). On page 42 of that article, Mr. Hoffman says:

> … a schism is emerging between two camps of environmentalist: the dark greens and the bright greens. The dark green ENGOs - such as Greenpeace USA and (another NGO) - seek radical change to solve environmental problems, often by confronting corporations.

Possibility of collaboration? Let's consider what Mr. Hoffman says later on in the same article, where he further classifies Greenpeace as an "Isolate" type of ENGO. Beginning on page 46 of the article, he says:

> By refusing to partner with corporations, Isolates are able to maintain a sense of purity … although Greenpeace and (another NGO) both make it clear that they do not work with corporations, their motivations are different. Greenpeace is more oppositional, avoiding direct ties with businesses because their mission is defined more by conflict.

(Author's Note: The parenthetical edits are mine.)

Possibility of collaboration? As the Brits would say … "not bloody likely."

In achieving their agenda, Greenpeace is about conflict and confrontation, not collaboration. Such a "pugnacious" positioning is one of the ways Greenpeace positions its brand, and sets itself apart from its own "competition." If Greenpeace was not confrontational, would they be known for protest actions such as draping a banner over Mount Rushmore, [124] or scaling the Canadian parliament building, [125] or for disrupting a Nestlé shareholders meeting by rappelling down from the ceiling with leaflets and banners flying?

No, Mr. Brabeck-Letmathe. I think your attempt to enlist the assistance of Greenpeace, though well-intentioned, is probably just a waste of time, and an act that Greenpeace may consider to be a strategic weakness, one which may increase further protest vitriol at a later date.

Fanning the Flames of Anti-Corporatism?

April 19, 2010

Categories: Anti-Corporatism, Ideas

Anti-corporatism is a necessary condition to the success of anti-corporate digital activism. The reason is self-evident. And last Friday, April 16, 2010, the U.S. federal government added some heat to the flames of anti-corporatism.

Whether or not the fraud charges filed by the U.S. Securities & Exchange Commission [126] (SEC) against Goldman Sachs have any merit is immaterial to the issue I'm presenting here. Because the issue I'm presenting here is not the guilt or innocence of that corporation in the matter about to be adjudicated or, more likely, negotiated. The issue that I'm presenting here is that of government-generated anti-corporatism, designed for political reasons.

The announcement of this charge, at this time, can appear to be a politically-motivated and opportunistic tactic. The SEC has, according to the Wall Street Journal, [127] been working on this case for 18 months and just now, days before the U.S. Senate takes up debate on a financial reform bill, decides to announce its charges against Goldman Sachs. This timing seems just a little too coincidental to me.

But coincidental or not, in passing any financial reform, the government must attempt to feed the flames of anti-corporatism. Not doing so would not help their case to pass such legislation. And with a recent Pew Research Center survey [128] saying that only 22% of Americans trust their federal government, the people on Capitol Hill will need any help they can get in progressing their less-than-business-friendly agendas.

Announcing the Goldman Sachs charges at any time will certainly contribute to anti-corporate sentiment. But by doing so now, in conjunction with the opening of a legislative debate on financial reform, this action would seem to be more effective in generating anti-corporate sentiment than waiting for a time when Congress is debating, say, some overarching foreign policy issue, unrelated to business.

What does this mean for corporations in general? Well, many things. But from the perspective of this blog, that of analyzing "irregular competitors," it means that currently corporations will need to be even more on guard for instances of digital activism against their brands and company. NGOs and activists will recognize that now is a time of "hotter than normal" anti-corporatism. They may see this current event as an "opportunity" and adjust plans for their future online protests accordingly; that is to say, they may perform these online protests sooner than later.

Just another "fringe benefit" from the folks in the District of Columbia.

Greenwashing? How About "Fact-Washing?"

April 20, 2010

Categories: Irregular Competition - Friends of the Earth, Research - Questionable

In a recent article entitled "Friends of the Earth fire back at corportate 'greenwashing'," [129] Metronews.ca writer, Romina Mc Guinness, filed a story about how Friends of the Earth (FOE) has pointed out various incidents of what they, FOE, believe to be corporate greenwashing. Well, this story really isn't news. Stories about corporate greenwashing pop up in the news now and again. Many of them emanate either from FOE, or Greenpeace, or another ENGO.

No, what I found interesting about this story, other than the fact that they misspelled the word "corporate" in their story title (yes, that new word "corportate" is theirs, not mine), is the way that Romina put a "foundation" of facts under her story.

After listing several instances of greenwashing, as per a FOE source which she listed in the article, Romina lists a greenwashing claim of her own, saying how "even coal companies are claiming to be environmentally friendly." As an example she cites German power-provider, E.ON, who she says "has plans to build coal-powered plants, yet in its advertising campaigns, the company focuses on its renewable power sourcing schemes." Then she says, "The facts speak for themselves — energy website electricityinfo.org states that between April 2008 and March 2009 E.ON's portfolio was: coal 43.4 per cent, natural gas 45.2 per cent, nuclear 6.2 per cent and renewables a tiny 0.3 per cent."

Well, the phrase "the facts speak for themselves" got me curious. I thought, "Who are these facts that are speaking for themselves and, by the way, who the heck is electricityinfo.org?" So, I did a bit of digging. It wasn't difficult to find the answers to my questions.

I did a "Whois" inquiry on the domain "electricityinfo.org." That Whois information [130] gave me a company name of "IT Power Ltd." A quick Google search gave me a link to IT Power Ltd, [131] to whose Web site I went. To be double-sure I was at the correct destination, I checked IT Power's contact page and verified that their phone number was the same as that listed in the Whois info. On IT Power's site, I went to their "About" page [132] which told me the following:

> *IT Power is a leading international energy consultancy which specialises in sustainable energy technologies and policy, and related economic, financial, commercial and environmental work.*

This source has an economic and financial interest in sustainable technologies. Fine. But is this an objective source of information that a news writer should use when trying to make a case regarding greenwashing?

I don't think so.

Now, IT Power's information may be exactly correct. Their information may be perfectly fine. Then again, it may not be. As a reader of Romina's article, I don't really know for sure. But my issue isn't with IT Power's information. My issue is with Romina's use of that information in her article. If she wants to convince me of her argument, if she wants me to believe that "the facts speak for themselves," then she needs to give me some facts, from an objective and impartial source, one with no "skin" in the environmental arena.

People Who Live in Glass Houses …

April 27, 2010

Categories: Hypocrisy, Irregular Competition - Greenpeace, The Battle for Meaning, Truth

On February 17, 2010, there was an article posted on a Greenpeace sponsored Web site named PolluterWatch.com. The article, "Polluters Charles and David Koch don't deny it: they fund front groups to deny climate science," [134] dealt with Greenpeace's ongoing battle with Koch Industries over the company's reported financing of various research organizations who, according to Greenpeace, "deny" climate change and "obfuscate the truth about climate science."

Well, I don't want to insert myself into the battle over climate change and who or what causes it. I don't have the scientific background or the technical qualifications to represent myself properly in that fight. But in that fight, I'm of the opinion that Greenpeace, and many other environmental NGOs, don't have the background or qualifications to make a proper argument. I say that because in my research on these organizations, I've noticed that many of them periodically take great liberties with how they present information, and thus represent "truth." It is into that fight that I want to insert myself because I have the background and the qualifications to represent myself in this "battle for meaning," and how semantics is used as a weapon in that battle. My qualifications are strong here. In fact, I've written a book about that battle.

In my analyses of how various NGOs conduct this battle for meaning, I've noticed that Greenpeace, among others, is often "semantically-challenged" and this post on PolluterWatch.com represents at least one example of these challenges with which they deal.

The article, which I reference above, begins with these two paragraphs:

> *On Friday, I had the pleasure of receiving a surprising e-mail from the head of communications for Koch Industries, a massive oil and chemical corporation and the second-largest privately held company in America.*
>
> *The e-mail was from the chief spokesperson for Koch Industries, a woman named Melissa. To my shock, Melissa didn't deny that the corporation does in fact pay an industry front group millions of dollars to perpetuate the dirty energy economy and obfuscate the truth about climate science.*

My first issue with this article is who is "I?" This article is written in the first person. Yet, nowhere in the article, or on the page, is the author's name. Why not? However, identification can be made, although the author doesn't make it as simple as it should be. In the article's fifth paragraph, the author discusses an op-ed article that he posted on CapeCodToday.com, [135] and links to that article. Once the link is followed, the reader can determine that, apparently, this post on PolluterWatch.com is made by David Pomerantz, a Greenpeace field organizer based in Boston.

The anonymity of this "byline-less" PolluterWatch.com article doesn't significantly impact the battle for meaning. There are more important issues here, like my second issue with this article which is semantics. Specifically, I'm talking about conceptual semantics which deals with the construction of meaning. In this PolluterWatch.com article, what impacts that fight for meaning is the phrase, "Melissa didn't deny that the corporation does in fact pay an industry front group millions of dollars to perpetuate the dirty energy economy and obfuscate the truth about climate science."

Huh?

It seems very odd that a company, any company, would not deny such a claim.

The way that sentence is phrased made me continue reading. (That was probably David's intent.) The PolluterWatch.com article continues and explains that, in her email, the Koch spokesperson engaged David over another issue posed within the CapeCodToday.com article, an alleged Koch association with an organization called Freedomworks. In the PolluterWatch.com article, David "concludes:"

> *The larger point is that while Melissa took great pains to dissociate her bosses from Freedomworks, she took no issue with my description of the Kochs' "providing millions of dollars designed to perpetuate the dirty energy economy and obfuscate the science of global warming.*

> *Well, I'm glad that's settled! The first step is always admitting you have a problem, so it's good that Koch Industries has officially acknowledged that they fund front groups to deny climate science.*

First, if Melissa took "great pains," she wouldn't have emailed David. She would have called him. But let's put that semantical exaggeration aside and get to the second semantical issue which is that not addressing something is not an acknowledgement. If you look up "acknowledgement" in the dictionary, you will see that, in its various definitions, an acknowledgement requires the performance of an action. For an acknowledgement to occur, there must a positive action, not a lack of action. There was, at least according to the PolluterWatch.com article, no action here in the form of an admission. And to represent the lack of an active acknowledgement as an acknowledgement is a clear obfuscation of "facts," a behavior of which Greenpeace accuses Koch Industries within the PolluterWatch.com article itself. Such representations only serve to weaken the argument that David is trying to win.

People who live in glass houses shouldn't throw bricks. And if they do, what does that say about them?

To me, it says that, in addition to being hypocritical, behaving in this manner simply makes Greenpeace appear that they are trying too hard. If Greenpeace has a good case, a sound argument, then that case will make itself without the semantical histrionics.

Nice Work … If You Can Get It? Friends of the Earth Does.

April 29, 2010

Categories: Activism, Irregular Competition - Friends of the Earth, NGOs, Research

The International Policy Network (IPN) [138] is a research organization based in the United Kingdom. On their "About" page they list their mission as to:

> *Promote the advancement of learning by research into economic and political science and the publication of such research.*

Last month, March 2010, they published such research in a report titled "Friends of the EU: The Costs of a Taxpayer-Funded Green Lobby." [139] In the Executive Summary of this report, IPN states:

> *Environmental non-governmental organisations (NGOs) have enormous influence in the European Union. However, some of the most vocal green groups are actually funded directly by the EU to lobby it.*

Nice work, if you can get it? Absolutely. And it seems that in Europe they can. One of the beneficiaries of such governmental largess is Friends of the Earth Europe (FoEE). On page 8 of the IPN report, in Table 2: Sources of Funding and Lobbying Expenditures, IPN shows that for 2008, FoEE had income of approximately €1.5 million. Of that amount, over 50%, or €790,000, came in the form of a grant from DG ENVI, which stands for Directorate General Environmental, the environmental commission of the European Union. And during that same year, FoEE reported to the EU that FoEE spent €696,000 to lobby the government of the European Union.

Indeed, nice work, if you can get it. And it's looks like Friends of the Earth doesn't have too much trouble in doing so.

Implications?

Generally, this means that the taxpayers of the European Union pay advocacy groups to lobby their government for changes deemed important by the advocacy group, and not necessarily the taxpayers.

Specifically, as related to the theme of this blog, this "nice work" means that European companies pay, via their taxes, for NGOs to campaign against them. And with, essentially, all the lobbying budget of FoEE picked up by the taxpayers of Europe, this leaves plenty of revenue left over for FoEE, and other lucky European NGOs, to apply to their online protest campaigns. Theoretically, at least, this means that FoEE's digital activism is taxpayer supported.

This is an important tidbit of information to keep in mind for the next time that NGOs complain about governmental tax breaks for certain corporations.

Ignorance is No Stranger to Twitter

April 29, 2010

Categories: Activism, Crowd Behavior, Humor, Protests in Social Media

Here's a quick post about one of the most ignorant, and silly, digital activist initiatives I've seen. In yesterday's Vanity Fair was an article entitled "Misinformed Activists Boycott Brooklyn's AriZona Beverages." [140] You probably already realize where I'm heading.

According to the story, unorganized activist boycott actions have been taking place on Twitter with people announcing that, due to their take on the controversial new immigration law in Arizona, they would no longer be consuming Arizona Iced Tea. But Arizona Iced Tea is made in Brooklyn, New York, about 2500 miles away from Arizona.

Enough said here, but if you'd like a little more detail, then please check out the Vanity Fair article. [141]

Chapter Nine - The Meme Marches On ... And On
———————— Take-Aways ————————

With "Living on a Meme - Part 2," this chapter opened with further examination in the title article of this book about how those who think there should be more truth on the Internet often succumb to the disease of meme propagation. And in this article, we also see how the memes of anti-corporatism and anti-wealth wind not very cleverly into the writer's "argument," with no proof or supporting statements, of course. If there were supporting references, well then, it probably wouldn't be meme. There is much faulty evidence in that critiqued article, indeed.

Continuing with the idea of no support for an argument, in "Greenpeace Chooses Wrong Success Indicator" and "Greenpeace Did Not Influence Stock Price in The Kit Kat Incident," I continued the examination of faulty evidence and how it supports irregular competition's memes by discussing how Greenpeace creates the meme of success in social media protest, no matter what the outcome. In these two essays, I showed how Greenpeace falsely claimed victory in a protest campaign against Nestlé. Declaring victory in such a manner is misleading to the average recipient of the message because the average person may not know how to analyze such arguments, no less even make the effort to question such memes as those examined in these essays.

Perhaps that is partially on what Greenpeace counts? The lack of challenge? Maybe so, but even though they count on meme, I awarded that irregular competitor a fairly high rating in the Irregular Competition Threat Index. I did that not because I think Greenpeace is so clever, but mainly because I feel that most average folks on the social web don't challenge meme. Because Greenpeace people are meme meisters, these communicational manipulators, hypocritical as they can be at times as was explored in "Greenpeace Hypocritical in Social Web Action," require watching and awareness. And if a company, with which Greenpeace competes, turns its back even for a moment, I think that we'll see results such as was evidenced in the essay "The Kit Kat Incident as a Harbinger." When Greenpeace has that meme going in the virtual world, it doesn't seem that they won't try to capitalize on it in the real world.

The meme marches on. It is not only perpetrated by irregular competition as you and I have discussed throughout this book, but the mainstream press also occasionally jumps into the game. In "Greenwashing? How About 'Fact-Washing?'," you can see an example of how the meme of certain irregular competitors is carried into mainstream media and taken as truth. Are the mainstream media, and non-mainstream media as discussed in "People Who Live in Glass Houses … ," also irregular competitors? I'll be exploring that thought further in future publications.

I've yet seen no sign that the meme-ing by irregular competition will abate. I fear that with the expansion of social media usage, meme mangling by irregular competition will carry on, and some of it will be taxpayer supported as we discussed in "Nice Work … If You Can Get It? Friends of the Earth Does." If irregular competition's meme-ing is fueled by the tax paying public, which it is in the European Union and, at least indirectly, in the United States, absent meme-ing's exposure for exactly what it is, there would seem little reason to believe that it will decrease. And in such case, we'll be exposed to more nonsense such as that pointed out in "Ignorance is No Stranger to Twitter."

CHAPTER TEN

The Perfect
Meme Storm

EXCLUSIVE
Friends of the Earth Doesn't "Get" Twitter - Part 1

May 3, 2010

Categories: Irregular Competition - Friends of the Earth, Research - Cases Studies - Friends of the Earth Studies - Social Media Campaign Analysis

As you know, I periodically review, in a case study format, the strengths and weaknesses of various irregular competitors. Today, with this post, I begin a case study series on how Friends of the Earth (FOE) uses digital tools in the pursuit of its agenda. In today's post, you and I will take a look at how one division of this organization, Friends of the Earth International, uses Twitter. Subsequent posts will look at how other FOE divisions use the tools available to support their online activism. All of this work will ultimately yield a FOE ranking in the Irregular Competition Threat Index.

As you may or may not know, Friends of the Earth, one of the world's largest environmental NGOs (ENGO), per the Friends of the Earth International Web site, [142] is divided into 77 national organizations, maintaining affiliations with over 5,000 activist groups on "every continent." (I wonder if "every continent" includes Antartica?) The organization also claims over 2 million members worldwide. [143] Friends of the Earth International (FOEI) is the central organization, based in The Netherlands.

These are impressive statistics. So, you would think that with over 2 million members, and affiliations with 5,000 local activist groups, FOEI would do an impressive job with their Twitter strategy.

Let's take a look.

On Thursday, April 22, 2010, at approximately 2PM EDT in the United States, I went to the FOEI Twitter page. [144] That date is significant. Why? Because April 22 was Earth Day. The implication is obvious and, because of that implication, before arriving at the FOEI Twitter page, I expected to be greeted with a plethora of tweets.

I was wrong.

There were no tweets from FOEI on Earth Day. Astounding. No tweets? How could that be?

Such a performance, or non-performance, must mean that FOEI doesn't "get" Twitter. They've not yet realized the power of this new digital tool and virtual environment. Indeed, even their "Twitter stats" imply that they don't understand this medium, which in many ways is perfect for an organization such as theirs.

On my Earth Day visit to the FOEI Twitter page, the organization had a paltry 469 followers and FOEI was following only 43. For an organization the size of FOE, these numbers are anemic, and confirm that FOE just doesn't "get it."

What does this deficiency in Twitter strategy imply for the "private politics" opponents of FOEI? What does this mean to the corporations which FOEI targets in their campaigns? Well, it may indicate that FOEI is not a powerful irregular competitor. With only this brief look into the FOE social media strategy, I shouldn't make an overall assessment yet. And therefore I won't be awarding them, yet, a ranking on the Irregular Competition Threat Index. But, I will rank them later, after you and I have looked more at how they perform in the digital arena.

The next post in this FOE series will be on Thursday, May 6, 2010. If you are reading this before May 6 and would like to be notified when the article posts, simply subscribe to the FREE RSS feed by clicking here. If you are reading this after May 6, simply click here to go to Part 2 of "Friends of the Earth Doesn't 'Get' Twitter."

EXCLUSIVE
Rainforest Action Network Twitter Campaign Fails … So Far

May 5, 2010

Categories: Irregular Competition - Rainforest Action Network - Threat Index, Protests in Social Media, Research - Case Studies - Rainforest Action Network Studies - Social Media Campaign Analysis

Just a quick note on a developing anti-corporate social media campaign.

On Monday, May 3, 2010, Rainforest Action Network (RAN) released a report entitled "Cargill's Problems with Palm Oil." [145] This is the latest shot in the palm oil battle between several NGOs and commercial consumers of palm oil. To support the RAN promotion of the release of this report, RAN made a tweet on May 4, 2010. Here is the text of the tweet: [146]

> *New Report: #Cargill destroys an area of rainforest in #Indonesia the size of Disney World! http://ran.org/cargillreport*

As of 3:15 PM today, May 5, 2010, about 24 hours after RAN released this tweet, it has been picked up verbatim and re-tweeted, using the hashtag, by only 14 people on Twitter. You may check by clicking here [147] on the progress of that re-tweeting. (Please note that the content of the tweet may have been issued in other forms. I am only checking, right now, on the verbatim re-tweet using the hashtag. This check would help to indicate the amount of support that RAN has in the Twittersphere.)

Such propagation does not indicate very much strength in the RAN Twitter strategy, and is consistent with my ranking, so far, of RAN on the Irregular Competition Threat Index, which, as of April 28, currently stands at a "5" on a scale of "1" to "10."

EXCLUSIVE
Friends of the Earth Doesn't "Get" Twitter - Part 2

May 6, 2010

Categories: Irregular Competition - Friends of the Earth - Threat Index, Research - Cases Studies - Friends of the Earth Studies - Social Media Campaign Analysis

In the Part 1 of "Friends of the Earth Doesn't 'Get' Twitter," I took a look at the strengths and weaknesses of the Twitter strategy of Friends of the Earth International (FOEI), the central organization of environmental NGO (ENGO) Friends of the Earth (FOE). In that post, I reviewed FOEI's usage of Twitter on a critical day for FOEI, April 22, 2010 - Earth Day, and found it, quite frankly, sad. On that date, a very important one for any ENGO, FOEI issued no tweets. None. Astounding.

Astoundingly poor.

Today, in Part 2 of "Friends of the Earth Doesn't 'Get' Twitter," you and I are going to take a look to see if the American division of FOE, which is Friends of the Earth US (FOE-US), understands Twitter any better than their international division.

As I said in Part 1, on the most recent Earth Day, Thursday, April 22, 2010, at about 2PM EDT, I went to the Twitter page for FOEI, and I also went to the Twitter page for FOE-US. [148] What I found on the Twitter page for FOE-US, at that time, wasn't much more exciting than what I found on the Twitter page for FOEI. On such a critical day for an environmental advocacy group such as FOE, on the afternoon of Earth Day, I found only 5 tweets from FOE-US. Five tweets. That's all.

And of those five tweets, two of them were re-tweets, one of which was a re-tweet from Greenpeace. So, effectively, FOE-US came up with only three original tweets of their own on that important day for the ENGO movement. This situation demonstrates that FOE-US likely does not realize the value of the Twitter environment, a value which is almost tailor-made for an organization such as an ENGO. This lack of value realization is also demonstrated by their follower stats.

When I went to the FOE-US page on Earth Day, the FOE-US Twitter stats were: 5,099 followers with FOE-US following 233. Now, although a list of 5,099 followers might not seem bad, for an organization the size of FOE-US, that level of followers is not great. To put this in perspective, consider that on that same date, my level of Twitter followers was close to 4,000. [149] No. 5,099 is not impressive for the US division of a global ENGO. But what stands out even more is the relationship between the follower level and the following level.

On Earth Day, FOE-US was following only 233, with 5,099 followers. With following and follower numbers this far out of balance, these stats mean, no scream, that FOE-US is not using Twitter to engage their 5,099 followers. If FOE-US realized the value of the Twitter environment, they would be using it to engage their 5,099 followers in a conversation. And that would mean that FOE-US would need to be listening to those followers, which would mean that FOE-US would need to be following everyone who is following them.

With stats of this proportion, and with, effectively, only three tweets on Earth Day, it's clear that, just like FOEI, FOE-US doesn't "get" Twitter, either.

What's that expression about "the apple doesn't fall far from the tree?"

As I mentioned in Part 1 of "Friends of the Earth Doesn't 'Get' Twitter," it's still a bit too early in this case study series, assessing the digital activism capabilities of FOE, to assign them a ranking in the Irregular Competition Threat Index. But I will do so later in this case study series on Friends of the Earth.

The next post in this case study series will be next Thursday, May 13, 2010. If you are reading this before May 13, and would like to receive that post automatically, just click here to subscribe to the FREE RSS feed. Or, if you are reading this after May 13, 2010, you may simply click here and go directly to the next post in this FOE case study series.

EXCLUSIVE
Rainforest Action Network Twitter Campaign Fails … Still

May 6, 2010

Categories: Irregular Competition - Rainforest Action Network - Threat Index, Protests in Social Media, Research - Case Studies - Rainforest Action Network Studies - Social Media Campaign Analysis

Yesterday, I updated you about a Rainforest Action Network (RAN) Twitter campaign that was designed to support the recent release of their "Cargill's Problems with Palm Oil Report." [150] Just another battle in the overall palm oil crude war. In yesterday's post, "Rainforest Action Network Twitter Campaign Fails … So Far," I observed that after about 24 hours from the first RAN tweet, designed to support and promote the release of the Cargill report, only 14 people had picked up the tweet and re-tweeted it, on a verbatim basis, with a hashtag identifying the subject. Here is the text of the tweet: [151]

> *New Report: #Cargill destroys an area of rainforest in #Indonesia the size of Disney World! http://ran.org/cargillreport*

A fourteen person re-tweet is not a very impressive level of involvement in a social media campaign.

Today, I checked to see if they were making any progress. I was curious to see if RAN supporters were "going crazy" and re-tweeting the RAN message like mad. Twenty-four hours later, RAN has increased their re-tweeting by 50%. Yes, now that re-tweet is up to 21 people participating. You may check their progress by clicking here. [152]

As I said in yesterday's post on this subject, this level of re-tweeting doesn't say much for RAN's appreciation of Twitter strategy. Such lack of Twitter understanding makes me leave my Irregular Competition Threat Index rating for RAN at "5." (Ten is the highest threat level ranking; please see my post the "Irregular Competition Threat Index," in Chapter Seven, for more information.)

Danone Fights Digital Slurs in an Interesting Way

May 11, 2010

Categories: Activism, Tactics, Threats

In Argentina, Danone countered online slurs against their brand, Actimel (which is known as DanActive in the United States), in an interesting way. Instead of simply and only refuting those slurs, which they did, in addition Danone decided to demonstrate how elusive truth can be in the virtual environment, showing that what you read online isn't always true.

A recent Ad Age article, titled "Danone Fights Damaging Viral Slurs in Argentina," [153] detailed various email rumors which denigrated the Actimel brand. According to the article, the company responded with some of the traditional tactics such as responding to each slur found on various Web sites. The company even went a step further by making a TV commercial which addressed the online attack. But the company went very much further when it decided to demonstrate how everything online shouldn't be believed. To do so, it set up a site called Creador de Rumores (Creator of Rumors). [154] (The site, assembled by digital shop Sinus, appears to be no longer active. Venturing to the site redirects one to the site of the digital shop.)

Per the Ad Age article, visitors to the site could create and start rumors about themselves. Visitors chose from a pre-selected list of rumors such as winning the lottery or going on tour with a British rock band. The Ad Age article doesn't provide any information on how well Danone made its point about the ease of virtual rumor mongering and if that point was absorbed by the general public, but the article did report that in the first month of the campaign (which per the article I believe was February 2010) over 40,000 people visited the site and initiated about 100,000 rumors.

Certainly this is a novel way to tackle the problem of online activism based in falsehood and it's a tactic that can be added to the irregular competition playbook. But like any tactic, it's one that should not be applied in isolation.

EXCLUSIVE
Friends of the Earth Doesn't "Get" Facebook, Either

May 13, 2010

Categories: Irregular Competition - Friends of the Earth - Threat Index, Research - Case Studies - Friends of the Earth Studies - Social Media Campaign Analysis

Recently, in a post entitled "Friends of the Earth Doesn't 'Get' Twitter," Part 1 and Part 2, I reviewed Friends of the Earth's (FOE) usage of Twitter on Earth Day 2010. Earth Day is a critical day for any environmental NGO, yet, as you and I saw in those two posts, neither Friends of the Earth - US (FOE-US) nor Friends of the Earth International (FOEI) made strategic use of the Twitter environment (no pun intended) on that important ENGO date.

Today, you and I will take a look at how Friends of the Earth, both the International and U.S. division, employed Facebook on that critical ENGO date.

On Earth Day 2010, April 22, at about 2PM EDT, I went to the Facebook pages for FOE-US and for FOEI. [155, 156] At that time of day, on Earth Day, FOE-US had only eight Facebook posts made on Earth Day. Only two of those eight were from FOE-US itself, and one of those two was a Twitter tweet from Greenpeace. I mentioned this Greenpeace re-tweet in Part 2 of "Friends of the Earth Doesn't 'Get' Twitter." It seems that FOE-US used this re-tweet not only on their Twitter page, but also on their Facebook page. At this same time, on Earth Day, FOEI had no Facebook page posts made on Earth Day.

This is extremely poor usage of Facebook, especially on such a significant day.

Such online behavior shows that FOE has little understanding of the potential effectiveness of social media as a tool of online activism. What drives my point home even further is the level of "friends" each division of FOE has on their Facebook fan pages.

On Earth Day, FOE-US had 12,566 "friends" while FOEI had 4,860 "friends." (By "friends," I refer to the numbers of people who "liked" the page. Facebook "fans" are not applicable in this particular analysis.) Now, considering that FOEI boasts over 2 million members worldwide (in all national divisions), [157] these friends levels are not particularly impressive. Yet, these numbers represent a large enough audience that, if either FOE-US or FOEI understood the power of social media, they would want to engage with those Facebook friends on Earth Day. The engagement was not made on Earth Day, indicating that FOE does not understand Facebook. This lack of engagement, also seen in the Twitter analysis mentioned previously, may also indicate that FOE does not understand the power of social media in general.

So, given these reviews of FOE's usage of two critical social media environments, Twitter (as discussed in "Friends of the Earth Doesn't 'Get' Twitter," Part 1 and Part 2) and Facebook, I will rate FOE at a "4" on the Irregular Competition Threat Index (ICTI). (The ICTI runs from "1" to "10," with "10" being of the highest threat level.) However, as I continue to study FOE, I reserve the right to change their ranking after further reviews.

To see those later reviews, you may click here to subscribe to the FREE RSS feed to receive the updates automatically.

EXCLUSIVE
Rainforest Action Network … Does Indoctrination Count?

May 18, 2010

Categories: Activism, Indoctrination, Irregular Competition - Rainforest Action Network, Research - Case Studies - Rainforest Action Network Studies - RAN and Children, Tactics

Today's post is the first in a case study series of articles about how Rainforest

Action Network uses children in their anti-corporate campaign strategy. To follow this series, simply subscribe to the free RSS feed or periodically check under the "RAN and Children" category listing over in right-hand column. Starting off this series is an article about children and posters.

Recently, Rainforest Action Network (RAN) ran an Earth Day poster contest.[158] Among the 400 posters submitted by school children from across the United States, per RAN, many were aimed at General Mills, which also happens to be a corporation targeted by RAN in its palm oil and deforestation campaigns. Doesn't it seem rather coincidental that in a poster contest sponsored by RAN that many children would submit posters, of an anti-corporate nature, criticizing a specific target of RAN? From RAN's Web site page [159] about the poster contest:

> *Many of the posters also called on one of America's most famous cereal brands, General Mills, to stop destroying rainforests for palm oil. Youth in Minneapolis delivered these posters to General Mills on Wednesday, April 28 in honor of youth working together for Earth Day from around the world. We have uploaded photos of this delivery to our online gallery.* [160]

The above referenced link to the RAN online gallery refers to a page in the RAN Flickr account. You may go to that page by clicking here. [161] On that Flickr page, along with photos of the poster delivery, you will find the following text:

> *Through art and poetry, kids expressed their love of cereals like Cheerios and Lucky Charms but lamented the fact that they have palm oil in them, thereby causing rainforest destruction and species extinction (dead orangutans in my breakfast cereal?!).*

I'm curious. How is it that grammar school kids know these sorts of issues exist? Are these kids doing independent research on these issues? Do they know both sides of the argument? Additionally, how is it that a grammar school kid would choose to put the following words in one of the anti-General Mills posters?

> *Dear General Mills ... You, Alone are the murder of the trees, Killing, The birds & the bees, cutting, Them down throwing them there, "Pfft, they're just orangutans, they don't care." Because Right Now, You say "Pfft" to humanity, And say "Pfft" to all thats there, You deney the*

right of breatnig clean air, No matter what you'll do this still, As long as your signed with Cargill.

Note: Direct quote from a poster as shown on the RAN Web site. Click here to see the poster image [162] or click here [163] to go to the RAN page showing this referenced poster as one of the honorable mentions in the contest.

And on the poster described above, on the word "Mills" the letter "M" is crossed out and a "K" is written in.

Maybe in addition to art instruction, these kids should be getting some spelling lessons? That's a different issue. Let's continue on this one.

How is it that school children can mount such vitriol, which amazingly parallels that in theme from RAN campaigns against General Mills? And how is it that school children would know that General Mills would have a contract with Cargill or even what Cargill is?

Concerning the ongoing palm oil disputes and disagreements over what contributes to deforestation, I don't know if Rainforest Action Network has a legitimate case against General Mills or not. I'm not picking a side in that battle, and if you read this blog regularly you already know that I often don't pick a side in these scientific arguments. But, where I do often pick a side is in the validity of an argument or, as is the case here, in the decency of an argument.

What I am picking a side on here is in the simple decency in making an argument. Grammar school children are not yet of an age where they can develop critical thinking skills and form an opinion on complex issues via the initiative of their own inquiries. I would think, and hope, that if RAN had enough confidence in their position on palm oil and deforestation, as it relates to their dispute with General Mills, that their issue would be strong enough to speak for itself rather than enlisting, and perhaps indoctrinating, impressionable children into that dispute.

In the Long Run ... We're All Dead.

May 20, 2010

Categories: Crowd Behavior, Ideas, Truth

A few weeks ago, I was a panelist at the 10th Annual Symposium on Communication, The Future of Communication, held at Bernard Baruch College, City University of New York, in the Big Apple. The panel's topic, "More than Friending: Social Media and Communication in Business and Education," [164] provided for a lively discussion about social media and its impact on business and education and how the two institutions overlap and complement each other.

In one section of the discussion, one of the panelists brought up the topic of crowd sourcing and alluded to its reliability in determining "truth." And to recall a line from that American "classic" film about the absurdities of modern business, Office Space, I said to him that "I was going to have to sort of go ahead and kind of disagree with him there," or words to that effect. (To make for an interesting and entertaining discussion, all the panelists had agreed ahead of time to be somewhat "feisty" in the panel discussion. Although, now that I think about it, this lead-in was a lot more silly than feisty. Well, perhaps at least it was entertaining.)

To make my point that crowd sourcing was not as reliable as many propose that it is, I drew upon an example from the offline world. I said to test the validity of the crowd sourcing theory, one could simply ask liberals how valid crowd sourcing was during the elections that gave the United States the presidency of George W. Bush or, conversely, one could ask conservatives how valid crowd sourcing was in the most recent presidential election that has given us Barack Obama. The other panelist countered with the theory that in the "long-run" crowd sourcing was a more accurate representation of "truth" than crowd sourcing in the "short-run." Until now, I hadn't remembered this quote by John Maynard Keynes, [165] the early 20th century British economist, "In the long-run, we're all dead." Had I recalled this quote during the panel discussion, it might have been even more "feisty," or entertaining, for the audience.

The Keynes quote points out that, yes, perhaps everything "evens" out fairly in the long-run, but the long-run may be too long. Specific to our panel discussion about truth in social media, if in the long-run the truth will out, crowd sourcing may be a valid approach to arriving at the "truth." But, what's the long-run? Is social media old enough to even have a "long-run?" We may need to wait too long for the truth to win within Web 2.0. By that time, we'd all be dead, and the truth wouldn't matter.

An idea to keep in mind for the next time we're perusing the world of Web 2.0.

Activist vs. Activist

May 25, 2010

Category: Activism

After reading the CNN.com article "Activists Call Foul on KFC Bucket Campaign," [166] I was reminded of the Spy vs. Spy cartoon [167] from Mad Magazine. [168] (Was there any pun intended on that usage of the word "foul?") The article describes a contribution campaign that KFC has initiated, donating 50 cents for every sale of a specially-marked, pink bucket of chicken. The contributions go to the advocacy, activist group Susan G. Komen for the Cure, a well-known group fighting breast cancer.

Seems all very well and good. But Barbara Brenner, the executive director of Breast Cancer Action (BCA), described as a "watch dog group" compelling changes "to end breast cancer" doesn't quite agree. The CNN article describes Ms. Brenner as saying KFC is "pinkwashing" by putting a pink, cancer-awareness ribbon on products that are "bad for health." Now, this is the kind of dispute that goes on daily between companies and activist groups. KFC, among other companies, are quite accustomed to this. But, what sets this story apart from other stories of activist vs. company and what makes this story interesting is that in this dispute BCA takes a shot at the Komen organization, another activist group. A quote from the CNN article:

> 'This will keep them (Komen) in business for years. They talk about a cure, but this this partnership will create more breast cancer. And Komen knows this,' said Brenner on the assumed relationship between fast food, excess weight and cancer risk.
>
> Brenner went on to say, 'Komen puts the responsibility for health in individuals' hands, but some people don't have the option to take care

of themselves. Say you don't have the money or choice -- KFC is making money in the poorest communities.'

Komen's director of communication, Andrea Rader, tells CNN the claims are 'ludicrous.'

Activist vs. Activist.

And I must agree with Ms. Rader, the BCA claims are ludicrous. Why?

In the second paragraph of the above quote, Ms. Brenner is saying that if a person doesn't "have the money" to take care of themselves, then they'll just "pig out" on KFC through ignorance. Ludicrous, indeed. If a person doesn't "have the money," as Ms. Brenner says, then why would they go to KFC to buy food which is, pound for pound, more expensive than what you can find in most aisles of any supermarket? If they didn't "have the money," then they could not do so. BCA certainly appears to have a very low opinion of people's abilities to think for themselves. I can't believe that the people to which BCA refers can be that ignorant.

However, this ignorance card is one that I've seen activists play well over the years. But in this case of activist vs. activist, this play just doesn't make the grade.

Now, maybe we can get an Activist. vs. Activist cartoon series going?

Rainforest Action Network, Child Actors, & Private Politics

May 26, 2010

Categories: Activism, Indoctrination, Irregular Competition - Rainforest Action Network, Research - Case Studies - Rainforest Action Network Studies - RAN and Children, Tactics

My article from last week, "Rainforest Action Network ... Does Indoctrination Count,?" drew a bit of attention on this blog. That article was the first in a case study series on how Rainforest Action Network involves children in its various anti-corporate campaigns. Today's post is the second article in that series.

Below you'll see a link to a Rainforest Action Network video [169] that appears on YouTube.com, in the Rainforest Action Network channel. [170] This video involves a toddler, to the seeming confusion of his mother, in declaring, toward the end of this 48 second video, that he doesn't want any "rainforest destruction" in his cereal.

I'm assuming that this young man was a child actor hired for this specific RAN video. I assume this because I don't realistically believe that any toddler is going to utter the words "rainforest destruction" of their own choosing. So, my question becomes:

Is using child actors appropriate in a politically-motivated campaign?

And, yes, this is politics. Private politics is the process of "collective interactions between parties attempting to advance their interests that do not rely on the law, public order, or the state." (Source: Contention and Corporate Social Responsibility, p. 30.) [171] NGOs practice private politics when they engage a company to get the company to change its behavior. In the RAN campaign of which this video is a part, RAN is attempting to affect a change in General Mills' (the maker of Cheerios) purchases of palm oil, an ingredient in their cereals.

Concerning the above question, you've probably guessed my opinion, especially if you have read the previous post in this case study series, "Rainforest Action Network ... Does Indoctrination Count?"

To be alerted about more posts in this case study series, "Rainforest Action Network and Children," simply subscribe to the FREE RSS feed. Just click on the icon on the left or in the top right hand corner of this page.

Chapter Ten - The Perfect Meme Storm
———— Take-Aways ————

The problem of meme manglers wanting to "change reality" so that they may advance their agenda is real. People encounter it everyday, many times without even knowing it. To keep their brand and company images on track, corporations need to fight this activity. We saw in the "Danone Fights Digital Slurs in an Interesting Way" article an interesting methodology for doing just that and for making the public aware that they can't believe everything, or maybe even a lot of what, they read from the Internet. I hope that we see more of these approaches to reality in the future.

The discussions of the less than impressive usage of Twitter and Facebook by Rainforest Action Network and Friends of the Earth were not intended to be misleading. In "Friends of the Earth Doesn't 'Get' Twitter," we discussed how FOEI showed bad Twitter usage on Earth Day. Their problem in using this social media venue, as well as Facebook as discussed in "Friends of the Earth Doesn't "Get" Facebook, Either," was just not limited to Earth Day, but can extend to every other day. What we found in these essays demonstrates that FOE doesn't want to use these venues for conversation, just broadcasting; although they missed their big Earth Day chance to broadcast many memes. Who knows why. Maybe they were just too busy with Earth Day office parties and forgot about the meme mangling opportunity that was staring them in the face.

And this same regard for Twitter was demonstrated in "Rainforest Action Network Twitter Campaign Fails … So Far" where RAN neglected to use Twitter to promote the publication of one of their protest "reports." This is a behavior that they definitely did not learn from their Greenpeace siblings as we saw exhibited in The Kit Kat Incident previously discussed.

But as I said above, don't be misled. In these instances, this lack of employment of Twitter or Facebook doesn't mean that they don't or can't mangle a meme with the best of them in other communications venues. These observations simply mean that the meme manglers resources are limited and that they pick the battle in which they think they can spread their memes most effectively. An example of that choice is given in the "Rainforest Action Network … Does Indoctrination Count?" essay.

The "Does Indoctrination Count" essay began a series, which extends into the next chapter, on Rainforest Action Network and how it appears, to me at least, that they are indoctrinating children into RAN's way of thinking, with some help from the public school system. Now, some readers may disagree with my choice of the word "indoctrination." I understand that. Those readers may think it sounds too dictatorial, with images of Stalin and Hitler coming to mind. I don't use the word within that context of totalitarianism. Rather I use the word within the context of its dictionary definition, which is shown near the end of the "Rainforest Action Network ... More Indoctrination?" essay appearing in the next chapter. This RAN approach of "educating" the children I think we can characterize as a "perfect meme storm." Why? Because the approach exploits and leverages some of the anti-corporate meme floating around in the culture, as previously discussed, and the approach operates from the position of RAN, as an ENGO, having a "moral shield;" that anything they do is perceived as "good." These two forces come together to legitimatize and support the transmission of one-sided information to persons who are not yet capable of critical thinking. For RAN, this confluence of storm forces is "perfect" (even if they don't use Twitter well) because it seemingly guarantees that their audience will carry forward the meme desired by RAN. And that is a meme that will help RAN, and other organizations like it, not only transmit their one-sided messages, but it is a meme which will also help these organizations to build other memes upon which they can support other one-sided positions in their "privately political" campaigns.

CHAPTER ELEVEN

Kudos Don't Last Long

Greenpeace Wants You to "Have It Their Way"

June 1, 2010

Categories: Irregular Competition - Greenpeace, Research - Case Studies - Greenpeace Studies

Currently, I'm reading a terrific book entitled *Good Cop, Bad Cop - Environmental NGOs and their Strategies toward Business.* [174] The title accurately describes the subject matter within the book. Edited by Thomas P. Lyon, the book is a collection of essays written by various experts within the field of the "private politics" between environmental NGOs (ENGOs) and business. In addition to articles by experts in sociology, economics, and political science, with each giving their own specialized view of ENGO and business engagement strategies, there are also articles by business and ENGO executives.

One of the articles in the book is entitled "Greenpeace" and is written by Kert Davies, who is listed in the book as being the research director for Greenpeace. Again, the title accurately describes the content. (Although, the book does not say if Kert is the research director for Greenpeace International, Greenpeace UK, Greenpeace Canada, etc.) In his article, Kert gives an historic overview of Greenpeace, and discusses its objectives and focus along with the organizational structure of that ENGO, as well as other topics. Toward the end of his article, Kert details some case studies describing some direct actions in which Greenpeace has engaged various corporations. One of those cases studies is titled the "ExxonSecrets Campaign."

The ExxonSecrets campaign was a direct action against Exxon Mobil that started in 2001. Kert's article states, on page 205 of Good Cop, that "the primary objective of this campaign was to remove or lessen corporate interference in U.S. climate policy … a key strategy was to put ExxonMobil in a negative light as a laggard among corporations, thereby motivating other companies to take proactive measures to avoid similar treatment."

Although Kert's article is not precisely clear on this next item, apparently one of the factors driving this Greenpeace direct action was a "leaked document" from the American Petroleum Institute (API), which Kert says was the subject of a New York Times front page article in April 1998. (I've read that New York Times article and will comment on it in the next paragraph.) Per Kert's article, the "leaked document" indicated that Exxon had participated in the development of a group which would run a multi-million dollar, multi-year campaign "to promote contrary scientific opinions and raise … uncertainty among the public …" Also, per Kert's article,

> the leaked document stated, "Victory Will Be Achieved When … Average citizens 'understand' (recognize) uncertainties in climate science; recognition of uncertainties becomes part of conventional wisdom" and "Media 'understands' (recognizes) uncertainties in climate science.

More is to be learned about this group. Referring back to that New York Times article, which was entitled "Industry Group Plans to Battle Climate Treaty" (by John H. Cushman, Jr., New York Times, April 26, 1998, p. A1) and aside from the article, in my opinion, being somewhat polemic in its perspective toward the global warming debate, the Times article stated that "the industry group said it wanted to develop a 'sound scientific alternative' to the Intergovernmental Panel on Climate Change (the IPCC), which was then in 1998, and still is, a group of scientists which advises the United Nations on issues of global warming.

Whether the arguments over the science are right or wrong is not an issue in which I wish to become involved. As I've stated on this blog many times, I don't have the qualifications or background to engage in an argument over the scientific facts of climate change. But I do have the qualifications and background to engage in an argument over the issue of freedom of thought and the pursuit of truth. And that is exactly the issue that I am raising in this post.

Now, I have no illusions that Exxon was participating in the development of this industry group solely for the purpose of inviting an open and balanced debate. I don't think that Exxon or most other corporations, including the corporation that is Greenpeace, are quite that altruistic. But, what's wrong with recognizing "uncertainties" in climate science? Wouldn't that recognition inspire such debate?

In this instance, it doesn't matter if the objective of Exxon was to inspire open and balanced debate or not. My point is that contribution to open debate would have been a by-product of the Exxon process. More light would have been shed on the subject of global warming, allowing free-thinking individuals to decide where the truth lies.

Allowing individuals to come to their own conclusions benefits society, but this is apparently not a perspective that is shared by Greenpeace. Indeed, in the third paragraph of this post (above), relative to the ExxonSecrets campaign, we saw that by Greenpeace's own admission "the primary objective of this campaign was to remove or lessen corporate interference in U.S. climate policy." Do they mean "interference" or do they mean that they simply object to "input" from stakeholders that do not share Greenpeace's version of truth?

If Greenpeace actually believed in the strength and validity of its position in the climate debate, and if they would have more faith in the intellectual capacity of the general public and in its freedom to reach its own decisions, they would welcome, or even invite, alternative views and not take measures to discourage those views or take actions to put opponents in a "negative light."

So, learning from what's been presented, it seems that Greenpeace wants you to "have it their way."

Choose Competition Strategy, Not Customer Strategy

June 3, 2010

Categories: Activism, Protests in Social Media - The Kit Kat Incident, Strategy, Threats

In a Forbes article from a couple weeks ago, "When It Comes to Social Media, Many Marketers Jump the Gun," [175] Jeremiah Owyang, web-strategist extraordinaire, discussed the March-April 2010 Greenpeace assault on Nestlé, much of which was conducted within social media. I discussed this social media attack in an article series entitled "The Kit Kat Incident."

Jeremiah, in his Forbes article, makes the point that Nestlé was unprepared for this assault. Of this there is no doubt. Much of the popular press on this event also pointed out this fault. As a suggested remedy for this unpreparedness, in his article Jeremiah outlines how marketers may prepare a social media marketing program to prepare for:

> *... opportunities to connect with customers ...*

Generally, I agree with what Jeremiah is proposing. Preparation is paramount.

Proaction is preferred to reaction. And the steps that Jeremiah outlines in his article will get marketers moving toward that proaction. But, specifically and with particular regard to Jeremiah's pairing of what I labeled "The Kit Kat Incident" together with the idea of using social media marketing, what I find unsettling is that, in his prescriptive remedy, he seems to be categorizing those involved in the assault on Nestlé along with customers. Indeed, in his article, for the first step of his plan "to help marketers prepare for social media interactions," he says:

Have a strong understanding of your customers.

Those involved in the Kit Kat assault are not customers. They are not consumers.

They are competitors. Irregular competitors.

And they must be regarded as such.

For three weeks, I watched the Greenpeace assault conducted against Nestlé. These attackers were not there to register complaints as would customers or consumers. These people were present to attack the name of the corporation. Period. And nothing would dissuade them from that. They were "tasked" with that mission by Greenpeace. Customer/consumer "nice-talk" was not going to quell their actions. In the early days of the attack, I saw how the Nestlé corporate Facebook page administrator attempted to assuage the "crowds" attacking the Nestlé name. It was clear, from his/her writings, that that administrator regarded those in the "crowd" as customers or consumers and attempted to interact with them as such. In fact, they were not customers or consumers. What they were was a crowd with a mission. Understanding them as customers or consumers would lead to the wrong web 2.0 strategy selection, proactive or reactive. Understanding them as a crowd, a protest crowd, would lead to better strategic selections.

So, although Jeremiah proposes using social media marketing strategy, one typically directed at customers/consumers, to quell or preclude the ire of a protest crowd such as that in the Greenpeace/Nestlé incident he cites, I think he might be suggesting a "cookie cutter" approach to a situation that requires the selection of a competition strategy, not a customer strategy.

This Time ... Kudos to Greenpeace

June 8, 2010

Categories: Activism, Irregular Competition - Greenpeace, Tactics

At a symposium I recently attended, someone asked me, "Why are you against Greepeace?" My reply was that I am not against Greenpeace as an organization; I am only against some of the actions that they take, specifically the ones which are destructive in a literal and figurative sense. However, occasionally other of their actions can be quite constructive, such as this one.

According to an article on DelawareOnline.com, [176] a couple of weeks ago, Greenpeace sailed one of their blimps around and over the two Du Pont chemical plants that line the Upper Delaware Bay, between New Jersey and Pennsylvania. Per the article, one of the objectives of the flight was to point out potential security problems at those plants. Sailing a blimp unchallenged and only 500 feet over chemical plants highlights a very big security problem. The implications, in this post-9/11 era, are obvious. The article also pointed out other security problems, occurring a few weeks prior to the blimp ride, such as this one on terra firma:

> ... Greenpeace members repeatedly drove around and entered the parking lots of both DuPont plants without being questioned.

Since Du Pont doesn't have a private air force to secure the space over its plants, I can understand why the blimp was able to penetrate the plant's air space. (Please note that I said that I understand ... but that's not to say that I agree.) But as far as the breaches of the parking lot go, there's no excuse. I'm not saying that every company's parking lot should be secured, but for companies handling sensitive materials, such as chemicals, I think extra precautions must be taken. Hiring some guards to secure a parking lot is much simpler than creating a private air force to secure the air space above.

So, this time, on this particular direct action I will have to send some kudos to Greenpeace. Greenpeace's main skill lies in publicity generation. I look at them as actually more of a publicity machine than an environmental NGO. And on this publicity stunt, they performed in a constructive manner.

Greenpeace, CNN, and Sloppy Research

June 10, 2010

Categories: Irregular Competition - Greenpeace, Protests in Social Media - The Kit Kat Incident, Semantical Terrorism

On May 24, 2010, CNN.com ran a story entitled "Social Media Can Help Save the Planet, says Greenpeace Boss." [177] There are two problems in this article. The first problem is with the accuracy of the reporting. The second problem is with how Greenpeace now looks at social media. The first problem you and I will discuss today in this post. The second problem you and I will discuss in next Tuesday's post entitled "Greenpeace ... Will You Use 'Semantical Terrorism' in Social Media?"

Regarding the first problem, the CNN article recalled the social media campaign that Greenpeace ran against Nestlé earlier this year. (For a review of this campaign, you may read my article series entitled "The Kit Kat Incident.") The CNN article states that "Central to the Greenpeace campaign was an online video posted in March -- a mock Kit Kat chocolate bar advert that shows an office worker biting into a bloody orangutan's finger instead of a piece of chocolate." The article then states "Less than a month after the video was first shown, Nestlé stopped all purchase of palm oil from Sinar Mas, one company Greenpeace claimed was causing deforestation in Indonesia." The implication is that the social media campaign, extending over several weeks and led by the video, was responsible for causing Nestlé's reaction.

That's not exactly correct.

I studied The Kit Kat Incident in great detail and watched it as it unfolded over several weeks. The protracted campaign was not the cause of Nestlé's acquiescence to Greenpeace's demands. How do I know that? I know that because on the same day that the Greenpeace social media campaign began, literally within hours, Nestlé agreed to the terms set out by Greenpeace. The extensive and prolonged social media campaign was not the cause of the shift in Nestlé behavior, although Greenpeace claims it to be, and most of the mainstream media through sloppy research backs them up. In support of this point, you may read the chronology of this event, well-researched and linked to supporting documents, by going to my article entitled "The Kit Kat Incident and an Abuse of Power," with particular attention given to the section entitled "The Acquiescent Result."

Yet, Greenpeace appears to be congratulating themselves on a social media campaign well-run. (Actually, tactically it could have been better run and my Kit Kat article series points out some of their gaping mistakes.) But, this is not to say that such a campaign could be ineffective. Quite the contrary. And in next Tuesday's post, "Greenpeace … Will You Use 'Semantical Terrorism' in Social Media?," you and I will discuss how Greenpeace now appears to view this version of an online strategy.

If you are reading this prior to next Tuesday, June 15, 2010, then please subscribe to the FREE RSS feed so that you will receive that article automatically. If you are reading this after June 15, 2010, then simply click here to be taken to "Greenpeace … Will You Use 'Semantical Terrorism' in Social Media?"

Greenpeace … Will You Use "Semantical Terrorism" in Social Media?

June 15, 2010

Categories: Ideas, Irregular Competition - Greenpeace, Semantical Terrorism, Strategy, Tactics, The Battle for Meaning

In last Thursday's post, entitled "Greenpeace, CNN, and Sloppy Research," I referenced a May 24, 2010 CNN.com article "Social Media Can Help Save the Planet, Says Greenpeace Boss" and said that there were two problems in that CNN article. The first problem, sloppy research, you and I discussed last Thursday. Today, you and I will discuss the second problem, that of "semantical terrorism."

The term "semantical terrorism" occurred to me while participating as a panelist at a recent symposium held at Bernard Baruch College in NYC. While participating on the panel "More than Friending: Social Media and Communication in Business and Education," I was describing to the audience what I do. One of the other panelists, Alan Levine, Vice President, NMC Community and CTO, The New Media Consortium, looked at me and said something like "Oh, so you're a counter-terrorist." I paused for a moment, then agreed adding a modifying statement that "semantical counter-terrorist" would probably be more applicable. So, I will credit Alan with the inspiration for the term that we will discuss today.

In my work, I analyze advocacy groups (NGOs, activists, etc.) who perform anti-corporate actions. My primary area of analysis is on their actions in both online and offline media. That analysis is focused on how these irregular competitors "mangle the meaning" and "diddle the definition" of the corporate images owned by the companies they target. In fact, I have written a book on this subject, this "battle for meaning." (For further details, please see *Insidious Competition - The Battle for Meaning and the Corporate Image* which is scheduled to publish very soon.) And it's in this battle for meaning that "semantical terrorism" is performed by irregular competitors, who threaten damage, either overtly or tacitly, to the images of corporations who don't go along with the NGO or activist agenda.

A battle in semantical terrorism it truly is and in the CNN article referenced above, I will point out how Greenpeace has showed their intention to use this tactic to meet their future objectives.

In the second to last paragraph of that article, Greenpeace's executive director, Kumi Naidoo, says that although Greenpeace has a dialogue going on with a number of companies "if talk does not deliver the results, we have to create the possibility for millions of people who care about the environment to send a clear message." He doesn't directly state that the option is semantical terrorism, but I believe his implication is clear; that if negotiations don't bring Greenpeace its desired results, then they will entreat millions of people to essentially "trash" the image of the targeted company. Greenpeace supporters have a reputation for exaggeration. And based on what I've seen Greenpeace supporters do previously in social media, based on how I've seen those supporters go off the central issue of the campaign, I can say that I expect many of those "clear messages" would not be based in fact, but rather in innuendo and insinuation. (For more on this, please see my research into the Greenpeace-engineered social media protest that I dubbed "The Kit Kat Incident.") Such action would constitute a systematic approach toward coercion, a definition which correlates with that commonly accepted for the word "terrorism," and would be anchored in the manipulation of meaning, i.e., semantics.

So, the answer to the question posed in today's title, "Greenpeace … Will You Use 'Semantical Terrorism' in Social Media?," appears to be a "yes" and thereby all corporations should be put on notice.

EXCLUSIVE
Rainforest Action Network ... More Indoctrination?

June 17, 2010

Categories: Activism, Anti-Corporatism, Indoctrination, Irregular Competition - Rainforest Action Network, Research - Case Studies - Rainforest Action Network Studies - RAN and Children, Tactics

This is the third article in a series about how Rainforest Action Network (RAN) involves children in its campaigns against corporations. To see the other two preceding articles, you may click here.

In my continuing research on this topic, I recently reviewed RAN's Web site where I found the following information:

> *A first grade class at Mill Hill Elementary School in Southport, CT raised $523 for the RAN Protect An Acre program by selling ice pops. The class also held lunch time screenings, open to the whole school, of the RAN video Forest Family Forever.* [178]

The mention of that RAN video piqued my interest. Knowing that RAN is a market activist organization, one that employs anti-corporate actions (click here, [179] then go to page 8 on the RAN PDF document for their self-characterization as anti-corporate activists), I decided to watch this video to learn how RAN portrays companies to children. You may watch this video as well. Forest Family Forever is posted on the RAN Web site. [180] Here is what I found.

Findings

Written from a child's perspective, this animated feature involves two characters, a 1,000 year-old grandfather tree with his sapling grandson growing next to him. Interestingly, the visual perspective in viewing both characters is that which would be seen from a child's point of view when standing on the forest floor. Lots of color is involved, nice music, too. Many of the elements that Disney has found so successful are used.

After the characters are established, the conversation between the grandfather and the grandson turns to the state of the rainforest. The grandfather explains what a rainforest is as well as its overall function in the planetary ecosystem.

Then the conversation turns to how the rainforest is being disrespected by humans. The grandfather 1,000 year-old tree says to the sapling grandson:

Many humans only see us rainforests as ways to make money. In order to make lots and lots of money, they formed companies that take things out of the rainforest in a harmful way. Nothing wrong with companies making money, mind you. But when they destroy the rainforest to do it, it creates big problems for everyone.

During this point in their conversation, the viewer is shown scenes of industrial actions taking place in the forest. None of those scenes are as visually pleasant as the bucolic scenes with which we were presented during the opening part of the video. And when the grandpa utters the words "lots and lots of money," the phrase is said in a very low register, with dark overtones.

The sapling then says to the grandfather tree, "Grandpa, those humans sound like a bunch of saps." (The script is filled with such puns.)

The grandfather then says, "Hold on there, sonny. Not all humans hurt the rainforest." It's then that the video shows various activists at demonstrations. Those activists are holding save the rainforest signs. It's then that the grandpa says, "There are many humans waking up and remembering that they are part of our forest family." The sapling questions, "How are they doing that?" The grandpa replies, "A bunch of different ways. Some humans are telling companies to stop destroying the rainforest. They write letters and choose not to buy that company's products." When the grandpa says the words "they write letters," the viewer is shown a small boy writing a letter.

The grandpa then suggests to the sapling that other ways to save the rainforest are by using recycled paper, but grandpa does not state that it is various companies who produce that recycled paper.

Conclusion

Generally, in Forest Family Forever, companies are framed negatively, and not positively. The intent behind using visually unpleasant scenes connected to the industrial actions and the lowering of the vocal tone when the words "lots and lots of money" is clear. This is a one-sided perspective.

Indeed, if RAN was interested in presenting a balanced view of corporations and their effects on the rainforest, both those of a positive and negative nature, they had ample opportunity. One such opportunity to present the positives is in the discussion of the manufacture of recycled products. During the conversation about recycled products, the opportunity was available for a discussion about how various companies produce those recycled products and about how various companies approach usage of the forest with a more "sustainable" viewpoint than others. But RAN does not avail itself of the opportunity to present a more balanced view of commerce. The recycled products are discussed as if they magically appear without the consideration of environmentally conscious companies.

The only contextual and visual reference to grandpa's own phrase of "not all humans hurt the rainforest" is to that of activists. In this feature, shown to small children, the only humans who are positioned as concerned with the rainforest are activists.

When producing materials for young minds, great care should be given to presenting those young and impressionable minds with both sides of a story. Naturally (pun intended ;-)), I realize that RAN is a political action group, engaging in "private politics" against corporations of their own selection. And I would be naive not to realize that such groups do not have a balance of the issues as their concern. But when one-sided information is presented to people who have not yet developed the capacity for critical thinking or the ability to seek out alternative information, such action can be defined as indoctrination. [181]

And when indoctrination is performed on children, it is especially distasteful.

EXCLUSIVE
Rainforest Action Network ... One-Sided Teacher Resources?

June 22, 2010

Categories: Activism, Indoctrination, Irregular Competition - Rainforest Action Network, Research - Case Studies - Rainforest Action Network Studies - RAN and Children - Questionable, Tactics

Today's post is the fourth article in a series about how Rainforest Action

Network (RAN) involves children in its campaigns against companies. To see the previous three articles, simply click here. Today's article will not only point to another instance of RAN engaging children in its anti-corporate campaigns, but this article will also point out that RAN targets teachers for incorporation into its private politics against companies. (For those of you that have not yet read the previous articles, private politics is the process of "collective interactions between parties attempting to advance their interests that do not rely on the law, public order, or the state." (Source: Contention and Corporate Social Responsibility, p. 30) [182] These types of interactions commonly take place between non-governmental organizations (NGOs) and public corporations.)

Introduction

RAN has a portion of its main Web site devoted to resources for children. This section, titled "Rainforest Heroes," [183] has an extensive amount of content. On the home page of this section, the visiting child will be greeted with a selection of six departments: 1) Kid's Action, 2) Heroes Corner, 3) Jungle Gym, 4) About Rainforests, 5) Protect An Acre, and 6) Teacher's Lounge. Today we are going to review the Teacher's Lounge, [184] which, of course, is targeted at teachers rather than children at whom the other five sections are targeted.

When the teacher clicks on Teacher's Lounge, he or she will arrive at a page where four more links await. Those links are: Kid's Action Toolkit, Forest Family Forever video, Factsheets, and Teacher's Resources. Today you and I will discuss the Teacher's Resources area, [185] and we'll discuss some of the other three links in future posts. (As I mentioned, this site has extensive content.) There the teacher is greeted with eight more links. (I did say that this site has extensive content; didn't I?) For the sake of brevity, I'll just say here that if you would like to see what all eight of those links are, then please click here. [186] The link that we'll be concerned with in this post is the link Rainforests Forever! - Curriculum Supplement for Grades 3-6 which leads the teacher out to RAN's main site. There the teacher is greeted with four more selections, all of which you may see by clicking here. [187] The selection among those four that I'll be discussing is "Agribusiness in the Rainforest" [188] which is billed on that page as an "Educator Resource."

This "Agribusiness in the Rainforest" page lists, as per the page's sub-title, "case studies on agribusiness's impact on rainforest communities."

Findings

Many of the statements in these case studies are not supported. To have a look for yourself, please click here. [189] RAN makes various unsupported claims about specific companies committing acts of pollution in specific foreign countries and undocumented claims concerning corporate actions that are against local host nation law. However, not all statements in these case studies are undocumented.

At the bottom of the page, [190] RAN cites 14 footnote sources. Indeed, there are 14 footnotes throughout these short cases studies extending over approximately 1,800 words. Here is a list of the sources they cite, along with the number of times each source is cited in the case studies.

1. Brazzil Magazine (used twice, the same article each time)
2. Grupo de Reflexion Rural (used seven times, the same article each time)
3. In These Times
4. The Nation
5. Center for Environmental Law and Community Rights - CELCOR
6. MOPIC Report

So, over 14 footnotes, they have actually cited only six different sources. And among those 14 footnotes, fully half of them, the seven times one article from Grupo de Reflexion Rural was used, are from one source.

Analysis

As can be seen from the above findings, the diversity of these sources is very narrow. Narrow sourcing usually doesn't present a very wide perspective on the problem examined and signals the danger of a one-sided argument. To examine just how narrowly concentrated the information is, let's discuss the nature of these sources. Who are these six sources?

1. Brazzil Magazine - a news, politics, and culture magazine in Brazil.[191]
2. Grupo de Reflexion Rural - a South American political action group, appears to be similar in orientation to RAN. [192]
3. In These Times - an economics and politics news magazine who describe themselves as "a nonprofit and independent newsmagazine

committed to political and economic democracy and opposed to the dominance of transnational corporations and the tyranny of marketplace values over human values." [193]

4. The Nation - an American news, culture, politics, and economics magazine which describes itself as a publication that will "make an earnest effort to bring to the discussion of political and social questions a really critical spirit, and to wage war upon the vices of violence, exaggeration, and misrepresentation by which so much of the political writing of the day is marred." [194]

5. Center for Environmental Law and Community Rights - CELCOR - an organization about which I couldn't locate much information other than they are an NGO based in Papua New Guinea

6. MOPIC Report - unable to locate any reliable information on just what this source is.

What I see here are five sources whose objectivity in presenting a balanced view, or reliability, is in question. Perhaps the only source that I would call close to being "reliable" relative to those listed would be The Nation.

Conclusion

So, I believe I have demonstrated that the sources used by RAN for the case studies that they offer as "Educator Resources" are far from objective, and very potentially highly-slanted. Yet, RAN offers this type of research as a foundation for teachers' lesson plans. Lessons that RAN would like to be imparted to children. Can we call this an attempt at indoctrination? Where indoctrination [195] means an attempt to influence with one-sided information? In my opinion, the answer is yes. Your opinion may differ. Comments on either opinion will be published below.

I hope that if any teachers use these resources, that they realize the limitations in the perspectives of these case studies, and point out to their students the limited sourcing, and then provide their students with information from more objective, and balanced sources so that the students have a chance at reaching their own conclusions. When it comes to teaching students, the quality of the information imparted is imperative.

Isn't that what school should be about?

•

EXCLUSIVE
Rainforest Action Network, Youth, and the Double-Standard

June 24, 2010

Categories: Activism, Indoctrination, Irregular Competition - Rainforest Action Network, Research - Case Studies - Rainforest Action Network Studies - RAN and Children, Tactics

This is the fifth article in a series about how Rainforest Action Network (RAN) involves children in its campaigns against corporations. To see any of the other four preceding articles, you may click here.

As I mentioned in the fourth article in this series, "Rainforest Action Network … One-Sided Teacher Resources?," RAN has quite an extensive amount of content on its Web site targeted at children. One section of its Web site is dedicated to older children, a demographic that we commonly refer to as "youth." That section of their site is named RYSE (RAN Youth Sustaining the Earth). [196] Among many of the resources available to youth on the RYSE site is the RAN Pressure Drop Primer. [197]

The RAN Pressure Drop Primer is a document, per page 5 of that same document, that is geared toward "student activists." In fact, RAN wants to involve youth in their anti-corporate campaigns and says so on page 8 of the Primer. A quote from that page is:

> *We believe corporations hold most of the power in our societies, so challenging their power is central to our organizing.*

Toward that goal, the Primer explains to the student activist what RAN is about and provides information on how to start a local RAN chapter. To facilitate the creation of those chapters, on page 29 through 35 of the RAN Pressure Drop Primer, [198] RAN provides forms to be filled out, and signed, by those establishing the local RAN group. (There are, of course, many legal requirements to be met in establishing those local groups, to say nothing of the legal difficulties involved in having minors establish such groups. But those are different issues which, for now, I'll set aside.) On page 34 of the Primer is the RAN Name Use Licensing Agreement. Two of the terms in the licensing agreement are:

1. Group will not permit any unlicensed use of the RAN name and will notify RAN immediately if such use occurs.
2. Group will use the name and logo provided by RAN and will not make any changes without prior authorization from RAN.

Certainly it makes good sense to take steps to protect your logo and brand name.

Yet, RAN has no hesitation in violating the spirit of its own rules by making unauthorized use of the brand names and logos of those companies they target in their anti-corporate campaigns. One example of such brand name and logo abuse may be seen on RAN's own Web site. [199] In this example, RAN uses the General Mills logo in a way that depicts the "G" as a buzz saw cutting down a tree. Somehow I don't think that General Mills gave RAN permission for this use of their brand name or logo.

Hypocrisy and double-standards are not proper things to teach youth. And doing so creates a lesson in disrespect in the minds of the people who will someday be in charge of our society.

Rainforest Action Network … Shock and Kiddy Paper

June 24, 2010

Categories: Activism, Indoctrination, Irregular Competition - Rainforest Action Network, Research - Case Studies - Rainforest Action Network Studies - RAN and Children, Tactics

This is the sixth post in the continuing series about Rainforest Action Network (RAN) and how it involves children in its campaigns against companies.

Today's post is a short one.

Recently RAN released a report regarding their assertion of how children's book publishers use paper that is linked to the destruction of the rainforest. [200] Well, as are many of RAN's reports arguable, so is this one. But I am not, today, commenting on the validity of the information within their report or on the integrity of their research processes. My post today is made simply to draw your attention to RAN's strategic choice of the continued employment of children into their anti-corporate campaigns.

Why would RAN choose children's books about which to write such a report? Why not, say pulp fiction books? Or how about romance novels? Or mysteries? Or graphic novels? Or even porno magazines? Why not? Because those other genres don't carry the presumed innocence that children's books carry, the very innocence that is attached to children themselves. There isn't as much shock involved in stating that, say for example, mystery novels use paper that is contributing to deforestation of the rainforest. No. Focusing on the children's genre attracts a lot more media attention than would focusing on most other genres. And residing within that attention is the shock that RAN wishes to strategically leverage for their purposes.

Truly shocking only if their report is correct. But is it? Or are they creating shock in kiddy paper? You may take a look here at their report and then decide for yourself. [201] And after reading that report, you might want to regard it within the context of the findings that I have made regarding how RAN uses children in its private political campaigns against companies.

Are the Days of Cheesy Street Theater Over?

June 29, 2010

Categories: Irregular Competition - Greenpeace, NGOs, Strategy, Trends

Earlier this month, in a Guardian Online article titled "Should the media be more supportive of corporate moves towards sustainability?," it was revealed that the new head of Greenpeace International, Kumi Naidoo, "has decided to work in partnership with companies rather than only criticise them from the outside." [202] This is big news. Very big news.

Greenpeace has been perhaps best known within the field of environmental non-governmental organizations (ENGOs) as one of the few ENGOs that consistently takes an adversarial approach and refuses to work in partnerships with corporations. Consider this. When you think about Greenpeace, probably some of the first thoughts that come to mind are their publicity-grabbing antics and their reputation as "environmental rebels." Will that rep now begin to be diluted?

There are many other ENGOs that, long ago, adopted the strategy of cooperation rather than confrontation: CERES, Conservation International, The Nature Conservancy, World Wildlife Fund, to name some. (See "Shades of Green," by Andrew Hoffman, Stanford Social Innovation Review, Spring 2009 [203]) Now it seems that, based on Kumi's announcement, Greenpeace is beginning to move in that direction, as well. But, it appears that Greenpeace will not transform themselves overnight. From what Kumi said, it seems that Greenpeace will, at least for the time being, pursue a bifurcated strategy of cooperation and confrontation. Such a two-pronged approach might be difficult to pull-off. The cooperation side might leave them vulnerable to the co-optation of their confrontation side, damaging their brand and that environmental rebel rep to which I referred above.

And if that environmental rebel rep was to be damaged, one question would pop into my mind. On whom will we depend when we want some entertainment from cheesy street theater?

Chapter Eleven - Kudos Don't Last Long
———— Take-Aways ————

This chapter opened with "Greenpeace Wants You to 'Have It Their Way' " which discusses another meme incident from that ENGO. This piece presents another example of how irregular competitors position the "truth" and live on a meme, or potential lie or at best half-truth, to advance their agenda. When I see these sorts of behaviors from irregular competition, I wonder that if the case of the irregular competitor is so strong, why is it that the meme mangling can't be forsaken? Why is it that the case can't stand on its own merits and withstand alternative views?

I pose that question as a rhetorical, which is really, of course, more of a statement. And my opinion raised by this "statement" is particularly relevant when it comes to competing head-to-head against irregular competitors. In "Choose Competition Strategy, Not Customer Strategy," I maintain that the competition in social media must be countered by keeping the special characteristics of irregular competition in mind, particularly with how they construct and exploit a meme, either of their own making or of the making of others. Irregular competitors are not customers and should not be dealt with as customers are within social media. To do so would constitute an improper assessment of the competitive situation. Yet, we should not eschew customer management strategy entirely. There is one adage from customer management strategy that could be slightly adopted to interacting with irregular competitors. The adage I have in mind is "The customer is always right." We can adapt that to our specialized interactions with irregular competitors and say "The irregular competitor is not always wrong."

Corporations do many good things and many stupid things. The same goes for irregular competitors. I highlighted one of those good things from an irregular competitor. It was the action taken by Greenpeace as summarized in the article "This Time ... Kudos to Greenpeace." I'm not 100% negative on irregular competitors; neither am I 100% positive on corporations. To be either would mean that I either succumb to or ignore the memes, rather than questioning them and searching for the truth. So, when an irregular competitor performs an action that helps get at the truth, instead of obscure it, I like to point that out. Such as it was with the "Kudos" article. Unfortunately for the truth, my kudos didn't last long.

The kudos didn't last long because, per "Greenpeace, CNN, and Sloppy

Research," the ENGO, supported this time by the mainstream media, went right back to bending the truth. I further discussed this mangling of the truth as "semantical terrorism" in "Greenpeace … Will You Use 'Semantical Terrorism' in Social Media?" Because in their interactions with corporations, that's really what it is. A terrorism of sorts, but one that involves only words as weapons and their bent meanings as the first in a long line of casualties.

From the concept of semantical terrorism, we then moved back to the topic of the indoctrination of children, but this time with a more in-depth discussion. In the essays, "Rainforest Action Network … More Indoctrination?," "Rainforest Action Network … One-Sided Teacher Resources?," "Rainforest Action Network, Youth, and the Double-Standard," and "Rainforest Action Network … Shock and Kiddy Paper," I laid out a case as to why I think what Rainforest Action Network is doing is really indoctrination. You may agree or you may disagree that incorporating children into private politics against corporations constitutes indoctrination. If the latter, I would ask that before you dismiss the case as "crazy," you first check the definition of "indoctrination," and then imagine the case as not involving Rainforest Action Network or any other type of organization that uses the "moral shield" to protect its agenda. Imagine instead that the case simply involves a generic organization, one that does not perpetrate or live on memes and then see if you feel the same.

CHAPTER TWELVE

And the Beat Goes On

High Seas Romance Raises
Greenpeace's Threat Rating

July 8, 2010

Categories: Irregular Competition - Greenpeace - Threat Index

Now you can be a virtual "whale warrior" or "high seas pirate," depending upon your point of view.

Paradox Interactive, a PC interactive game publisher, announced that the next installment in their Ship Simulator series will be Ship Simulator Extremes, a game that will allow players to assume a virtual captaincy on missions upon the high seas. [204] One of the modules in the game will allow players to "captain" Greenpeace's, as yet unlaunched, Rainbow Warrior III, due to be launched in the physical world during October 2011.

Per Ecorazzi.com, the new game will allow players to hunt down whalers and experience other intense situations, in a virtual, danger-free environment of course. [205]

Partnering with this interactive game publisher to publicize their new vessel, is a very clever tactic employed by Greenpeace in the digital space. This organization, among many irregular competitors, truly understands how to make use of virtual environments for their own political agenda. By making the Rainbow Warrior III "available" to almost anyone who wants to play activist on their PC, it legitimizes the controversy of a political action, enticing armchair activists with simulated danger and elevating the brand image of Greenpeace. At the same time, it may satisfy the "activist jones" ordinary "joes" may have and preclude them from entering into any real-life activism, a potential downside for any activist group.

In either case, this development certainly represents another example of Greenpeace's understanding of how to apply the digital space in their activist campaigns. As such, this development spurs me to add another point to Greenpeace's Irregular Competition Threat Index rating. Per my last post on Greenpeace's status in this ranking, they stood at 7.5 (where a 10 represents the highest level of threat). Today, I'll pop them up to 8.5; that's what a little nautical allure can do for a ranking.

But, watch for further changes in their status, in either direction.

More Sloppy Research from Greenpeace

July 13, 2010

Categories: Irregular Competition - Greenpeace, Research - Questionable

Recently I reviewed a new chemical plant inspection report authored by Greenpeace. This one is titled "Greenpeace Security Inspection Report: Kuehne Chemical, South Kearny, NJ." [206] I was looking forward to a clever, and relatively objective, report like the one Greenpeace filed concerning the Du Pont facilities in southwestern New Jersey and southeastern Pennsylvania which I reviewed in my blog article "This Time … Kudos to Greenpeace." But they disappointed me.

All that this eight page Kuehne report amounts to is just a waste of space that rehashes old information known for years by the public. The original "research" done for this "report" is basically non-existent. Greenpeace tries to present original research on pages 5, 6, and 7 of this document, but they squandered the opportunity in this thing they call a report. On those pages appear photos of the Kuehne facility, all taken from public property such as next to the front gate and from a highway bridge spanning the facility. I thought, because they were able to get such public access, that they were going to make a point about security threats, similar to the way they made their points in the report about the Du Pont facilities. Instead, next to photos showing their close approach, they listed captions such as:

> *These pictures were taken from the pedestrian walkway on the Pulaski Skyway. There is a fence on the skyway that runs part of the length of the facility and is meant to add security to the facility but, as demonstrated by the photo, when standing on either side of the fence, one has a clear, unobstructed view of the facility. This facility failed inspection because it puts 12 million people at risk including inhabitants of New York City.*

Not only did they just take a lazy short-cut by applying these same three sentences to three of the six pictures taken of the plant from public property, but they didn't even explain the third sentence, "This facility failed inspection because it puts 12 million people at risk including inhabitants of New York City." (Incidentally, this sentence, and direct variations, was lackadaisically applied to all six photos.) Well, why is there a risk? Just because the plant is there? Explain please. Give us your rationale.

But they didn't explain. They didn't give a rationale. They simply made another unfounded statement, something at which Greenpeace, sadly, has become all too adept.

What a disappointment.

And, oh yes. On page 5 of this "report" PDF, Greenpeace makes an unreferenced statement that the Kuehne plant had eight chlorine release accidents in the time period of 2000-2010. But on the Greenpeace report summary lead-in page, from which one would download this "report" PDF, Greenpeace says that for the time period 2000-2010 there were ten chlorine release accidents, of course again unreferenced. Well, which is it? Eight or ten? And from where do these variable numbers come, anyway?

Sloppy. So sloppy. Too sloppy.

Although in this blog, I observe strategic and tactical weaknesses of various NGOs and activist groups, I do believe that groups such as Greenpeace can contribute benefits to society. But with sloppy research such as this, they just squander the opportunity, sub-optimize society, and help no one.

EXCLUSIVE
Indoctrination Flows in School?

July 15, 2010

Categories: Activism, Anti-Corporate, Indoctrination, Irregular Competition - Corporate Accountability International - Rainforest Action Network

If you are a regular reader of this site, you'll know that I have been recently researching and writing about how Rainforest Action Network (RAN) is involved in, what I believe to be, the indoctrination of children in anti-corporatism. Now, this anti-corporate indoctrination may or may not be RAN's main objective in the programs that they have for schoolchildren and in the material that they make available for school teachers. Yet, I believe that the teaching and subsequent support of anti-corporate beliefs are a possible result of the employment of the RAN teaching material that I have reviewed. You are, of course, free to come to your own conclusions after reviewing these articles.

Introduction

Indoctrination against commerce, and any benefits it may provide society, their effect may be. But, it doesn't appear that they are the only NGO moving in this direction. Recently I read about students at Atlantic City (NJ) High School, who participated in a water taste test to see if they could discern the difference between tap water and bottled water. How is a water taste test anti-corporate in nature? Well, on the face of it, it isn't. But let's dig deeper. The article I read, from the Press of Atlantic City, [207] as written by Diane D'Amico, said:

> *The taste test was organized by students in Regina Banner's Advanced Placement environment class after they watched a documentary called 'Flow' about global water availability.*

The article's mention of a documentary piqued my curiosity. So, I obtained a copy of *Flow* via my local public library. I watched the entire 84 minute film. Here is some of what I found in the film:

Findings

In the first 37 minutes of the film, the experts interviewed were as follows:

1. Paul Schwartz, national policy coordinator of Clean Water Action
2. Erik Olson, former senior attorney with the Natural Resources Defense Council (NRDC) - who accuses various governments around the world of "making deals" with various corporate interests
3. William Marks, author of *The Holy Order of Water* [208]
4. Vandana Shiva, physicist and environmental activist - who says "everyone of these chemicals was designed for warfare" and saying that now they (the chemicals) are in our drinking water (It wasn't clear to me to what chemicals she was referring in her statement.)
5. Tyrone Hayes, a biologist from the University of California at Berkeley
6. A French man speaking of various water pollution problems by using unsupported statements. This man was not identified until about 20 minutes later in the film. Then he was identified as Jean-Luc Touly, a former accountant for Vivendi, a provider of water systems in foreign countries
7. Marcela Olivera, a Bolivian activist

8. Maude Barlow, author of *Blue Gold*. [209] Only her book's main title was shown with her name. On a later Google search, I found that the subtitle of her book is The Fight to Stop the Corporate Theft of the World's Water. Within the first 21 minutes, Maude says "developing countries are being forced to hand over their basic control of water systems to multinational corporations." She disparages the water company efforts with no supporting or referenced facts. Then at minute 34:49 she says "the market is amoral."

9. Gerard Mestrallet, CEO of Suez, a water systems provider in foreign countries. He is seen describing that his company is a provider of water systems.

10. Oscar Olivera, leader of 2000 Cochabamba "Water Wars," an activist group [210]

11. David Hemson, research director, Human Sciences Research Council, South Africa's "statutory research agency" [211]

12. Michel Camdessus, former Director of the International Monetary Fund - who said that to get more water to more people the know-how of the private sector must be employed

13. Shelly Brime, of the Concerned Citizen's Group

14. Patrick Cully, executive director of the International Rivers Network - who directly and generally bashes private industry's ability to cost-effectively provide water services

15. Gigi Kellett, from Corporate Accountability International - who appears in the film while conducting a water taste test at a school

Other general findings were, summarized:

- Various unreferenced statements, presented in a graphic format with a globe image in the background, about birth defects due to water pollution in various parts of the world.
- Ominous, minor key music playing throughout the film.
- Corporate water system providers being described as a "corporate takeover of water."
- Corporate water companies are called "corrupt" several times with no evidence provided or referenced.
- Corporate water companies are generally framed as greedy entities. There was no balanced look at any benefits that these water companies may provide compared to the costs incurred.

Near the end of the film, I found the following information:

- A graphic appears saying: "We are launching a petition asking the United Nations to add the 'right to water' to the Universal Declaration of Human Rights. Please join us."
- Then after that graphic appears Wenonah Hunter, executive director of Food & Water Watch, who says that "we need an organized army of water activists in every (U.S.) congressional district."

Here is the film's full title that appears on the front of the film's DVD box:

FLOW - How Did a Handful of Corporations Steal Our Water?

As with all DVDs, on the back of the box is some marketing copy to help sell the product. Here is some information from that marketing copy as it appears on the rear of the film's DVD box:

Salina (the films' director, Irena Salina) builds a case against the growing privatization of the world's dwindling fresh water supply with an unflinching focus on politics, pollution, human rights, and the emergence of a domineering world water cartel ... the film introduces many of the governmental and corporate culprits behind the water grab.

Also printed on the back of the box, under "Special Features" in the film, is listed:

Call to Resistance: Key first steps to action and links to important allies in the fight to preserve access to safe, affordable water.

Now, let's discuss these findings.

Analysis

Of the 15 experts interviewed in the first 37 minutes of the film, to me it appears clear that at least ten of them are activists. Their status as activists is clear based upon their title or, in the case of the authors, based upon the nature of their writings, which I have reviewed online. Two people are clearly not shown as activists, #9 Mestrallet and #12 Camdessus, while the advocacy status of the other three is unclear based upon their title. Yet, it seemed to be that from what these three people discussed in the film, they had somewhat of an activist agenda. Most of their statements were generalized criticisms with no foundation presented. So, here we see that at least two-thirds of the experts appearing in the first 37 minutes of the film were activists pursuing an advocacy agenda. This sets the tone for the remaining 47 minutes of the film.

The general findings show that corporations, and for-profit organizations in general, were portrayed in a negative manner. The claims of corruption and "greed" were not substantiated and were not referenced, and as such were unproven, and perhaps unfounded.

The calls to action, the graphic that describes the petition and the statement of the director of Food & Water Watch, are without doubt politically-based and activist in nature.

The film's subtitle is sensational, putting corporations, at large, in a negative light. Such a subtitle indicates that the "information" within the film will likely be subjective and one-sided. Indeed, such an anti-corporatist view is evident, and reinforced, within the marketing copy on the back of the DVD box. Phrases such as "builds a case against … privatization" and "governmental and corporate culprits" support a prejudicial view against commerce and tell the box's reader that what they are about to view will not be a balanced and considered analysis. And if there is still further doubt as to whether the film in the box is activist oriented, the "Special Features" phrase "Call to Resistance: Key first steps to action" should be an overwhelming clue.

Conclusion

Based on these findings, there appears to be little doubt that the film *Flow* is an activist oriented piece. The objective of the film is to call upon viewers to join in a cause which is portrayed with a polemic perspective. The issue of global water supply, in an ever-expanding world population, is a complex one; far more complex than that which is portrayed in this one-sided film. It may very well be that all or some of the "information" presented in the film is indeed true. But the manner of its portrayal, as reviewed above, its lack of balance and its one-sidedness, leads a critical viewer to doubt its veracity.

A definition of indoctrination is the teaching of a one-sided belief or ideology.[212] Is this another example of activist indoctrination in our schools? I certainly hope not. But whether it is or not is unclear. Certainly my hope is that after the students in Atlantic City High School viewed this film, their teacher led them in a discussion about the film's perspective and provided them with alternate views, providing balance, and including a look at how private industry can be of great help in solving the problem of quenching the world's thirst.

A balanced view is what a responsible society needs to provide for its children, who have not yet attained the ability to seek out vetted information on their own and who have not yet developed the ability for critical thinking. To do less is simply short-changing the future.

The Keys to "Anti-Slacktivism" Might Burn Corporations in the Butt

July 20, 2010

Categories: Activism, Protests in Social Media, Tactics, Threats

The ways to transition from slacktivism to digital activism have been debated in the social web for a while now. Recently, there was another entry in the on-going debate.

In an Ad Age Digital article, "How to Get the Social-Media Generation Behind Your Cause," Ann Marie Kerwin writes about a TBWA Chiat Day study, "Social Activism 2.0," that recommends various ways marketers can get young adults to break the divide between slacktivism (e.g., merely hitting a "like" button on a Facebook "Cause" page) and activism (e.g., first-person involvement in corporate cause-marketing efforts via donations of money or volunteered time). To attempt to bridge this gap, summarizing, the article says the study recommends:

- Make the cause "fun" for young participants.
- Make participating in the cause "social."
- Make prospective participants believe that they will "make a difference" by participating.
- Make it "easy" to participate.

These are certainly good words of advice for getting anyone to do anything that you want them to do, and as such really aren't much of a revelation. Yet, if corporations take the advice to heart, they may indeed succeed in helping young adults break that barrier between slacktivism and activism. But, I don't want to let this idea go stale. In that article there is some other information that is a bit more enlightening, and can provide a different insight.

Per the study, 75% of young adults (ages 20-29) think that corporations have the resources to assist social causes, while 60% believe that corporations have the knowledge to support such efforts. Hmmm. This sounds like a market segment that can be primed and ignited for activism, especially digital activism, involving corporations. For sure, those corporations would want that behavior directed at cause-marketing programs of their own selection and creation. But once you light the fire of activism, controlling it can be difficult. The United States discovered how this "wildfire" phenomenon can turn around after it supported the Afghani Mujahideen in their 1980s battle against the Soviet Union. The Mujahideen later turned around to fight against the nation who helped make that victory against the Soviet Union possible.

The phrase "be careful what you wish for" comes to mind. Corporations should understand that, if they help break that slacktivism/activism wall in support of cause-marketing, the energy penetrating that wall can be easily converted into anti-corporate activism, (i.e., irregular competition) especially given that 75% of the demographic segment targeted believes that corporations have the resources to assist in social causes.

Perhaps a "burnt butt" is better saved by not lighting the fire?

EXCLUSIVE
Who Is Really the Prey in Predatory Marketing?

July 22, 2010

Categories: Anti-Corporatism, Irregular Competition - Corporate Accountability

A few weeks ago Corporate Accountability International (CAI) released a press statement, "Suit Mc Donald's Cue to Stop Predatory Marketing," announcing that their partner, the Center for Science in the Public Interest (CSPI), threatened a lawsuit against Mc Donald's if the company did not cease using toy promotions in the sales of its Happy Meals. [213] There were two claims in the press release: 1) that the practice of toy-related promotions violated several state consumer protection laws, and, 2) that such promotional practices were "predatory marketing."

As to the first claim, if indeed these practices do violate state laws where the toy promotions take place, then wouldn't a complaint to the state consumer protection board be more expedient? Probably. But taking such a route would not generate as much publicity for CSPI or CAI, nor afford them the opportunity to "hold court" in the media through the issuance of press statements such as the one cited above. As to the second claim, let's talk about who's actually being "preyed" upon here, if anyone.

The press release states that "predatory marketing is no less than exploitative." Well, yes, that is semantically correct. If you look up the word "predatory" in the dictionary, you will see that the word "exploit" is used in the definition.[214] So, saying other than "predatory marketing is no less than exploitative" wouldn't be correct. (For more about predatory marketing and the exploitation of children in a non-commercial sense, see my article series on the Rainforest Action Network and Children.) But by making the claim of predatory marketing, and tying the correct definition to it (the word "exploitative"), CAI ignites the shock value that they seek, and implies that children have the right to choose what they eat and are represented as victims of an over-bearing marketing machine. This, of course, might seem repugnant to the casual observer. That's the idea. However, let's dig a little deeper.

Children don't have the right to choose what they eat.

When was the last time you saw a ten year-old pull into a parking spot at Mickey D's, hop out, amble up to the counter, smack a fiver on the counter, and order up a Happy Meal, with toys, please? Such an action would indicate, on the surface, an ability to drive and earn money. But less tongue-in-cheek and looking deeper down, that action would demonstrate that there is a person who has the ability to make a reasonable decision given all the other alternatives for available sustenance and has made that decision based on all known options and information.

No, you probably haven't seen children take all these actions. Yet, you have seen their co-opted proxies take these actions. Co-opted proxies? Read that as "parents."

You have seen parents driving a car loaded with kids, probably some of them overweight, pull into a Mickey D's parking spot, amble up to the counter, smack a fiver on the counter, and order up a Happy Meal, with toys, please. These are likely parents who have been harangued all day by the tykes who want that taste of cow flesh and the cheap toys that come with it. These are parents who don't want to be "hated" by their rug rats or who don't want their kids to grow up with complexes.

So, they give in. They give in to the marketing aimed at the kids. They give in to the desires generated in the minds of those kids by those marketing programs. The parents become co-opted because they are the ones with the keys to the car, with the moolah in their pockets, and because they are the ones that can make it all happen for junior. And they become co-opted by their progeny under pain of a guilt-trip, the key to exploiting a parent. (If you've spent any time as either a parent or a child, you'll understand what I mean.)

So, who is actually being "preyed" upon here?

Is it the children as CAI and CSPI claim in their press statement? Or is it the parents? Parents who are expected, as adults, with the responsibility of raising tomorrow's adults, to have the capacity to make reasonable decisions, to have the fortitude to do what is best for their children, and who have the ability and authority to just say "no." Or is it all the rest of us? Those who CAI and CSPI would have believe that Mc Donald's is the "problem" that causes children to make "poor" decisions.

You know my opinion. What's yours?

Another "Piece of Crap" Report by Greenpeace

August 3, 2010

Categories: Irregular Competition - Greenpeace, Research - Questionable

On this blog I have several times written about the questionable "research" that sometimes issues from the Greenpeace offices. To have a look at those other posts, simply click here. Today's post is another entry in that series of articles.

Greenpeace's latest installment in their string of sloppy research is their ranking of U.S. supermarkets in the debate over selling sustainable seafood. This "report" is entitled "Carting Away the Oceans" and may be seen by clicking here. [215] This document devotes much space to critiquing various supermarket chains regarding their individual sustainable seafood policies (pages 12 to 34 of "Carting Away the Oceans"). The document also reserves quite a bit of room for Greenpeace to claim victory in this supermarket campaign which they have conducted for the last few years (page 4 of "Carting Away the Oceans"), even though those claims of victory are unsubstantiated.

On those pages referenced above, as well as on others in this document, Greenpeace mentions repeatedly the "red list species" and refers to them as unsustainable. Yet, in this document it does not comprehensively list the species on the "red list," which is apparently a list of Greenpeace's own making, nor, and most importantly, does Greenpeace demonstrate in the document why those "red list" species are "unsustainable" in an objective sense (i.e., in the opinion of third-party experts) or even in a subjective sense (i.e., in the opinion of Greenpeace). There is not a hint of scientific evidence, objective or otherwise, as to why Greenpeace thinks certain species are endangered. This document is not referenced and has no sources cited, other than the occasional mention of Greenpeace surveys which were used to rank the supermarket chains in the sales of sustainable seafood.

In other words, the reader is expected to accept, on face-value only, Greenpeace's assertions and rankings in this document. The degree of that acceptance would, of course, vary by reader and, I think, be determined by the value of the Greenpeace brand held in that reader's mind. The higher the brand image in the mind of the reader than the more believability this document would hold.

Given the transparency and information-rich environment that we now experience via social media, an environment that organizations like Greenpeace use to attack their corporate opponents, it will be interesting to see if the public catches on to the lack of substance in this Greenpeace document or in others produced by that organization.

Chapter Twelve - And the Beat Goes On
———— Take-Aways ————

In this final chapter of *Living on a Meme - How Anti-Corporate Activists Bend the Truth, and You, to Get What They Want*, we see the meme generation from Greenpeace marching on. The article "High Seas Romance Raises Greenpeace's Threat Rating" exposes a new approach in Greenpeace's campaign to romanticize what it is that they do and thereby build a meme in the process. Perhaps their hope is that if all the "armchair activists" out there will be enticed by the prospect of doing some "virtual good," then the video game excitement will generate positive sentiment toward Greenpeace, reinforcing the meme propagation in which they engage via other media. This sort of "slacktivism" is certainly an interesting approach and, as I opined in the piece, it is one that could actually have a counter-productive effect on the NGO.

Counter-production via slacktivism, indeed, is an idea that was also explored in "The Keys to 'Anti-Slacktivism' Might Burn Corporations in the Butt." But in that article I spoke about how corporations could be "burned" in the reverse direction by trying to use the activist-spirit killing tendencies that are often attributed to slacktivism or, as some call it, clicktivism. As of now, this type of "ism" and virtual approach to activism in the real world is still too new to be certain of which way it will turn. Will slacktivism be a boon or a bust to real-world activism? No one really knows. But, vigilance often pays off. So, companies need to be aware of these approaches to activism and how they may effect corporate engagement with irregular competition.

Again the memes rolled on in the irregularly competitive research methodologies examined in the essays "More Sloppy Research from Greenpeace" and "Another 'Piece of Crap' Report by Greenpeace." In other parts of this book, I've addressed my observations of Greenpeace's tendency to feature reports based on questionable sourcing or methodologies. These two pieces simply highlight more instances of what I have observed and imply that it's likely that in the future Greenpeace will not depart from what I consider to be poor research and poor reporting practices.

The article "Who Is Really the Prey in Predatory Marketing?" raises a point that not only corporate managers need to consider when battling irregular competition, but brings to light a question that needs to be considered by the general public when engaging with NGO and activist ideas, or the groups themselves. Based on the research that I have done in the area of irregular competition, some of which is touched upon in this book, it is my opinion that many, far too many, NGOs and activist groups depend on the meme of predation, that corporations are preying upon "helpless" groups, and those groups need the NGOs and activists to save them from being consumed as prey. In my observations of and research into this tactic, the NGOs and activists rarely support the predation meme and, perhaps, simply hope that the emotionality of this meme will carry their protest agendas to completion. It is a tactic that I believe, given the meme of anti-corporatism as support, can be very effective.

CONCLUSION

So, as I said back in Chapter One Take-Aways, "Something is happening here, but you don't know what it is, do you, Mister Jones?" I hope by now you are no longer a "Mr. Jones." I hope that you are beginning to get an idea of what is happening here. It was my intention in this book as an exploratory work into the idea of irregular competition that you would begin to realize the power and impact of this new form of competition to business.

We live in a world that is changing more rapidly than it has changed before. It will likely change more rapidly tomorrow. Doesn't it always? The high-speed velocity and virality of information in today's social online world affect the very veracity of what it is that we experience in that world, impacting the truths that we learn on a daily basis. NGOs and activists adversarial to business have learned this and have embraced the concept wholeheartedly. By mangling memes and manipulating meanings, so simple to do within the social web, these virtual actors leverage and contribute to a vitriolity against companies. In so doing, they are simultaneously employing, leveraging, and augmenting something deeper operating in social media, where the mangling of memes is as easy as sitting down at a computer.

Throughout this book, you and I have discussed examples of memes used by irregular competition, and that discussion of memes is by no means comprehensive. Yet, we have at least started moving toward an understanding of how to cope with this new 21st century competitor. We have seen how through a passive or engaged process of meme mangling the semantical extortion or semantical terrorism will likely continue to exert its influence in the marketplace.

In *Living on a Meme - How Anti-Corporate Activists Bend the Truth, and You, to Get What They Want*, we have discussed the following memes of irregular competitors:

A By-No-Means Exhaustive List of Irregular Competition Memes Reviewed in this Book

1. presidential support for activism,
2. "we are all socialists now,"
3. a "highly profitable" health insurance industry,
4. altruistic benefits behind free food for all,
5. 100% and complete transparency in business,
6. the protection of children (which could actually mean the exploitation of children),

7. activist as archetypical hero,
8. general anti-corporatism; that corporations are responsible for everything bad in your life including your own obesity (probably the most important meme on which to base other memes),
9. "mea culpa," self-flagellating anti-corporatism,
10. corporate executives taking as compensation too high a percentage of their organization's revenue (often propagated by NGOs themselves),
11. success in social media protest - no matter what the actual outcome,
12. a corporation not meeting the "demands" of an activist when indeed the corporation has done just that,
13. the meme that heavy industry is dirty and destructive to society - regardless of what that industry does to mitigate its own negatives,
14. predation by corporations upon a naive public; a public that is told by irregular competitors that it is naive and that it has a weak personal willpower

These memes, and others we haven't discussed, serve to support at least three overarching themes employed by irregular competitors.

1. Corporations are bad, wrong, and led by mean spirited "fat cats" who have no interest in "doing right" by the common man.
2. Socialism is good, better, needed, and more fair. Business leaders and corporations who have taken risk and invested their own ingenuity, time, and money should be freely sharing their knowledge and wealth.
3. Society can't trust corporations, or the government to watch them, and that individuals are powerless against corporations, so the NGO or activist is needed to protect the public's interest.

As we've seen in this book, these themes are played as background, supported, and leveraged by various NGOs and activist groups so that they can bend reality in the hopes of enlisting support, whether that support be psychological, financial, or behavioral.

All of these memes support and progress the agendas of anti-corporate NGOs and activists. And the memes listed here are just some of the highlights. These are some of the memes that anti-corporate activist organizations live on and, so that they may continue to pursue their agendas, they want you to live on these memes, too, which they are happy to feed you ad nauseum.

There are many more memes. We've only just scratched the surface. Look for more irregular competitor memes in future editions of *Living on a Meme* or stop by my Web site at Telofski.com.

Why is it important to know all of this? It's important to know all of this because of what I said back in the Chapter Six Take-Away. When irregular competitors, adopt "name and shame" tactics, exploit memes unfairly, subjectively, and falsely, interpreting, supporting, and leveraging those memes to fit their own agenda and not the agenda of the customer, benefit to society is not served. It is then that benefit is only served to special interest with "semantical extortion" or "semantical terrorism" driving companies rather than the will of the customer.

If companies are to combat the untruths propagated by these memes, untruths that can negatively affect not only their business but also the lives of their employees (Maybe you are one of them?) and customers and the economic system in general, then business must understand what irregular competition is doing and how it is doing it. This book is a step toward that understanding.

Thanks for reading.

ABOUT THE AUTHOR

Thanks for reading my fifth book, *Living on a Meme - How Anti-Corporate Activists Bend the Truth, and You, to Get What They Want,* and thanks for wanting to learn more about my background.

I am a competitive strategy and intelligence analyst. At my consulting practice, I specialize in the analysis of non-traditional competitors, which I define as "irregular competition." As you know from reading this book, by irregular competition, a term I coined, I refer specifically to NGO and activist organizations which are adversarial toward business. In recent years, these organizations have begun to have a greater influence on not only the corporate image, but also on how corporations operate day to day. In my work, I specialize in critical and independent analysis of irregular competitors and how they impact businesses from within both Web 1.0 and Web 2.0 environments as well as from within mainstream media.

Before I began to study irregular competitors I performed similar work, but it concerned more "regular" competitors. I founded and headed The Becker Research Company, Inc., one of America's premier competitive intelligence consultancies. Working with Fortune 100 clients, I helped them predict competitive actions from their regular, "garden-variety" competitors, reducing surprises and assisting them in maintaining or increasing market share.

After Becker Research, but prior to my current consulting practice, I founded and operated eBusiness Analysts, a Web 1.0 strategy firm. When everyone was crazy for e-commerce, I advised various clients on a reasoned and measured approach to conducting business on the Internet. It was during that time that I wrote my second book which is entitled *Dangerous Competition*, available via major online booksellers.

Prior to Becker Research, my previous experience in strategic counseling came from my work in a U.S. Department of Commerce program, the Trade Adjustment Assistance Center. As a Strategic Planning Officer in the TAAC, I designed strategic plans and advised American manufacturers who were adversely affected by foreign competitors.

Before my work for the USDOC, I was a professor of economics and marketing at Monmouth University and at Georgian Court University.

My educational resume sports a B.A. in Communications & Sociology from Rutgers University, and a M.B.A. in Marketing from Rider University. Because of my unique experience and educational background, I believe in analyzing both the soft and hard sides of business. I believe this because without knowing both, I think that a business analyst is really just wasting his or her client's time.

If you would like to follow my work, I blog about it regularly at www.Telofski.com.

Your comments or questions about *Living on a Meme - How Anti-Corporate Activists Bend the Truth, and You, to Get What They Want* are welcome. You may send them to Richard@Telofski.com.

Thanks for reading me and I look forward to hearing from you.

REFERENCES

1. Stecklow, Steve, "How Web of Activists Gives Coke Problems in India," *Global Policy Forum*, June 7, 2005, http://www.globalpolicy. org/component/content/article/176/31337.html, accessed August 21, 2009

2. http://press.meetup.com/archives/000456.html, accessed September 1, 2009

3. Neff, Jack, "Crashing Motrin-Gate: A Social-Media Case Study," *Advertising Age*, November 24, 2008, http://adage.com/ article?article_id=132787, accessed September 1, 2009

4. "Activism, Social Class, and the Digital Divide," *Education and Class*, October 3, 2008, http://educationandclass.com/2008/10/03/activism-social-class-and-the-digital-divide/, accessed September 15, 2009

5. Mooney, Allison, "Web Sites Donate Ad Space for Social Good," *Advertising Age*, October 21, 2009, http://adage.com/goodworks/ post?article_id=139815

6. http://www.publisherswithapurpose.com/, accessed October 22, 2009

7. Borelli, Tom, "Nike, Starbucks and Other Team Up With the Left to Sell Cap-and-Trade," Fox Forum, *FoxNews.com*, October 15, 2009, http://www.foxnews.com/opinion/2009/10/15/tom-borelli-cap-trade-apollo-ceres/, accessed October 27, 2009

8. http://en.wikipedia.org/wiki/Us_Tareyton_smokers_would_rather_ fight_than_switch!, accessed October 27, 2009

9. Hall, Mike, "Health Care Action: Union Activists Visit Congress, Deliver Letters from Consumers,"October 7, 2009, http://blog.aflcio. org/2009/10/07/health-care-action-union-activists-visit-congress-deliver-letters-from-consumers/, accessed October 29, 2009

10. Conniff, Ruth, "Health Care Reform on the Homestretch," *The Progressive*, September 15, 2009, http://www.progressive.org/ rc091509.html, accessed October 29th, 2009

11. "Top industries: Most profitable - 2008," *Fortune*, from the July 20, 2009 issue, http://money.cnn.com/magazines/fortune/global500/2009/ performers/industries/profits/, accessed October 29, 2009

12. "UN Agency Promotes Global Governance of Food Policies," *GlobalGovernanceWatch.org*, http://www.globalgovernancewatch. org/on_the_issues/food-for-thought-un-agency-promotes-global-governance-of-food-policies, accessed November 3, 2009

13. http://www.fao.org/, accessed November 2, 2009

14. "Methodological Toolbox on the Right to Food," Food and Agricultural Organization of the United Nations, http://www.fao.org/righttofood/publi_02_en.htm, accessed November 3, 2009

15. "Guide on Legislating for the Right to Food," Food and Agricultural Organization of the United Nations, 2009, http://www.fao.org/righttofood/publi09/guide_on_legislating.pfd, accessed November 3, 2009

16. Cienfuegos, Paul, "Paradigm Shift: Challenging Corporate Authority," p. 175. In *The Global Activist's Manual - Local Ways to Change the World*, edited by Prokosch, Mike, and Laura Raymond, New York, New York: Nation Books, 2002

17. Skies, Kellee K., "Buying Local -- Isn't it really about Social and Environmental Responsibility?," *Fast Company*, June 20, 2008, http://www.fastcompany.com/blog/kellee-k-sikes/business-social-responsibility/buying-local-isn't-it-really-about-social-and-env, accessed November 11, 2009

18. Peyton, David, "Chevron's Headache: NGOs and Film Raise Profile of 27 Billion Dollar Case," *NGO Watch* - American Enterprise Institute & The Federalist Society, November 6, 2009, http://www.globalgovernancewatch.org/ngo_watch/chevrons-headache-ngos-and-film-raise-profile-of-27-billion-dollar-case-3, accessed November 12, 2009

19. Atwood, John, "Government Usurps Charitable Giving and Nature," *American Chronicle*, August 6, 2009, http://www.americanchronicle.com/articles/view/113208, accessed November 18, 2009

20. Judge, Clark S., and Richard Torrenzano, "Capitalism by Proxy Fight," *The Wall Street Journal*, November 22, 2009, http://online.wsj.com/article/SB100014240529702034401045744047800125924 04.html, accessed November 30, 2009

21. Tuna, Cari, "Proxy-Voting Advocates Pool Resources on the Web," *The Wall Street Journal*, November 23, 2009, http://online.wsj.com/article/SB10001424052748704533904574548051210200852.html, accessed November 30, 2009

22. Clark & Torrenzano, op. cit.

23. Laudicina, Paul, *World Out of Balance*, New York, New York: Mc Graw-Hill, 2005

24. Wilson, J. Justin, "Obesity activists a public health threat," *The Daily Camera* (Boulder, Colorado), December 5, 2009, http://www.dailycamera.com/c_i13928221, accessed December 11, 2009

25. Calories per Pound of Fat, http://www.weightlossforall.com/calories-per-pound.htm, accessed December 11, 2009

26. Soule, Sarah, *Contention and Corporate Social Responsibility*, New York, New York: Cambridge University Press, 2009

27. Saunders, Debra J., "When scientists behave like bullies," *San Francisco Chronicle*, December 1, 2009, http://www.sfgate.com/cgi-bin/article.cgi?file=/c/a/2009/11/30/EDV01ASHN5.DTL, accessed December 21, 2009

28. "Anti-Corporate Gift Guide," *Million Dollar Swim*, December 15, 2009, http://milliondollarswim.blogspot.com/2009/12/anti-corporate-gift-guide.html, accessed December 23, 2009

29. Clark, Stephen, "Wireless Company Mixes Liberal Politics With Business," *FoxNews.com*, December 16, 2009, http://www.foxnews.com/politics/2009/12/12/wireless-company-mixes-liberal-politics-business/, accessed January 5, 2010

30. Laudicina, op. cit.

31. Jessica Rabbit defined - http://en.wikipedia.org/wiki/List_of_Who_Framed_Roger_Rabbit_characters#Jessica_Rabbit, accessed January 14, 2010

32. Schwartz, Ariel, "What Will Wal-Mart's Sustainability Index Look Like?," *Fast Company*, July 16, 2009, http://www.fastcompany.com/blog/ariel-schwartz/sustainability/what-will-wal-marts-sustainability-index-look, accessed January 21, 2010

33. Walmart Sustainability Index, http://walmartstores.com/Sustainability/9292.aspx, accessed January 21, 2010

34. Ibid.

35. Ryan, Tom, "Wal-Mart Classifies Customers for Growth," *Retail Wire*, as seen on *Supply Chain Digest*, March 27, 2007, http://www.scdigest.com/assets/newsViews/07-03-27-2.php?cid=977&ctype=content, January 21, 2010

36. Weston, Liz Pulliam, "National Bank of Wal-Mart?," *MSN Money*, http://moneycentral.msn.com/content/Banking/Betterbanking/P109171.asp, January 21, 2010

37. Mallaby, Sebastian, "Progressive Wal-Mart. Really.," *The Washington Post*, November 28, 2005, http://www.washingtonpost.com/wp-dyn/content/article/2005/11/27/AR2005112700687.html, accessed January 21, 2010

38. "Bush Job Approval - 34%," *Zogby.com*, August 16, 2006, http://www.zogby.com/News/readnews.cfm?ID=1157, accessed January 21, 2010

39. Mallaby, op. cit.

40. Gouge, Pallavi, "Wal-Mart's Jim and Laura: The Real Story," *Business Week*, October 9, 2006, http://www.businessweek.com/bwdaily/dnflash/content/oct2006/db20061009_579137.htm, accessed January 26, 2010

41. Plambeck, Erica and Lyn Denend, "Wal-Mart's Sustainability Strategy," *Harvard Business Review*, April 17, 2007, http://hbr.org/product/wal-mart-s-sustainability-strategy/an/OIT71-PDF-ENG, access January 26, 2010

42. Mc Causland, Christianna, "Onetime foes, companies and activists find ways to cooperate," *The Christian Science Monitor*, December 28, 2009, http://www.csmonitor.com/Money/2009/1228/Onetime-foes-companies-and-activists-find-ways-to-cooperate, accessed January 26, 2010

43. Slacktivism defined, http://www.urbandictionary.com/define.php?term=slacktivism, accessed January 28, 2010

44. Mc Causland, op. cit.

45. http://twitter.com/RichardTelofski

46. Osborne, Evan, *The Rise of the Anti-Corporate Movement - Corporations and the People Who Hate Them*, Stanford, California: Stanford University Press, 2007

47. Henderson, David, *The Role of Business in the Modern World - Progress, Pressures and Prospects for the Market Economy*, London: The Institute of Economic Affairs, 2004

48. Hart, Stuart and Sanjay Sharma, "Engaging Fringe Stakeholders for Competitive Imagination," *Academy of Management Executive*, Vol. 18, No. 1, 2004, p. 7.

49. Library Review for When Corporations Rule the World as seen on Amazon.com at http://www.amazon.com/When-Corporations-World-David-Korten/dp/1887208046/ref=sr_1_1?ie=UTF8&s=books &qid=1264449248&sr=8-1, accessed July 23, 2010

50. http://www.corporatewatch.org/

51. Corporate Watch About page, http://www.corporatewatch. org/?lid=58, accessed January 27, 2010

52. CorporateWatch.org visitor statistics at http://siteanalytics.compete. com/corporatewatch.org/, accessed February 16, 2010

53. http://www.change.org/

54. http://www.change.org - About Page, accessed January 28, 2010

55. Creative Commons License Page - http://creativecommons.org/ about/licenses/, accessed January 28, 2010

56. Change.org FAQ - http://www.change.org/info/faqs, accessed January 28, 2010

57. California Secretary of State Website - http://kepler.sos.ca.gov/, accessed January 28, 2010

58. California Secretary of State Website Field Descriptions and Status Definitions - http://www.sos.ca.gov/business/be/cbs-field-status-definitions.htm, accessed January 28, 2010

59. State of Delaware, Department of State, Division of Corporations Website - https://delecorp.delaware.gov/tin/GINameSearch.jsp, accessed January 28, 2010

60. State of Delaware, Department of State, Division of Corporations Website, Field Definitions - https://delecorp.delaware.gov/tin/ FieldDesc.jsp#ENTITY%20TYPE, accessed January 28, 2010

61. http://www.alexa.com/siteinfo/change.org, accessed January 29, 2010

62. http://siteanalytics.compete.com/change.org/, accessed January 29, 2010

63. Change.org Facebook Fan page - http://www.facebook.com/change. org, accessed January 29, 2010

64. Change.org Facebook fan blogs - http://www.facebook.com/change. org?v=app_7146470109, accessed January 29, 2010

65. Change.org Facebook Take Action area - http://www.facebook.com/ change.org?v=app_4949752878, accessed January 29, 2010

66. Change.org Web site Take Action area - http://www.change. org/petitions, accessed January 29, 2010

67. Change.org Twitter page - http://twitter.com/change, accessed January 29, 2010

68. Friends of the Earth Web site - http://www.foe.org/meet-eric-hoffman

69. Friends of the Earth US - http://www.foe.org

70. Gaylord, Chris, "Dispute Finder: Making the call on Web 'facts'," *The Christian Science Monitor*, October 13, 2009, http://www. csmonitor.com/Innovation/Responsible-Tech/2009/1013/dispute-finder-making-the-call-on-web-facts, accessed February 25, 2010

71. Universal Mc Cann, "When Did We Start Trusting Strangers," http://www.universalmccann.com/global/knowledge/view?id=34, accessed February 25, 2010

72. Memorandum For The Heads Of Executive Departments and Agencies, http://www.whitehouse.gov/the-press-office/presidential-memorandum-establishing-a-task-force-childhood-obesity, accessed March 1, 2010

73. Irregular Competition Defined, http://www.telofski.com/blog/irregular-competition-defined/, accessed March 9, 2010

74. Ibid.

75. Rainforest Action Network Twitter page, http://twitter.com/ran, accessed March 9, 2010

76. InsidiousCompetition.com, accessed March 10, 2010

77. "Divided SEC proposes investor access plan," http://inform.com/business/divided-sec-proposes-investor-access-plan-531407a, accessed March 10, 2010

78. Chase Community Giving Facebook fan page, http://www.facebook. com/ChaseCommunityGiving?v=wall&ref=ts#!/ChaseCommunityGi ving?v=wall&ref=tsp, accessed March 16, 2010

79. "The Trouble with Trusting Complex Science," *The Guardian*, March 8, 2010, http://www.guardian.co.uk/commentisfree/cif-green/2010/mar/08/belief-in-climate-change-science, accessed March 25, 2010

80. "Caught Red-Handed: How Nestlé's Use of Palm Oil is Having a Devastating Impact on Rainforest, The Climate and Orangutans," *Greenpeace US*, http://www.greenpeace.org/international/en/publications/reports/caught-red-handed-how-nestle/, accessed March 26, 2010

81. "The Nestlé-Greenpeace clash: a chronology," *Social Media Influence,* http://socialmediainfluence.com/2010/03/24/the-nestle-greenpeace-clash-a-chronology/, March 26, 2010

82. Nestlé Facebook fan page, http://www.facebook.com/Nestle, accessed March 26, 2010

83. Kit Kat Facebook fan page, http://www.facebook.com/kitkat, accessed March 26, 2010

84. "What We Can Learn from Nestlé's Facebook Drama." Communications Executive Council, *Insider,* http://cecinsider.exbdblogs.com/2010/03/22/what-we-can-learn-from-nestle's-facebook-drama/, accessed March 26, 2010

85. Cluetrain, http://www.Cluetrain.com, accessed March 26, 2010

86. "Caught Red-Handed: How Nestlé's Use of Palm Oil is Having a Devastating Impact on Rainforest, The Climate and Orangutans," Greenpeace US, http://www.greenpeace.org/raw/content/international/press/reports/caught-red-handed-how-nestle.pdf

87. "Update on deforestation and palm oil," Nestlé, http://www.nestle.com/MediaCenter/SpeechesAndStatements/AllSpeechesAndStatements/statement_Palm_oil.htm, accessed March 26, 2010

88. "Nestle respond to Greenpeace Campaign..but don't say much..," *Sian Sophia Investigates,* http://siansophia89.wordpress.com/2010/03/17/nestle-respond-to-greenpeace-campaign-but-dont-say-much/, accessed March 26, 2010

89. Google search, http://www.google.com/search?client=safari&rls=en&q=We+have+also+joined+other+major+purchasers+of+palm+oil+in+making+sure+that+companies,+such+as+Cargill,+understand+our+demands+for+palm+oil+which+is+not+sourced+from+suppliers+which+destroy+rainforests.&ie=UTF-8&oe=UTF-8, accessed March 26, 2010

90. Because of Nestlé changing their Web site and not leaving an archive of previous stories, a discontinuity of sources, similar to that pointed out in the Updated Note earlier in the article, occurs at this note point. However, a related story, "Nestlé sets timetable for palm oil decision," *The Guardian*, March 19, 2010, significant to the timing of Nestle's reaction, and supported the overall contention of the article, was found during the compilation of *Living on a Meme - Year One*. It may be seen at http://www.guardian.co.uk/sustainable-business/nestle-cargill-palmoil, accessed March 26, 2010

91. "Nestlé: You're not fooling anyone," Greenpeace Web site, http://weblog.greenpeace.org/climate/2010/03/nestle_not_fooling_anyone.html, March 26, 2010

92. Kit Kat bar information, http://en.wikipedia.org/wiki/Kit_Kat, accessed March 26, 2010

93. "Ask Nestlé to give rainforests a break," http://www.greenpeace.org/international/campaigns/climate-change/kitkat/, accessed March 26, 2010

94. Taylor, Jim, "Technology: How Social Media Can Ruin Lives," http://drjimtaylor.com/blog/2010/03/technology-how-social-media-can-ruin-lives/, accessed March 30, 2010

95. "Ask Nestlé to give rainforests a break," Op. Cit.

96. "Caught Red-Handed," Op. Cit.

97. "Caught Red-Handed," Ibid.

98. Taylor, Jim, "Anti-corporate vs. Anti-government Anger: Who to Trust?," San Francisco Chronicle, March 8, 2010, http://www.sfgate.com/cgi-bin/blogs/jtaylor/detail??blogid=180&entry_id=58633, accessed April 1, 2010

99. Ibid.

100. Taylor, Jim, "Technology: How Social Media Can Ruin Lives," Op Cit.

101. "Who Pays Income Taxes," National Taxpayers Union, http://www.ntu.org/tax-basics/who-pays-income-taxes.html, accessed April 1, 2010

102. Taylor, Jim, "Technology: How Social Media Can Ruin Lives," Op Cit.

103. "Your Kit Kat Campaigns," Greenpeace Web site, http://weblog.greenpeace.org/climate/2010/03/your_kit_kat_campaigns.html, accessed April 2, 2010

104. http://www.marketwatch.com/investing/stock/NSRG.Y, accessed April 2, 2010

105. http://finance.yahoo.com/

106. http://en.wikipedia.org/wiki/American_Depositary_Receipt, accessed April 2, 2010

107. "Ask Nestlé to give rainforests a break," Op. Cit.

108. "Your Kit Kat Campaigns," Op. Cit.

109. Ibid.

110. http://www.marketwatch.com/investing/stock/NSRG.Y

111. Wang, Shirley, "J&J Pulls Online Motrin Ad After Social-Media Backlash," *The Wall Street Journal*, November 18, 2008, http://online.wsj.com/article/SB122697440743636123.html?mod=googlenews_wsj, accessed April 8, 2010

112. "Your Kit Kat Campaigns," Op. Cit.

113. Steel, Emily, "Nestlé Takes a Beating on Social-Media Sites," *The Wall Street Journal*, March 29, 2010, http://online.wsj.com/article/SB10001424052702304434404575149883850508158.html, April 15, 2010

114. Hickman, Leo, "Greenpeace could learn a simple lesson on manners from George Washington," *The Guardian*, April 6, 2010, http://www.guardian.co.uk/environment/blog/2010/apr/06/greenpeace-gene-hashmi-climate-sceptics, accessed April 15, 2010

115. "Your Kit Kat Campaigns," Op. Cit.

116. http://www.telofski.com/blog/category/protests-in-social-media/the-kit-kat-incident/

117. Taylor, Scott, "Parliament protest ends; questions remain," *The Toronto Sun*, December 7, 2009, http://www.torontosun.com/news/canada/2009/12/07/12065051-qmi.html, accessed April 16, 2010

118. "Greenpeace activists drop in on Nestle shareholder meeting," http://www.youtube.com/watch?v=hREuFFE4cB4&feature=youtube_gdata, accessed April 16, 2010

119. Hance, Jeremy, "Nestle shareholder meeting interrupted by Greenpeace orangutans," *Mongabay.com*, April 15, 2010, http://news.mongabay.com/2010/0415-hance_nestle.html, accessed April 16, 2010

120. Fahrenthold, David, "Greenpeace Activists Arrested After Draping Banner on Mount Rushmore," *The Washington Post*, July 8, 2009, http://www.washingtonpost.com/wp-dyn/content/article/2009/07/08/AR2009070802246.html, accessed April 16, 2010

121. http://www.nestle.com/Resource.axd?Id=6AED7940-5140-4C34-BD16-FCF2C86E543F, accessed April 19, 2010

122. Ibid.

123. Hoffman, Andrew, "Shades of Green," *Stanford Social Innovation Review*, Spring 2009, pp. 40 - 49, http://www.ssireview.org/images/articles/2009SP_Feature_Hoffman.pdf, accessed April 19, 2010

124. Fahrenthold, Op. Cit.

125. Taylor, Scott, Op. Cit.

126. "US stock market, economy and companies update (April 16, 2010)," http://www.stockmarketsreview.com/reports/us_stock_market_economy_and_companies_update_20100416_4745/, accessed April 18, 2010

127. "The SEC vs. Goldman," *The Wall Street Journal*, April 19, 2010, http://online.wsj.com/article/SB10001424052702303491304575188352960427106.html, accessed April 19, 2010

128. Kohut, Andrew, "Americans Are More Skeptical of Washington," *The Wall Street Journal*, April 19, 2010, http://online.wsj.com/article/SB10001424052702303491304575187941408991442.html#articleTabs%3Darticle, accessed April 19, 2010

129. Mc Guinness, Romina, "Friends of the Earth fire back at corportate 'greenwashing'," Metro.com, April 5, 2010, http://www.metronews.ca/toronto/life/article/494834--friends-of-the-earth-fire-back-at-corportate-greenwashing, April 20, 2010

130. Whois information, https://www.networksolutions.com/whois-search/electricityinfo.org, accessed April 20, 2010

131. http://www.itpower.co.uk/Company, accessed April 20, 2010

132. Ibid.

133. http://www.youtube.com/watch?v=WaUZFWGQqco, accessed April 22, 2010

134. http://www.polluterwatch.com/2010/02/polluters-charles-and-david-koch-admit-it-they-fund-front-groups-to-deny-climate-science, accessed April 27, 2010

135. Pomerantz, David, "What The Alliance doesn't want Ken Salazar to know," Cape Cod Today, February 4, 2010, http://www.capecodtoday.com/blogs/index.php/2010/02/04/what-the-alliance-doesn-t-want-ken-salaz?blog=94, accessed April 27, 2010

136. http://www.youtube.com/watch?v=yPaO4JKp344, accessed April 28, 2010

137. http://www.telofski.com/blog/2010/04/22/whats-wrong-with-this-rainforest-action-network-video/, accessed April 28, 2010

138. http://policynetwork.net/, accessed April 29, 2010

139. http://www.policynetwork.net/sites/default/files/Friends_of_the_EU.pdf, accessed April 29, 2010

140. Weiner, Juli, "Misinformed Activists Boycott Brooklyn's AriZona Beverages," April 28, 2010, *Vanity Fair*, http://www.vanityfair.com/online/daily/2010/04/misinformed-activists-boycott-brooklyns-arizona-beverage-co.html, accessed April 29, 2010

141. Ibid.

142. http://www.foei.org/en/who-we-are, accessed May 3, 2010

143. Ibid.

144. http://twitter.com/foeint, accessed May 3, 2010

145. "Cargill's Problems With Palm Oil," Rainforest Action Network Web site, http://ran.org/cargillreport, accessed May 5, 2010

146. http://twitter.com/ran/statuses/13375603544, accessed May 5, 2010

147. http://search.twitter.com/search?q=%23Cargill+destroys+an+area+of+rainforest, accessed May 5, 2010

148. http://twitter.com/foe_us, accessed May 5, 2010

149. http://twitter.com/RichardTelofski, accessed May 5, 2010

150. "Cargill's Problems With Palm Oil," Op. Cit.

151. http://twitter.com/ran/statuses/13375603544, accessed May 5, 2010

152. http://search.twitter.com/search?q=%23Cargill+destroys+an+area+of+rainforest, accessed May 5, 2010

153. Cavalli, Patricia, "Danone Fights Damaging Viral Slurs in Argentina," Advertising Age, April 29, 2010, http://adage.com/globalnews/article?article_id=143598, accessed May 11, 2010

154. http://www.creadorderumores.com/, accessed May 11, 2010

155. Friends of the Earth US Facebook page, http://www.facebook.com/foe.us, May 13, 2010

156. Friends of the Earth International Facebook page, http://www.facebook.com/pages/Friends-of-the-Earth-International/12410115279?ref=tsp, accessed May 13, 2010

157. Friends of the Earth International Web site, http://www.foei.org/en/who-we-are, accessed May 13, 2010

158. Rainforest Action Network Web site, http://understory.ran.org/2010/04/28/winner-of-rans-2010-earth-day-poster-contest/, accessed May 18, 2010

159. Ibid.

160. Rainforest Action Network Flickr page, http://www.flickr.com/photos/rainforestactionnetwork/sets/72157623832930187/, accessed May 18, 2010

161. Ibid.

162. Rainforest Action Network Web site, http://understory.ran.org/wp-content/uploads/2010/04/850806927_RQict-M.jpg, accessed May 18, 2010

163. Rainforest Action Network Web site, http://understory.ran.org/2010/04/28/winner-of-rans-2010-earth-day-poster-contest/, accessed May 18, 2010

164. Bernard Baruch College, CUNY, Web site, http://blsciblogs.baruch.cuny.edu/symposium/the-program/afternoon-workshops/, accessed May 20, 2010

165. http://en.wikiquote.org/wiki/John_Maynard_Keynes

166. Kinsman, Kat, "Activists Call Foul on KFC Bucket Campaign, CNN.com, April 28, 2010, http://www.cnn.com/2010/LIVING/homestyle/04/28/kfc.pink.bucket.campaign/, accessed May 25, 2010

167. http://en.wikipedia.org/wiki/Spy_vs._Spy, accessed May 25, 2010

168. http://www.dccomics.com/mad/, accessed May 25, 2010

169. http://www.youtube.com/watch?v=ZbUQIahOvN0, accessed May 26, 2010

170. Rainforest Action Network YouTube channel, http://www.youtube.com/user/ranvideo, accessed May 26, 2010

171. Soule, Op. Cit.

172. Rainforest Action Network YouTube channel, Op. Cit.

173. Sahlin, Doug and Chris Botello, *YouTube for Dummies*, Wiley Publishing, Hoboken, New Jersey, 2007

174. Lyon, Thomas. Ed. *Good Cop Bad Cop*, RFF Press, Washington, DC, 2010

175. Owyang, Jeremiah. "When It Comes To Social Media, Many Marketers Jump The Gun," *Forbes.com*, May 17, 2010, http://www.forbes.com/2010/05/17/nestle-greenpeace-facebook-twitter-cmo-network-jeremiah-owyang.html, accessed June 3, 2010

176. http://www.delawareonline.com/article/20100522/NEWS02/5220323, accessed June 8, 2010

177. "Social media can help save the planet, says Greenpeace boss," *CNN.com*, May 24, 2010, http://www.cnn.com/2010/TECH/05/24/eco.greenpeace.nestle/, accessed June 10, 2010

178. Heroes Corner, Rainforest Action Network Web site, http://cms.ran.org/new/kidscorner/heroes_corner/, accessed June 17, 2010

179. Pressure Drop Primer, Rainforest Action Network Web site, http://ryse2.ran.org/wp-content/uploads/2010/01/pressure_drop_primer.pdf, accessed June 17, 2010

180. Forest Family Forever Video, Rainforest Action Network Web site, http://cms.ran.org/new/kidscorner/about_rainforests/forest_family_forever_video/, accessed June 17, 2010

181. Definition of "indoctrination," http://www.google.com/search?hl=en&client=safari&rls=en&defl=en&q=define:indoctrination&sa=X&ei=K4AGTK-eK4H88AbDmtj3Cw&ved=0CAgQkAE, accessed June 17, 2010

182. Soule, Op. Cit.

183. Kids Corner, Rainforest Action Network Web site, http://cms.ran.org/new/kidscorner/home/, accessed June 22, 2010

184. Teacher's Lounge, Rainforest Action Network Web site, http://cms. ran.org/new/kidscorner/teachers_lounge/, accessed June 22, 2010

185. Teacher's Resources, Rainforest Action Network Web site, http:// cms.ran.org/new/kidscorner/teachers_lounge/teachers_resources/, accessed June 22, 2010

186. Ibid.

187. Educator Resources, Rainforest Action Network Web site, http:// ran.org/category/resource-class/educator-resources, accessed June 22, 2010

188. Agribusiness in the Rainforest, Rainforest Action Network Web site, http://ran.org/content/agribusiness-rainforest, accessed June 22, 2010

189. Ibid.

190. Ibid.

191. *Brazzil Magazine*, http://www.brazzil.com/, accessed June 22, 2010

192. Grupo de Reflexion Rural, http://www.grr.org.ar/, accessed June 22, 2010

193. *In These Times*, http://www.inthesetimes.com/about/, accessed June 22, 2010

194. *The Nation*, http://www.thenation.com/about-and-contact, accessed June 22, 2010

195. Definition of "indoctrination," http://www.google.com/search?hl=en &client=safari&rls=en&defl=en&q=define:indoctrination&sa=X&ei =K4AGTK-eK4H88AbDmtj3Cw&ved=0CAgQkAE, accessed June 22, 2010

196. RAN Youth Sustaining the Earth, Rainforest Action Network Web site, http://ryse.ran.org/, accessed June 24, 2010

197. Pressure Drop Primer, Op. Cit.

198. Ibid.

199. Rainforest Action Network Web site, http://ran.org/content/problem-palm-oil, accessed June 24, 2010

200. Turning the Page on Rainforest Destruction, Rainforest Action Network Web site, http://understory.ran.org/wp-content/uploads/2010/05/Turning_The_Page_on_Rainforest_Destruction. pdf, accessed June 24, 2010

201. Ibid.

202. Confino, Jo. "Should the media be more supportive of corporate moves towards sustainability?," *The Guardian*, June 1, 2010, http://www.guardian.co.uk/sustainability/blog/7, accessed June 29, 2010

203. Hoffman, Andrew, "Shades of Green," Stanford Social Innovation Review, Spring 2009, pp. 40 - 49, http://www.ssireview.org/images/articles/2009SP_Feature_Hoffman.pdf, accessed June 29, 2010

204. http://www.shipsim.com/

205. Fortney, Daelyn. "New Game Allows Players To Pilot Greenpeace's Rainbow Warrior III," *Ecorazzi.com*, http://www.ecorazzi.com/2010/06/24/new-game-allows-players-to-pilot-greenpeaces-rainbow-warrior-iii/, accessed July 8, 2010

206. Greenpeace Web site, http://www.greenpeace.org/raw/content/usa/press-center/reports4/greenpeace-security-inspection-2.pdf, accessed July 13, 2010

207. D'Amico, Diane. "Atlantic City students pick tap water over bottled - barely - in blind taste test," The Press of Atlantic City, June 10, 2010, http://www.pressofatlanticcity.com/communities/atlantic-city_pleasantville_brigantine/article_04f4427e-74e1-11df-8352-001cc4c002e0.html, accessed July 15, 2010

208. Marks, William E. *The Holy Order of Water*, Bell Pond Books, 2001

209. Barlow, Maude. *Blue Gold*, New Press, 2003

210. http://en.wikipedia.org/wiki/2000_Cochabamba_protests, accessed July 15, 2010

211. Human Sciences Research Council Web site, http://www.hsrc.ac.za/, accessed July 15, 2010

212. Definition of "indoctrination," http://www.google.com/search?hl=en&client=safari&rls=en&defl=en&q=define:indoctrination&sa=X&ei=u7wkTMapNMG78gaKtfyxDw&ved=0CAgQkAE, accessed July 15, 2010

213. Corporate Accountability International Web site, http://www.stopcorporateabuse.org/statement-suit-mcdonalds-cue-stop-predatory-marketing-altogether, accessed July 22, 2010

214. Definition of "predatory," http://www.thefreedictionary.com/predatory

215. "Carting Away the Oceans," Greenpeace Web site, http://www.greenpeace.org/raw/content/usa/press-center/reports4/carting-away-the-oceans.pdf, accessed July 27, 2010

216. Ziobro, Paul. "McDonald's Blasts Criticism of Happy-Meal Toys," *The Wall Street Journal*, July 7, 2001, http://online.wsj.com/article/SB10001424052748704545004575352991417426552.html?mod=googlenews_wsj, accessed July 29, 2010

217. Statement, Corporate Accountability International Web site, http://www.stopcorporateabuse.org/statement-suit-mcdonalds-cue-stop-predatory-marketing-altogether, accessed July 29, 2010

218. Warner, Melanie. "Food Marketing to Kids: Why Ronald McDonald Will Survive But Happy Meal Toys May Not," *Bnet.com*, June 23, 2010, http://industry.bnet.com/food/10002557/food-marketing-to-kids-why-ronald-mcdonald-will-survive-but-the-happy-meal-may-not/, accessed July 29, 2010

INDEX

G

garden variety 2
General Mills 132, 135, 204, 205, 209, 229
George W. Bush 72, 206
GGW 26, 27
Global Activist's Manual 29, 263
GlobalGovernanceWatch.org 26, 262, 263
global warming 36, 50, 51, 103, 188, 215
Goldman Sachs 184
Goliath 21
good cop, bad cop 214
Google 10, 32, 79, 111, 139, 140, 142,
    156, 159, 186, 240, 268, 274–276
government 18, 26, 28, 32, 34, 35, 37, 38,
    53, 62, 67, 70, 74, 78, 96–98, 104,
    117, 124, 143, 146, 147, 152, 156,
    157, 159, 166, 179, 184, 190, 239,
    253, 263, 269
grammar 5, 79, 204, 205
Great Recession 158
Greenpeace x, xi, 65–69, 79, 80, 83, 90–93,
    119, 139, 149–152, 154–156,
    160–163, 168–176, 178–180,
    181–183, 185–189, 192, 199, 202,
    210, 214–221, 230–233, 236–238,
    246–248, 268–271, 274, 276, 277
Guardian 147, 179, 180, 230, 267, 269,
    270, 276
Guidestar 65, 66, 67, 105

H

hard target 100
Harvard Business Review 76, 265
hashtag 135, 198, 200
health care 19, 20, 23, 28, 58, 74, 103,
    158, 159, 262
health insurance 19, 20, 21, 23, 75, 158,
    252
hero 39, 41–44, 54, 225, 253, 274
Hershey 150, 155, 156, 163, 170
hissy-fit 74
hit the fan 62
hourly wages 75
human ancestors 42
humor 52, 60, 190
hypocrisy 179, 186, 229

I

ideas x, 1, 5, 12, 17, 34, 73, 83, 124, 144,
    180, 184, 206, 220, 248
implicit threat 88, 89
income tax 94, 115, 167, 168
indoctrination 203, 208–211, 222, 224,
    227–229, 233, 238, 239, 242,
    274–276
insidious competition i, xiii, 6, 12, 51, 55,
    65, 83, 131, 133, 134, 143, 144,
    221
Intergovernmental Panel on Climate Change
    215
International Monetary Fund 240
International Policy Network 189
in the news 66, 148, 185
intimidation 180
IPCC 215
IPN 189
irregular competition xi, xiii, 5, 12, 32,
    46–48, 54, 63, 65, 69, 75, 79, 83,
    90, 98, 99, 102–104, 110, 116,
    120, 128, 130–134, 137, 138, 143,
    149, 155, 160, 162, 163, 168, 172,
    178–180, 182, 185, 186, 189, 192,
    193, 196–198, 200–203, 208, 214,
    218–220, 222, 224, 228–230, 232,
    236–238, 244, 246, 248, 249, 252,
    254, 258, 267
irregular competitor xi, xi–xiii, 38, 47, 48,
    55, 83, 84, 90, 93, 98, 102–104,
    110, 114, 116, 120, 130, 131, 133,
    134, 137, 138, 143, 149, 151, 162,
    163, 178, 184, 192, 193, 196, 197,
    217, 221, 232, 236, 252–254, 258
irregular competitors xi, xi–xiii, 38, 55, 83,
    84, 90, 93, 98, 104, 120, 133, 143,
    162, 184, 192, 193, 196, 217, 221,
    232, 236, 252–254, 258
IRS 65, 66

J

Jacques Ellul 33
jobs program 73, 74, 75
John Kerry 72
Johnson & Johnson 176
journalistic castigations 148
JP Morgan Chase 132, 135, 138, 140, 141
Jungian psychology 42